SIGMUND FREUD

MODERN MASTERS

Already published

MODERN MASTERS

EDITED BY frank kermode

sigmund freud

richard wollheim

NEW YORK | THE VIKING PRESS

23835

ACKNOWLEDGMENTS

Basic Books, Inc., publishers, and The Hogarth Press Ltd.: From *The Collected Papers of Sigmund Freud*, edited by Ernest Jones, M.D. Basic Books, Inc., publishers, New York 1959. From *Three Essays on the Theory of Sexuality* by Sigmund Freud, translated and newly edited by James Strachey, 1962. Basic Books, Inc., publishers, 1962. Reprinted by permission.

Liveright Publishers: From *Introductory Lectures* by Sigmund Freud. Copyright © 1966 by Joan Riviere. From *Beyond the Pleasure Principle* by Sigmund Freud. Copyright © 1961 by James Strachey. From *The Future of an Illusion* by Sigmund Freud. All reprinted by permission of Liveright Publishers, New York.

W. W. Norton & Co., Inc.: From *The Ego and the Id* by Sigmund Freud. Translated by Joan Riviere. Revised and newly edited by James Strachey. Copyright © 1960 by James Strachey. From *Civilization and Its Discontents* by Sigmund Freud. Translated from the German and edited by James Strachey. Copyright © 1961 by James Strachey. From *New Introductory Lectures on Psychoanalysis* by Sigmund Freud. Newly translated and edited from the German by James Strachey. Copyright 1933 by Sigmund Freud. Copyright renewed 1961 by W. J. H. Sprott. Copyright © 1964, 1965 by James Strachey. Reprinted by permission of W. W. Norton & Co., Inc.

For Rupert and Bruno

Operating from a private medical practice in Vienna, which he maintained from Easter 1886 until he was forced into exile in 1938, Sigmund Freud, by the power of his writings and by the breadth and audacity of his speculations, revolutionized the thought, the lives, and the imagination of an age. He contradicted, and in some cases he reversed, the prevailing opinions, of the learned as well as of common people, on many of the issues of human existence and culture. He led people to think about their appetites and their intellectual powers, about self-knowledge and self-deceit, about the ends of life and about man's profoundest passions and about his most intimate or trivial failings, in ways that would have seemed to earlier generations at once scandalous and silly. It would be hard to find in the history of ideas, even in the history of religion, someone whose influence was so immediate, so broad, and so deep.

A heavy price has been paid for this achievement. In many of the consequences of the Freudian revolution, little trace can be found of Freud's own complex thought. His ideas were among the first victims of their success, and a generation brought up on them would be unable to say with any precision what they actually are. Furthermore, the fact has been lost sight of that, in revolutionizing the world, Freud revolutionized himself. Freud would probably have been a lesser thinker, most certainly he would have been a lesser man, if his ideas had come to him more easily.

That Freud's views have become largely obscured for us, and that his evolution as a thinker has received little recognition, are not unrelated. For, if ideas and hypotheses coming from very different periods in Freud's work are simply put together, the result in many cases is nonsense; in order to understand the individual ideas and hypotheses, it is often necessary to identify the situations to which they are a response or the problems they were devised to solve. With this in mind, I have set myself two aims in the writing of this study: first, to bring out what Freud actually said; and, secondly, to show the relevance of the chronological order in which he said it. To these ends I have, wherever possible, allowed Freud to speak for himself, and, insofar as the tasks are separable, I have preferred exposition to interpretation or evaluation. My first concern has been to set out Freud's account of the mind as this developed over the first half-century of psychoanalysis.

Freud's scientific career began in pathological medicine and in neurology, and it was attended with some success. But for an unlucky accident, he would have made himself famous as the discoverer of cocaine in its clinical use. However, the Freud that we know dates from the visit to Paris in the winter of 1885–1886, when he had the opportunity of working under the famous French physician Charcot with patients suffering from hysteria.

Charcot's great discovery, from Freud's point of view, was that certain types of hysterical patient could be cured of their symptoms by the use of hypnosis; conversely, that hypnosis could be used to induce in normal people the symptoms of hysteria. With these findings, clearer perhaps to pupil than to master, Charcot fired Freud's imagination. He started him off on a new career, and he endowed him with two gifts, which, transformed over the years by experience and by the ingenuity of Freud's mind, became the foundations of psychoanalysis. One was a form of therapy, which set out to remove the symptoms of a mental disorder through the use of words, and the other was a diagnosis, according to which the symptoms of the disorder were traceable to the influence of ideas.

The two parts of Freud's legacy from Charcot—the therapy and the diagnosis—are interrelated. It is because ideas help to form hysterical symptoms that hypnotic suggestion is effective against them: and the efficacy of hypnosis confirms the "ideogenic," or idea-made, character of hysteria. During the first decade of psychoanalysis, both therapy and diagnosis underwent a series of modifications—this will be the theme of Chapter I. But it is important to see how the two processes are connected, and how any change in the one leads to, or is the product of, a change in the other.

As far as the therapy is concerned, the first shift was from hypnotic suggestion, in which the patient is hypnotized and the physician then talks, giving the patient instructions which will rid him of a symptom, to the "cathartic method," in which the patient is hypnotized and then *he* talks, at once giving the physician information and ridding himself of the symptom: then the cathartic method gave way to free association, in which hypnosis is altogether abandoned and the patient no longer confines himself to the history of a particular symptom but says whatever comes into his head, thereby ranging over the various factors that have brought about his disorder. Parallel to these changes in therapy, inspiring and inspired by them, there were changes in the diagnostic account. For Freud was led to look further and further back in the patient's history for the ideas that made themselves felt in the symptoms of his mental disorder. The "traumatic event," as the moment is called from which the ideas derive, was eventually located in infancy, and—a more disturbing note—if the patient's associations were to be trusted, it was found invariably to have a sexual character.

In the light of Freud's later theory, perhaps the most striking aspect of his views at this date is an omission. There was emphasis upon the infantile, there was (somewhat reluctantly) emphasis upon the sexual, but one thing of which there was no mention in Freud's writings —nor, for that matter, any suspicion in his mind—was infantile sexuality. In the so-called "seduction theory," we can see the lengths to which Freud was prepared to go in accounting for the facts of mental disorder as he saw them without compromising the innocence of childhood. According to this theory, hysteria has its origins in an event that is both infantile and sexual but that happens to or is endured by the child. In other words, the middle-class Viennese who came to Freud's consulting room for relief from their nervous disorders had all been sexually assaulted by their fathers between the ages of six and eight.

Then, in 1897, in a letter to Wilhelm Fliess, his friend and mentor, Freud announced his disbelief in the theory. It was a confession of failure, and yet Freud could also recognize that it was a great moment of decision, that it marked a new beginning. "I have," he wrote "a feeling more of triumph than of defeat." It was not simply that Freud saw the implausibility of the seduction theory—that must always have stared him in the face—but he now felt that it was less implausible to credit the infant with wishes and impulses from which tradition and orthodoxy had tried so hard to protect it. The long painstaking researches into the sexual life of the child, as well as into the scope of sexuality, the findings of which form the subject of Chapter IV, begin.

However, with the admission of infantile sexuality, Freud was also led to a more general truth about the mind: to an awareness of the role of impulse and desire in so much human activity. The ideas that Freud, following Charcot, had held to be formative in mental disorder, he originally identified with memories. "Hysterics suffer mainly from reminiscences" is a famous phrase dating from the period when the cathartic method was firmly believed in. Gradually, however, Freud came to think of the ideas that account for disease as the representations of wish and impulse. From then onward, he saw the neurotic as suffering not from buried recollections, but from repressed desires. And in many aspects of normal life—in dreams, in errors, in jokes—as well as in the symptoms of the neurosis, Freud detected the agency of the appetitive side of the mind. The discovery of desire

in so many areas of behavior, where previously everything had been attributed to chance or to physical forces,
is considered in Chapter III.

Of course, even in the period when Freud thought that
it was ideas in the sense of memories that were effective
in mental disorder, he had recognized, indeed insisted,
that the ideas were not accessible to consciousness—at
any rate, as things stood. They were "unconscious." And,
when Freud came to think that it was ideas in the sense
not of memories but of desires that were the true agents
in the formation of a neurosis and its symptoms, he
thought of them in the same way: they too were unconscious. Indeed, the growing emphasis upon desire in
Freud's thought only helped him to clarify his concept
of the unconscious, as against earlier concepts. For,
though in earlier views of the mind, unconscious
mental phenomena had often been admitted alongside
conscious ones, the difference between the two types
had been thought to lie solely in their degrees of strength
or efficacy. Freud, however, from the beginning, was
dealing with ideas that were both unconscious and very
strong. The older distinction between conscious and unconscious ideas was accordingly recast by Freud as one
between conscious and preconscious; and to account for
his kind of unconscious idea, which was not only un-
admitted but inadmissible to consciousness, he postulated a prior act of repression, to which the idea had
fallen victim. In later life, and particularly in the psychoanalytic session, repression manifested itself in the
form of resistance. The conviction that the ideas that
made themselves felt in the neuroses had not merely
lapsed into a state of unconsciousness, but had been
forced there by repression, could only be strengthened
when these ideas were equated with desires. For desires,

unlike memories, have an urgency to them, they seek satisfaction, and some powerful explanation is needed why they are unavailable to consciousness.

From the beginning, then, the notions of the unconscious and repression (or resistance) were closely linked. It was through repression that ideas found their way into the unconscious: just as, through the lowering of resistance, in dreams or in therapy, they found their way out. However, the question had to be asked, If everything that is repressed is unconscious, is everything that is unconscious the consequence of repression? In the course of grappling with this question Freud came to formulate his conception of "the system *Ucs.*," or of the unconscious area of the mind as a system with its own rules and principles.

Freud's thinking on the topic of the unconscious, which culminated in the paper of 1915, one of the great "metapsychological" papers (originally twelve in number, of which only five survive) written in an astonishing bout of creativity over a period of five months in mid-1915, forms the subject of Chapter VI. And that chapter ends with the reflection that at the moment at which it seemed that Freud had worked out to his satisfaction the distinguishing criteria of conscious and unconscious, the distinction itself began to lose its interest for him: the central place that it had occupied for so long in psychoanalytic theory was now taken over by another distinction. During the last phase of Freud's thinking, which coincides with the last fifteen or twenty years of his life, it was the opposition of ego and id that was in the forefront of his attention.

Freud described the change as a shift in interest from the repressed to the repressing forces in the mind, and as a general characterization this gives an adequate account of his later work. The questions why and how repression comes about had always been with him, but a systematic investigation of the agency responsible for repression had to be postponed until the consequences of repression, as these manifest themselves in the neurosis, had been thoroughly studied. And, when Freud did embark on this new investigation, he found that he was not—as his earlier work might have led him to believe—simply turning away from the unconscious to the conscious. For, though the ego, as the repressing agency was called, was in large part conscious, insofar as it was responsible for repression it operated unconsciously. For this reason, as Freud moved over to a functional study of the mind or to the study of the interactions between various parts of the mind that inaugurate mental conflict, the distinction of conscious versus unconscious seemed to him less and less relevant.

In examining the ego as the repressing agency, Freud was led to ask how the ego came by the standards it enforced in repression. The question itself was not new, but what was peculiar to Freud's late phase was the determination to provide a genetic or developmental account—a history, as it were, within the history of the individual—for these standards. Identified originally as a "differentiating grade" in, or a "modification" of, the ego, the superego is treated as a deposit left behind in the infant's mind from its passionate but catastrophic relations with a loved parent.

In one respect Freud's characterization of the change that came over his work as it entered its last phase does not do justice to its range. For, alongside the study of the ego, the other great theme of this period certainly was concerned with the repressed forces of the mind. And that was Freud's discovery, and analysis, of the death instinct. Contrary to certain popular conceptions, Freud had never believed that the whole of man's instinctual endowment was sexual. His theory of the psychoneuroses rests on a duality of instinct. In his early period he said little about the nonsexual instincts, except to refer, quite conventionally, to hunger and thirst. In his middle period—at any rate, after 1910—he contrasted sexuality and the ego instincts, but he left the ego instincts curiously unspecified. Then, in 1920, in *Beyond the Pleasure Principle*, he announced the discovery of the death instinct, and, from then onward, the human psyche and, by extension, human society and human history are seen as the arenas for the warring instincts of Eros and Thanatos, of love and death. Freud's late work was, however, not without its unity, for the two themes of the ego and its development and of the reclassification of the instincts bear upon each other, and in Chapter VII I set out to trace how they connect.

Freud is generally thought of primarily as one who explored the workings of the abnormal mind. That is certainly a fair estimate of his life's work. The study of the neurosis—its nature, its cause and its cure, the subject of Chapter V—lies at the center of his achievement. However, for various reasons, Freud held that the study of the abnormal mind could be advanced solely within some more general theory of the mind; and, in order to have a thorough understanding of his theory of the neurosis, one should really see it in this larger setting. I have endeavored to do this in Chapter II. For all the importance that a general psychological theory had for Freud, there are only two works in which he tried to set one out. They stand at the two ends of his life's work, and both are unfinished. One is the *Outline of Psychoanalysis*, written at the age of eighty-two, and the other, which is the more elaborated account, is the brilliant and abstruse manuscript, composed during a few weeks in late 1895, and generally known as the "Scientific Project." I have concentrated on the earlier work because, though Freud never published it and never referred to it again, it casts a lengthy shadow over much of his work. The manuscript is, however, difficult, and as a result the chapter in which I deal with it requires a closer and more exacting attention than I would have wished to ask of the reader. However, so much of the interest in Freud's development currently centers in the "Project" that I felt that it would have been quite wrong to treat the subject in a more glancing fashion. Those whose interest in the history of psychoanalytic theory is less fundamental could quite legitimately omit the chapter or read it later.

In the last chapter I deal with Freud's views about society and human culture. This, I have felt, is perhaps the area where there is the greatest need to retrieve what Freud actually said from the many interpretations and partial readings to which his words have been subjected. Freud speculated both about the past and about the future of society. Two very big questions clearly intrigued him: How did human society originate? and, Is it ultimately worthwhile? Much of what Freud said on these issues is stimulating and original, but it does not add up to a social theory or a social ethic. Nor did he think so.

In his reflections on society Freud was influenced by two very general principles, which pulled him in somewhat different directions. They were a belief in the ultimate power of reason and rational argument, and a profoundly low opinion of human nature. He was not intimidated from referring, on several occasions, to the majority of human beings—as they were, or as society had formed them—as "worthless." In addition, Freud's thinking about politics was colored by two deeply held sentiments, which were characteristic of the man: a bitter antagonism to religion and all forms of religious authority, and a hatred of America.

To point out that Freud himself did not have a "political theory" is not to deny that his writings are and will remain one of the most fruitful sources upon which speculation about society can draw. In the writings of Erik Erikson and Alexander Mitscherlich, Freud's general theories have been put to interesting use.

On one subject I have said nothing in this study: Freud's views about art. What Freud actually says on the subject—as opposed, once again, to what can be legitimately derived from his thinking—is very fragmentary, and the task of separating off what is there from various accretions is not simple. I have dealt with the subject in "Freud and the Understanding of Art," *British Journal of Aesthetics*, X (1970), 211–224.

I have discussed the themes and topics of this book with many friends, colleagues, and pupils, and I would find it hard to thank them individually. I am grateful to Dr. Frederic Weiss for letting me see how well the "Rat Man" case lends itself to exposition of Freud's view of the neurosis, and for various suggestions. My wife, Mary Day, and Katherine Backhouse have given me invaluable help with the preparation of the text. And I owe a debt to Dr. Leslie Sohn but for whom I would not have the necessary qualification for writing either about Freud or about psychoanalysis.

CONTENTS

BIOGRAPHICAL NOTE

May 6, 1856	Sigmund Freud born.
1860	Arrives in Vienna.
1873	Enters university.
November 1882	Hears from Breuer of Anna O.
October 1885– February 1886	Works in Paris with Charcot.
1886	Starts private practice; marries Martha Bernays.
November 1887	Meets Wilhelm Fliess.
December 1887	Uses hypnotic suggestion.
1890	Begins to use cathartic method.
1892–1898	Development of free association.
1892	Writes "Preliminary Communication" jointly with Breuer.
1895	Publishes *Studies on Hysteria* and writes "Scientific Project"
March 1896	First use of term "psychoanalysis."
August 1897	Self-analysis begins.
1897	Rejection of "seduction theory," and awareness of infantile sexuality.

1898–1899	Writes *The Interpretation of Dreams* (published 1900).
October 1902	Wednesday-evening meetings begin.
1905	Publishes *Three Essays on Sexuality, Jokes and Their Relation to the Unconscious*, and Dora case-history.
1906–1913	Association with Jung.
October 1907– Spring 1909	"Rat Man's" analysis.
April 1908	First International Psychoanalytical Congress, Salzburg.
September 1909	Visits Clark University, Worcester, Mass., *Five Lectures* delivered.
February 1910– June 1914	"Wolf Man's" analysis.
1914	"On Narcissism"; first mention of the ego ideal, later the superego.
March–August 1915	Writes twelve metapsychological essays, of which only five survive.
1915–1917	*Introductory Lectures* delivered at Vienna University.
1919–1920	At work on *Beyond the Pleasure Principle*; the death instinct postulated.
April 1923	First operation for cancer. Publishes *The Ego and the Id*; the structural theory of the mind formulated.
July 1925	Writes *Inhibitions, Symptoms and Anxiety*.
May 1933	Freud's books burned in Berlin.
May 1936	Eightieth birthday: Fellowship of Royal Society, and many honors.
June 1938	Journey to London.
September 23, 1939	Death.

SIGMUND FREUD

The abbreviations used in the notes throughout the book are as follows:

The Origins of Psychoanalysis	Kris
Sigmund Freud: Life and Work	Jones
The Letters of Sigmund Freud and Arnold Zweig	Zweig
Standard Edition of *The Complete Psychological Works of Sigmund Freud*	Volume and page number only, e.g., II, 231

The First Phase

●

1

Sigmund Freud was born on May 6, 1856, in the small Moravian town of Freiberg, then in the Austro-Hungarian Empire, now in Czechoslovakia, where he was brought up, much as a country child, until 1859, when the family moved, first and briefly to Leipzig, then to Vienna. The long train journeys that this move involved—on one occasion, as he passed through Breslau, the gas jets, which were the first he had seen, put the young child in mind of souls burning in hell[1]—became the object of a number of early anxieties, and a phobia of traveling by train never altogether left him.

The family into which Freud was born was complex in its generations. His father, a wool merchant who never attained more than modest success, was forty at the time of Freud's birth; his

[1] Kris, p. 237.

mother, Jakob Freud's second wife, was twenty. By the first marriage, there were two grown-up half brothers, one of whom already had a son, John, who was to be Freud's childhood companion—his companion, as he was to put it, "in crime."[2] Ambivalence toward the father, in which hate mingled with fear and pity, as well as with love; a passionate and sensuous attachment to the mother; intense resentment of other brothers and sisters, both elders and new arrivals; and a ready displacement of feeling across the various members of the family circle, so that a much older brother might become scapegoat for the father, or, in the momentary absence of the mother, a nanny could draw upon herself the child's fears and jealousy—these were not merely to be the great themes of Freud's theory of the human condition, they were the overt experiences of his own childhood. "It is reasonable to suppose," Freud's biographer writes of his life's work, "that this restless search into the meaning of humanity and human relations was first generated in connection with the puzzling problems of his early family life."[3]

Neither at school nor at university did Freud give any clear indication of the direction that his life would take. There had been childhood dreams of becoming a general or a minister of state, and these had given way to a far-ranging curiosity about all aspects of human culture. Only a limited number of careers were open to a Viennese Jew, and when Freud decided to become a medical student—after, he says, listening to a public reading of Goethe's "Ode to Nature"—it was the desire to acquire knowledge rather than to alleviate suffering that drew him.

[2] Kris, p. 219.
[3] Jones, I, 33.

I

The first item in the Standard Edition of Freud's works is, suitably enough, the report that Freud submitted to the College of Professors in the Faculty of Medicine at Vienna University in April 1886, on his return from Paris, where he had been studying with Jean-Martin Charcot, the famous French professor of neurology and the director of the Salpêtrière, through the previous winter. Suitably enough: for the Standard Edition is, to give it its full title, the *Standard Edition of the Complete Psychological Works of Sigmund Freud*. At one point in his report Freud writes,

> Charcot used to say that, broadly speaking, the work of anatomy was finished and that the theory of the organic diseases of the nervous system might be said to be complete: what had next to be dealt with was the neuroses. This pronouncement may, no doubt, be regarded as no more than an expression of the turn which his own activities have taken.[4]

Or, we might say, of the turn that Freud's activities were about to take. For the visit to Paris was undoubtedly the turning point, the great turning point, in Freud's life. Till then concerned largely with histology or the anatomy of the nervous system, Freud now moved increasingly in the direction of psychopathology. It would be wrong to think of Freud as moving, for much of the way, in Charcot's footsteps. But that so great a scientist as Charcot should have seen fit to turn his attention to such matters as hysteria and hypnotism must have been a great source of inspiration and strength to someone with

[4] I, 10.

Freud's training and background. The two men had at least a common point of departure.

In his obituary of Charcot—Charcot died in 1893—Freud ascribes the peculiar character and authority of the man's work and of his contribution to science to the "good fortune"[5] whereby he combined anatomical knowledge and clinical experience. If we are to understand Freud's achievement, we must see how his ideas too evolved under these twin influences: we must observe how the clinical findings interacted with the presuppositions retained from neurology. It is often said that all that is good in Freud's work derives from the first source, and that this was contaminated or clouded by what accrued to him from the second source. Such a view is, I think, quite false: it is false in the estimate it offers of Freud's work, and it can also mislead us as to its character. To appreciate the work in its richness as it evolved, we must note how the clinical and theoretical sources flow together.

I shall make reference to the clinical findings as occasion arises—meaning by this phrase not only Freud's case-histories but also a number of studies in which he drew upon both primary and secondary material.[6] But, on the theoretical side, it is worth pointing out that Freud's first teacher, Ernst Brücke, the director of the

[5] III, 13.
[6] For the case histories, see those included in the *Studies on Hysteria* (1893–1895), the Dora case (largely written 1901, published 1905), the Rat Man case (1909) and the Wolf Man case (largely written 1914, published 1918). Studies based on written sources include the Leonardo da Vinci essay (1910) and the case of Senatspräsident Schreber (1911). A somewhat special position is occupied by the Little Hans case (1909), which was conducted by the boy's father but in consultation with Freud. *The Interpretation of Dreams* (1900) is in part a record of Freud's epic self-analysis.

Institute of Physiology, derived from the famous Berlin circle of scientists that included Emil Du Bois-Reymond and the great Hermann Helmholtz. This group, whose influence was far-reaching, was distinguished by its uncompromising opposition to vitalism—a fashionable mid-nineteenth-century doctrine, which held that special unobservable forces had to be introduced into the biological sciences in order to account for the phenomenon of living matter—and by its adherence to a rigorous mechanism. Years later Freud spoke of Brücke as the man "who carried more weight with me than anyone else in my whole life,"[7] and it would seem that it was above all in his theoretical standpoint that Freud continued to be Brücke's student. Though he freed himself from any crude form of mechanism, Freud always identified the scientific *Weltanschauung* with a total commitment to the principle of universal causality.

Charcot's influence on Freud was not merely exemplary. Freud was in Paris from October 13, 1885, to February 28, 1886, and for seventeen weeks of this period he was a regular attendant at Charcot's clinic. He listened to his lectures, he accompanied him on his ward visits through the Salpêtrière, he engaged himself to translate his writings into German, and he worked in his laboratory on the anatomy of the brain. But it was, of course, on the newfound topic of hysteria that Freud had most to learn from Charcot, and, specifically, there were three lessons that were to be of enduring value.

First, there was Charcot's rejection of the traditional diagnosis of hysteria, which went back to antiquity and which attributed the disease either to "imagination" or to an irritation of the womb or uterus (the Greek *hystera*

[7] XX, 253.

= womb). Ironically, it was Charcot's insistence on this point and his instatement of hysteria as a nervous disorder that for so long influenced Freud against any sexual etiology, or origin, for the neuroses. Secondly, there was Charcot's discovery that in the traumatic hysterias—i.e., hysterias consequent upon an accident (which had attracted the attention of doctors largely on account of the expensive court cases that centered round them)—the symptoms are delimited not in accordance with the anatomy of the nervous system but by reference to our ordinary concepts of the body. So, for instance, an hysteric will have a paralysis of the leg, in the sense of that limb as far up as its insertion into the hip, or of the arm, meaning that part of the body which is unclothed by a sleeveless dress, though neither of these areas corresponds to a neurophysiological grouping. Hysteria, as Freud was to put it, *"behaves as though anatomy did not exist, or as though it had no knowledge of it."*[8] Thirdly, Charcot revealed a close link between hysteria and hypnotism in that hysterical symptoms could be simulated in nonhysterics by hypnotic suggestion, and, conversely, the symptoms of traumatic hysterics could be removed or modified by hypnotic suggestion.

The second and third of these findings fit together in a startling and significant fashion, for they imply that in the case of a large number of hysterical symptoms, at any rate, ideas or concepts have agency: i.e., ideas are effective in the genesis, in the maintenance, and in the extirpation of the symptoms. The symptoms, that is, are "ideogenic." Precisely how aware Charcot himself was of the implications is unclear, and Freud gives differing accounts of the matter.[9] Moreover, the over-all or causal

[8] I, 169; cf. I, 48–49.
[9] Cf. I, 160, and XX, 13–14.

picture of hysteria to which Charcot subscribed was strictly physiological, not psychological. The capacity to develop the disease was essentially connected with a deterioration of the brain, which was hereditary. All other etiological factors were regarded as purely incidental or as *agents provocateurs*. Among these factors traumatic events might or might not figure. It was only if they did that the hysteria was traumatic and the symptoms "ideogenic." If Charcot's discovery of the role of ideas in neurotic disorder was to be vital for the history of psychoanalysis, in his own thinking it played a strictly limited role.

On his return from Paris, Freud established a practice in the nervous diseases, of which hysteria was one of the most important. Notices of the practice were sent out on Easter Sunday 1886, and it soon proved sufficiently lucrative for Freud to take a step he had delayed for over four years: in September 1886 he married Martha Bernays.

Meanwhile, in the face of official opposition, which thought such interests undignified, Freud endeavored to present Charcot's findings to his scientific colleagues. In his own practice, however, he seems at first to have relied entirely on current physical methods of treatment —hydrotherapy, electrotherapy, massage, and the Weir-Mitchell rest cure. It is only on December 2, 1887, that we find Freud writing to his new friend, Wilhelm Fliess, "I have plunged into hypnotism and have had all sorts of small but peculiar successes."[10]

Fliess was to be a great figure in Freud's life, but to understand the significance of hypnosis in Freud's clinical thinking, it is to another and older friend, no less

[10] Kris, p. 53.

an influence upon the course of his life and also to be outgrown, that we must turn. For when Freud did take up hypnosis, though he employed it in the classical manner that Charcot had shown was peculiarly appropriate to hysteria—in other words, for the removal of troublesome symptoms by counterinstructions—he also had another use for it. "From the very first," Freud wrote in the so-called *Autobiographical Study*, "I made use of hypnosis in *another* manner, apart from hypnotic suggestion."[11] To understand the reference, we must invoke the name of Josef Breuer. For Breuer was a well-known practicing doctor in Vienna with some repute as a scientist and teacher, who had, a number of years before, taken on treatment of a case which was in retrospect to achieve historical significance.

The patient, later known as "Anna O.," was, at the time of falling ill, twenty-one. She was a girl of high intellectual gifts, vivacious, imaginative, but also of a sharp and critical cast of mind. Emotionally and sexually she was quite immature, and, in an effort to enliven the monotonous existence to which she was condemned inside a puritanical family circle, she had resorted to systematic daydreaming, to what she called her "private theater," which, according to Breuer, was to have such a baneful influence on her health. In July 1880 her father fell ill of an abscess, and died in April 1881. Anna O. devoted herself to nursing him until she herself had to take to her bed, and it was a this point, in December 1880, that Breuer undertook her treatment.

The symptoms of which she complained were a rigid paralysis of the right side sometimes extending to the left, a severe nervous cough, an aversion to nourishment (for several weeks she was unable to drink and could

[11] XX, 19.

eat only fruit), and disturbances of sight and speech (for two weeks she was totally unable to speak her native language). In addition, there were conditions of consciousness which Breuer called *"absences,"* or, as the disease progressed and they became more systematic, a *"condition seconde,"* in which she was pursued by hallucinations and behaved in a "naughty" or violent fashion. The *absences* would be followed by a deep sleep from which she would emerge into an autohypnotic state for which she invented the word "clouds": in this state, she would mutter words as though they were part of the dialogue in an incident she was enacting. Out of this heterogeneous material there emerged a therapy, which can as truly be said to have devised itself as to have been constructed by Breuer. I shall trace the steps by which this happened.

On one occasion, between Breuer's visits, someone, overhearing some of the words Anna O. was muttering to herself, repeated them to her: Anna O. immediately joined in, and told a story in which these same words occurred; after that she woke up much calmer—and the next *absence* was evidently occupied by a fresh set of ideas. Breuer, on hearing of this, repeated the ruse with marked success. It was called the "talking cure," or "chimney-sweeping,"[12] and soon, if the cure was not employed, Anna O. would wake up in a disturbed state and would show every sign of an accumulation or clutter of stories. Her condition became a function of the time that had elapsed since the last talking cure. After her father's death the stories became more frightening, and the need for the cure increased. This was the first step.

Exactly a year after her father's death, Anna O.'s *absences* began to be dominated by memories of that

[12] II, 30. Both phrases are in English in the original.

year, which she then proceeded to relive, down to quite specific visual experiences, day by day. In addition, the events of the period from her father's illness to her own collapse—which was, Breuer was convinced, the incubation period of the hysteria—began to make themselves heard. And then something remarkable and unexpected occurred. Anna O. recited an event from this early period, and then a symptom disappeared. The symptom was her inability to drink, and the event was her going into her lady companion's room and seeing to her disgust her little dog drinking out of a glass. The second step in the evolution of the therapy was taken when Breuer, observing what had happened, set out to exploit it. Taking each symptom in turn, he asked Anna O., during her autohypnotic periods, when it had previously occurred, and with the answer the symptom disappeared. And when Breuer found that this method did not allow him as much time as he needed, he pushed the therapy a stage further by supplementing the autohypnotic periods with a period of hypnosis. On the progress of the treatment Breuer made two observations: first, that it was enough to jump over only one occurrence of a given symptom for the therapy to be inefficacious; secondly, that a symptom emerged with greatest force at the moment it was being talked away.

Gradually all the symptoms were traced back to determining causes during the early stages of nursing her father: and in each case the symptom bore the traces of, or had a conceptual link with, the event which was its cause. So, on the last day of the treatment—before "the untoward event,"[13] of which we shall hear more, and on which it abruptly terminated—the paralysis of her right side and her occasional loss of command over the

[13] XIV, 12.

German language were traced back to a hallucination she had experienced one night at her father's bedside while awaiting the arrival of a surgeon from Vienna. In her waking dream she had seen a snake approaching to bite her father. Her right arm, which was over the back of the chair, had gone to sleep and she couldn't move it. And when she tried to pray she could think of nothing until some English children's verses came to her.

What emerged from this case was that a symptom can be talked away; that this talking away occurs in a hypnotic condition; and that to be effective, it takes the form of reciting the originating cause of the symptom. From this two consequences seemed to follow, one rather more immediately than the other: that hypnosis can be employed in a diagnostic role, to discover the origin of a symptom, and that a symptom must have been ac-quired in a state of consciousness parallel to that in which it can be removed, i.e., a hypnoid state. And, finally, Breuer formed an over-all hypothesis: that, until cure is achieved, the symptoms may appear in normal consciousness but the stimulus remains "in the uncon-scious."[14] In other words, Breuer postulated a persistent causal factor, which he located in the mind, though not in consciousness.

Breuer told Freud of the incident in November 1882, and Freud, who was deeply impressed, in turn told Charcot of it during his stay in Paris, and it was (accord-ing to the *Autobiographical Study*) Charcot's evident lack of interest that damped Freud's enthusiasm; so that it was only when he was well engaged in his own practice

[14] II, 45. This is the first mention of the term, and the fact that it occurs in quotation marks may suggest, according to the editors of the Standard Edition, that it derives from Freud.

that he returned to the incident and began to employ hypnosis in the new or "cathartic manner," as opposed to suggestion.

There are five cases that we know Freud treated in this new way: that of Frau Emmy von N., said to be the first where the new method was used "to a large extent,"[15] which began in the early summer of either 1888 or 1889 and lasted a year; that of Fräulein Elizabeth von R., in the autumn of 1892, which Freud described as his "first full-length analysis of hysteria"[16]; that of Miss Lucy R., at the end of 1892; and two slightly later but undated cases, those of Katharina and Frau Cäcilie M. Our knowledge of these cases, and that of Anna O., derives from the fact that Freud managed to persuade Breuer, somewhat reluctantly, to cooperate in a joint work in which the various case histories would be written up and some more general chapters appended. Collaboration was slow and uneasy, and significantly, in the final version, each section appears over the signature of one or other of the two authors.

In March 1895, fourteen years after the case of Anna O., the work was published under the title *Studies on Hysteria*. But a "Preliminary Communication," later to serve as an introduction to the whole, had been put out jointly in early 1893. Based on the cases of Anna O. and Emmy von N., it does not go much beyond Breuer's original findings, but it brings them together in a neat formulation, which Freud was to repeat on a number of occasions as being *the* discovery of the period—"Hysterics suffer mainly from reminiscences."[17] The "Pre-

[15] II, 105*n*.
[16] II, 139.
[17] II, 7.

liminary Communication" also sets these findings inside a somewhat broader conception of mental functioning.

Hysteria arises because an event is experienced, probably painful in character, and the memory of it does not fade or lose its affect in any of the normal ways. These ways are listed as "abreaction" (which means, roughly, being flushed away by the attendant emotion), entering a complex of associations, or, simply, being forgotten. A memory holds out against these natural processes either because of the nature of the event, so that the person in trying to forget it represses it, which is a way of preserving it, or because of the nature of the person's psychic state when he experienced the event—he was in a hypnoid or semihypnoid state. Of these two possibilities it is the latter that is dominant in the "Preliminary Communication": the view, familiar from Charcot, that hypnosis is a kind of artificial hysteria is now balanced by the view that hysteria derives from self-induced hypnosis. The memories that are not worn away persist, but they remain inaccessible to normal consciousness and thus form a second consciousness, or *condition seconde*. Chronic hysterical symptoms or hysterical attacks are intrusions of this second state into normal consciousness, either through innervation of part of the body (a symptom) or through temporary control of the whole person (an attack); in either case, the hysterical phenomena reproduce the traumatic event or express memories of it. The trauma is not, as Charcot maintained, simply an *agent provocateur*, which releases the symptom, which then has a life of its own. It, or rather the memory of it, is an agent still at work: it acts as a "*directly* releasing cause." And the consequence of this— and also the evidence for it—is that if, under hypnosis, the pathogenic memory is got rid of through verbal expression, the hysterical phenomenon disappears. A complication is that every symptom has a multiple causation or is "overdetermined": it will contain references to more than one element of the trauma.

The theory as it stands is clearly bold, though still somewhat sparse. And Freud was most evidently to feel its inadequacies. Even by the time of Emmy von N. he thought that the nature of the symptom needed elaboration. How is the symptom related to the past event it derives from? But his most serious doubts related to what the theory had to say about the genesis of hysteria. Yet, strangely enough, the theory of the "Preliminary Communication" received its sharpest challenge, and underwent its first revision, at what must have seemed its securest part: its implications for therapy, or the role it assigned to hypnosis.

In the autumn of 1892 Freud undertook the treatment of Fräulein Elizabeth von R. She came to him originally complaining of pains in the leg and a difficulty in walking. The account she gave of her life indicated a series of family misfortunes—the death of her father, the marriage and subsequent alienation of one sister, the early death of another in pregnancy, the unaccountably difficult behavior of her widowed brother-in-law, the serious illness of her mother—but in none of this could Freud find a trauma fit to precipitate hysteria. So he decided to hypnotize his patient. But she would not be hypnotized. And, at much the same period, he also failed with Miss Lucy R., an English governess who was suffering from general fatigue and exhibited the curious symptom of being haunted by the smell of burnt pudding. Indeed, hypnosis would seem always to have had its difficulties for Freud: it was partly to improve his technique that he had in 1889 journeyed to Nancy to visit the great Bernheim, and Liébeault, the *doyen* of hypnotism.

On this occasion, Freud decided not to be deterred by failure. Instead, he made a fresh assumption, to the effect that his patients "knew everything that was of pathogenic significance and that it was only a question of obliging them to communicate it."[18] In his first effort to solve this question, Freud hit upon the so-called "pressure technique," in which he merely placed his hands upon the patient's forehead and told her she could remember everything. This method, which aimed at retaining the moral, while abandoning the causal, efficacy of hypnosis, was finally given up in 1900. Another method, of which we see the first traces in the Emmy von N. case, simply consisted in encouraging the patient to say whatever came into her head without constraint or forethought. The physician had finally abdicated the directive powers he had assumed as hypnotist, and the central diagnostic technique of psychoanalysis, later to be known as "free association," slowly came into being.

Initially the case of Elizabeth von R. responded to the new technique, and Freud began to hear of a young man, as yet unidentified, to whom she was evidently attracted, and who set up for her some conflict of duty. There were also occasions on which no results were forthcoming. The patient remained silent, and Freud had to ask himself whether this new method too had not its severe limitations. The editors of the Standard Edition dwell on the sense of drama that in retrospect invests Freud's decision to persist with free association despite its draw-

[18] II, 110.

backs. It "led him directly into the uncharted world which he was to spend his whole life in exploring."[19]

For Freud became convinced that, on each occasion when Elizabeth von R. remained silent or the flow of association dried up, there was some relevant fact which the patient knew but which, for some reason or other, she would not, or could not, bring out. This received confirmation from the fact that, when she overcame this inability, what she brought out was an idea which she found "incompatible," or repugnant to her moral being; the more reluctantly the idea emerged, the more incompatible it proved to be. So it turned out that the young man who attracted her was her brother-in-law, and that, at her sister's deathbed, the thought had struck her, "Now he is free again, and I can be his wife." This new phenomenon Freud described by saying that he was encountering *resistance*; and in the resistance to recalling a given idea to consciousness, he saw the converse of an earlier process of *defense* or *repression* in which that idea had been put out of consciousness. The words "defense" and "repression" are originally used interchangeably, though with the implication that repression is a specific form of defense. After a few years "repression" wins out, and we hear almost nothing of "defense" until *Inhibitions, Symptoms and Anxiety.*

In the "Preliminary Communication" there had already been a reference to defense—though not under that description—as one of the two ways in which an event can become traumatic. Later Freud suggested that the reference to hypnoid states (the other way) was due entirely to Breuer, and that the split between the two men came over these rival etiological hypotheses.[20]

[19] II, xvii.
[20] VII, 27*n*.

Whether this is historically correct or not—or whether the break came over the increasing emphasis Freud was to lay on sexuality, or whether it was not ultimately a temperamental clash, the audacity of Freud's mind as against the greater timidity of Breuer's—it is certainly true that the development of Freud's thought can be gauged by the degree to which, as he put it, the notion of defense "forced its way into the foreground."[21] The emphasis on defense is really the beginning of psychoanalysis, and the linkage of defense and resistance into a single concept—so that they become backward-looking and forward-looking criteria for one mental phenomenon —is one of the two things that are meant in talking of psychoanalysis as a *dynamic* theory of the mind. (The other we shall come to by the end of this chapter.) Once we see how this bringing together of an etiological hypothesis and a therapy at once radically alters the content, and yet retains the form, of the original hypnoid state— hypnosis theory, we can see the justice in both the estimates that Freud gave of the relations of psychoanalysis to hypnosis: that psychoanalysts are the "legitimate heirs"[22] of hypnosis, and that psychoanalysis proper "begins only with the new technique that dispenses with hypnosis."[23] And, somewhat more significantly, we can see what an absurd understatement it is to say, as I did just now, that Freud persisted with the new method *despite* its drawbacks.

With defense "in the foreground," several questions arose, each with ramifications enough to destroy the simple theory of the "Preliminary Communication," which was evidently in ruins in Freud's mind, if not in

[21] II, 285.
[22] XVI, 462.
[23] XIV, 16.

Breuer's, by the time that the main text of *Studies on Hysteria* came to be written. And now the wheel has turned full circle. Freud's original doubts had concerned what the theory said about the genesis of hysteria, and it was only the difficulties he encountered in applying the theory that led him to question the therapy; now these difficulties, when worked through, brought him back with a sharpened awareness to his original problem. For he had now three questions to resolve: What is defense? What is defense defense against? And, What are the consequences of defense? These questions, moreover, could not be answered in isolation, since a new answer to one precipitated a reconsideration of the others.

If we put together everything that Freud contributed to the *Studies on Hysteria*—after, that is, the "Preliminary Communication" and a paper that he wrote at the same time, "The Neuro-Psychoses of Defence," we find a picture somewhat like this: An event is experienced, and the experience involves an "incompatible idea." This idea is very often sexual in character. The person tries to forget the idea or to treat it as *"non arrivée."*[24] This effort fails, but there is an "approximate fulfillment of the task" if the incompatible idea can be robbed of the sum of excitation with which it is loaded, or its affect. The affect is then put to another use, and from here onward the various neuropsychoses, which include hysteria, obsessional neurosis, and hallucinatory confusion, follow their different paths.

In this new account four features deserve comment. First, the traumatic event was retained, in the Charcot-Breuer tradition, as the precipitating cause of the psychoneurosis. As to the other factor emphasized in that

[24] III, 48. The terms "psychoneurosis" and "neuropsychosis" are now used interchangeably.

tradition—the predisposition to neurosis—there was now some uncertainty. Freud at one point suggested that in the acquired hysteria—now equated with hysteria through defense—there need be no predisposition. His somewhat inconclusive remarks are, however, best seen as an attempt to free the notion of predisposition from one whole conception of the matter, with its emphasis on heredity, in order to replace it by another.

Secondly, the importance of sexuality is newfound. Originally, under the influence of Charcot, Freud too had depreciated sexuality as an influential factor. In an encyclopedia article on hysteria of 1888, he had written, "As regards what is often asserted to be the preponderant influence of abnormalities in the sexual sphere upon the development of hysteria, it must be said that its importance is as a rule over-estimated."[25] Freud's views changed slowly, very much against the grain, under two powerful influences. First, there was the study of the "actual neuroses"—that is, psychic disorders entirely attributable to current or ongoing factors. In a paper of 1895, Freud identified two such disorders—neurasthenia, which had previously been a blanket term, and anxiety neurosis—and he ascribed to each a sexual cause, but in a way that needs understanding. The origin of neurasthenia was said to lie in an impoverished form of sexual discharge, generally masturbation; the origin of anxiety neurosis in an incomplete form of sexual discharge, generally *coitus interruptus* or other chaste practices.[26] In other words, sexuality was introduced into the etiology of the actual neuroses—in contrast to the way in which it will figure in that of the psycho-neuroses—as something essentially physical, as a prod-

[25] I, 50.
[26] III, 109, 114, 150–51, 268.

uct which, if undischarged, can become toxic. Freud talked throughout of "sexual noxae." However, it should be noted that, though he treated failure of discharge as a physical phenomenon, he introduced psychological considerations to explain *why* discharge is either impoverished or incomplete. So, for instance, an elderly bachelor, who is led into excessive sexual performance by his young mistress, is said to achieve incomplete discharge because physical desire was only partially linked to psychical desire.[27] Again, masturbation is said to provide impoverished discharge because the link with psychical desire is effected at too low a psychic level. And, when Freud did move from a predominantly physical to a predominantly psychological theory of the role of sexuality, two features of this early theory remained: first, the connection of pathological states with lack of discharge of some kind or other, and secondly (a view that was to have a long and important history, only to be abandoned in 1926), the equation of anxiety with transformed sexuality. The other powerful influence in bringing Freud around to a new estimate of sexuality was his clinical practice in the various psychoneuroses; for he increasingly found that the trail of free association, in which he now put his trust, ended in sexual ideas.

This leads on to the third feature that deserves comment: the individuation of the different neuropsychoses. To follow the over-all account Freud gives of the varied consequences of defense, we need to grasp an underlying philosophical assumption that Freud retained throughout his work and which probably derives from the Viennese philosopher Franz Brentano, whose seminars he had attended as a student. And that assump-

[27] Kris, pp. 79, 93.

tion is that every mental state or condition can be analyzed into two components: an idea, which gives the mental state its object or what it is directed upon; and its charge of affect, which gives it its measure of strength or efficacy. Now, it is always the idea that draws down upon the mental state disapproval or that marks it out as "incompatible," but the disapproval is vented only if the idea is charged with affect. A weak idea can get by. Accordingly, what defense does is to effect the fissure of idea and affect within the repressed memory. Once this has been achieved, the various psychoneuroses can be explicated by following up the different fates or vicissitudes that befall these two elements. Freud's philosophical assumption about the nature of mental phenomena thus permits a singular neatness of classification and exposition.[28] In hysteria, the vital factor is "conversion," or the transformation of affect into some bodily manifestation, the precise nature or limit of which is, as we have seen, significantly determined by the idea: while the idea itself, or its memory trace, forms "the nucleus of a second psychical group." When the idea is reinforced with affect through a repetition or revival of the original experience, there is either an hysterical attack or else abreaction and the passing of the hysteria. The *Studies on Hysteria* abound in such cases. In obsessional neurosis, the capacity for conversion is absent. Accordingly, both affect and idea remain in the psychic field and pursue divergent though linked paths. The affect attaches itself to another idea, which is "falsely" or "freely" connected with it, so as to form a self-reproach, while the original idea is able to remain in consciousness, its very weakness assuring its immunity from further repression. Freud cited the case of a girl who, over-

[28] III, 45–60.

whelmed by feelings of guilt about masturbation, began to accuse herself of all manners of crime. Whenever she read of a case of counterfeiting or murder, she would ask herself whether it was not she who had done it. In hallucinatory confusion, idea and affect are simultaneously rejected, but at too heavy a price: the experience is treated as though it had never occurred, and along with it a piece of reality that is inseparable from it is also disposed of. Asylums, Freud said, are full of such cases: the woman whose baby has died and who rocks a piece of wood, or the jilted girl who is arrayed in her wedding dress. For them the phrase was invented, "the flight into psychosis."

All this, of course, is by way of description of the various psychoneuroses. In time the descriptions will be refined. But more important, they will be supplemented. Description will be supplemented by explanation: explanation of why one particular path is followed rather than another, why defense has the consequences it has. In a letter to Fliess dated May 30, 1896, Freud talked, quaintly, of "the choice of neurosis,"[29] and this problem —the phrase is not to be taken literally, of course— remained with him for years, receiving, each time he returned to it, a yet more complex resolution.

My final comment on Freud's theory at this stage is negative. It might be expected, particularly in view of Freud's earlier doubts on the matter, that, along with this extended classification of the neuroses, would have gone a deeper inquiry into the nature of the symptom. It is true that the introduction of free association permitted Freud to generalize Charcot's findings about the symptoms of traumatic hysteria—that they were ideogenic—over all the neuroses: for, under analysis, it

[29] Kris, p. 164. For its first use in print, see VII, 275.

emerged that the concept under which the symptom fell was invariably connected, if not directly, then associatively, with the traumatic event. But as to the nature of the symptom, Freud contented himself with a phrase, "mnemic symbol." This phrase does indicate some advance on the theory of the "Preliminary Communication." For the maxim employed there, "Hysterics suffer mainly from reminiscences," implies that symptoms are caused by overpreserved memories, so that, when the memories are abreacted, the symptoms will disappear. Psychological and physical phenomena are more intimately brought together when it is asserted that symptoms *are* memories.

For the next move forward in the theory, we must look to an interaction between two of the features I have picked out: typically, the new modifying the old. We have already noted that Freud, following Charcot and Breuer, retained the distinction between the predisposition to neurosis and the precipitating cause: though he reversed their relative importance, and even expressed some doubts about the ubiquity of the former. However, as the etiological importance of sexuality increases, the distinction between the two got blurred. The trauma, which Breuer had envisaged as being contained within narrow temporal limits, is now stretched out across time so that it becomes identical with the "history" of the patient—as also does the process of defense. Then, in "Further Remarks on the Neuro-Psychoses of Defence" (written in the winter of 1895–96), in "The Aetiology of Hysteria" (summer 1896), and in Draft K, despatched to Fliess on January 1, 1896, we find a startling etiology proposed: In all cases, the original traumatic event is a sexual experience in early childhood, i.e., before puberty, which is called "the primal scene" or "the sexual scene." The nature of the primal scene determines the choice of neurosis. In hysteria the primal scene is a passive sexual experience, or seduction, with an adult, sustained around the ages of five to seven: in obsessional neurosis it is an active sexual experience, or rape, with another child, carried out at a slightly later age. Furthermore, in all cases of obsessional neurosis there is a substratum of hysteria which is accounted for by the invariable priority of a passive over an active sexual experience. The causal efficacy of these events is, however, complicated: above all, it is deferred. *"The traumas of childhood operate in a deferred fashion."*[30] At the time of its occurrence the sexual experience, which, Freud insisted, always involves an actual irritation of the genitals, makes little impact and is forgotten. With the oncoming of puberty, however, a fresh experience (the "later trauma") revives it in memory, and this leads to repression. At first, the repression is comparatively successful, and all the patient exhibits are the primary symptoms of defense. Then the defense fails, and there is the "return of the repressed," which does not, however, enter consciousness. Further repression occurs, and the resultant symptoms, or the symptoms of the neurosis, are called "compromise formations." Beyond this, there can be secondary symptoms, in that the true character of the symptom, or that of which the symptom is a mnemic symbol, begins to show through, or the symptom itself becomes threatening, and, in either case, the symptom is defended against. Typically, an obsessional idea is followed by the construction of an obsessional ceremonial to ward off the idea.

The new account was obviously a leap forward in complexity, in sophistication, and in scope or empirical

[30] III, 167*n*.

richness. It thrust the history of the neurosis deep into the life of the individual, and it deployed for the first time a number of concepts that were to be retained in Freudian theory: "the return of the repressed," "compromise formation," "secondary defense." And yet, in the perspective of Freudian thought as it was to develop, perhaps the most striking feature of the account is something negative. For all its references to the infantile, for all its references to sexuality, one thing it totally omits is infantile sexuality. There is no admission that the infant has sexual impulses.

This point emerges clearly when we look at the matter the other way round, and see what Freud had to put into the account in order to make it adequate without appeal to infantile sexuality. There are two pieces of the account that fill this role. The first is that the sexual origins of the neurosis are said to lie in a passive sexual event endured by the infant at the hands of an adult. And, if in the case of obsessional neurosis reference is made to sexual activity, this activity is construed as a kind of mimicry, whereby the child does to others what was first done to it; in other words, Freud's insistence that obsessional neurosis invariably rests upon a substratum of hysteria has value not only for explaining the behavior of obsessional neurotics,[31] but also for safeguarding a hypothesis about the infant and his emotional development. We might express the point by saying that one way in which Freud tried to block the road to infantile sexuality was—though he tried hard not to think of it in this light—by invoking a quite scandalous hypothesis

[31] It is interesting that he clung to the empirical claim that "every obsessional neurosis seems to have a substratum of hysterical symptoms" (XX, 113) many years after its significance for theory had evaporated.

about the family life of the Viennese *bourgeoisie*. The second piece of the account that serves this purpose is the assertion that the effect of the "sexual" scene or, to put it more bluntly, of the seduction of the child by a parent—occurs at a distance, at a distance in time. "It is not the experiences themselves which act traumatically," Freud wrote, "but their revival as a *memory* after the subject has entered on sexuality."[32] In insisting that the memory is effective though the event is not, Freud believed he had sealed off any need to credit the infant with sexual responses.

However, it would be quite wrong to overlook the specific merits of the so-called seduction theory. In the first place, it insisted that symptoms must be traced back to events that possess "the suitability to serve as a determinant" or are endowed with adequate "traumatic force."[33] Too often, Freud thought, in the explanation of a disorder, events are invoked that are "at once innocuous and unrelated to the character of the hysterical symptom." No one could say this of infantile seductions. Secondly, the theory provided an answer to the question that was always to puzzle Freud: Why should ideas with a sexual content be found "incompatible" and repressed? Why should not sexuality be simply enjoyed, at any rate to the extent that the maturity of the person permitted? And the answer it gives is in terms of a discrepancy in excitement between the original event, which means little to the infant, and the memory, for which the adolescent is quite unprepared and to which he therefore reacts abnormally or pathologically. The implication is that against an original sexual experience

[32] III, 164.
[33] III, 193–94.

which the adolescent could take as such, he would be able to resort to normal defense.

2

A year and a half later, Freud was to make two momentous discoveries that would revolutionize his whole thinking. Both were originally disclosed in letters to Fliess, and they were only slowly assimilated into the published work.

The first, which is ultimately the more significant (and which, incidentally, is the other element in the characterization of the psychoanalytic theory of the mind as dynamic), is that the proper object or target of defense is not an event, but an impulse. Memories, in other words, are found "incompatible" and repressed not because of the events that they are of, but because of the impulses expressed in the events that they are of. On May 2, 1897, Freud wrote, "The psychical structures which in hysteria are subjected to repression are not properly speaking memories, . . . but impulses deriving from the primal scenes."[34] And then, on September 21, Freud produced his second discovery: "I will confide in you at once the great secret that has been slowly dawning on me in the last few months. I no longer believe in my *neurotica*."[35] In other words, the primal scenes were divested of any claim to historical accuracy, and the patients' recollections of seduction or rape were assigned not to truth, but to fiction. Many years later, Freud was to write, "My mistake was of the same kind as would be made by someone who believes that the legendary story of the early kings of Rome (as told by Livy) was his-

[34] Kris, p. 196.
[35] *Ibid.*, p. 215.

torical truth instead of what it is in fact—a reaction
against the memory of times and circumstances that
were insignificant and occasionally, perhaps, in-
glorious."[36] This remark may catch the drama of the
occasion but it goes wrong if it suggests that, at any
time when Freud accepted the seduction theory, he
overlooked, or was insensitive to, the "legendary" interpretations that could have been placed on his patients'
words. Rather, he had considered them, and rejected
them.

Several explanations have been offered of how Freud
came to abandon the seduction theory: his clinical experience, a partial analysis of his sister, or his epic self-
analysis which began in the summer of 1897, both of
which could have compromised his own parents in incestuous indulgence. But it is perhaps more important
to see how the seduction hypothesis was no longer
necessary, indeed was definitely constricting, once the
first of Freud's momentous discoveries had been made.
For, granted the existence of infantile impulses, what
could be more natural than to treat what were otherwise
implausible memories as expressions of those impulses?
Within a couple of years two terms—"screen-memory"
and "phantasy"—were coming to prominence in Freud's
writing and signify a new turn in his interests. For what
was implausible taken as a memory or as a guide to the
past becomes vastly illuminating when seen as an expression of impulse or as a guide to the recesses of the
mind.

So the two discoveries of 1897, linked as they are,
were gradually to make Freud rethink—to revise, to extend, to consolidate—his existing theory. The developmental account of the individual, the role and con-

[36] XX, 35.

sequences of repression, the nature of a symptom, the form of the therapeutic process, the conception of the mind—all are looked at again. I shall start with the last of these, with the conception of the mind, on which so far I have said little, but which was an area where Freud had already developed ideas.

Before we embark on this, one point should be noted. Freud was already, in the late 1890s, investigating the normal mind and its nonpathological workings in order to find a broader base for his theory of the neurosis. Specifically, there were two pieces of normal functioning which he was studying, each of which was to have a book to itself: dreams, to be treated of in the great *The Interpretation of Dreams* of 1900, and errors, to be treated of in the *Psychopathology of Everyday Life* of 1901. When Freud's work with mental illness comes to be overstressed, when his theory is said to be of limited value because of the narrow range of mental phenomena in which he took an interest, it is worth remembering that these books were two of the three which he took pains constantly to bring up to date. And one is his masterpiece.

The Theory of the Mind

ii

So far, we have considered Freud as an empirical
inquirer, as an experimentalist who sought the
characteristics and causes of mental disorder.
But this does not exhaust Freud's psychological
concerns, at this or at any other stage in his
career. For he was also interested in producing
an over-all theory of the mind. In part, the two
concerns are linked. Freud realized that it is only
inside some more general picture of the mind
that any specific account of mental malfunction-
ing will acquire plausibility, let alone explanation.
In this respect Freud's concern with theory derives, as much as his clinical work, from the
tradition of scientific thought in which he grew
up. In part, however, this concern can be seen
as the heir to his earliest desires for the most
comprehensive form of understanding open to
man; and on such occasions he was inclined to

identify his passion for theory, now contrasted to mere empirical or practical understanding, with the philosophical quest. So in a letter of April 4, 1896, we find him writing,

> When I was young, the only thing I longed for was philosophical knowledge, and now that I am going over from medicine to psychology I am in the process of attaining it. I have become a therapist against my will. . . .[1]

This letter was written to Wilhelm Fliess, and it is Freud's correspondence with Fliess, miraculously conserved through the Second World War and brought to light only in 1950, that is the best source for Freud's earliest theoretical endeavors. Fliess was a distinguished Berlin physician and biologist, and the first meeting between the two men took place in the autumn of 1887, arranged, ironically enough, by Breuer. Ironically: since Fliess was to supersede Breuer in Freud's friendship and esteem. For fifteen years the two men were in sustained correspondence, exchanging observations and hypotheses, meeting and holding what they called "conferences" whenever the mounting exigencies of professional and family life permitted. Ernest Jones, in his biography of Freud, has rightly called the years from 1887 to 1902 "the Fliess period." The abrupt way in which the friendship came to an end—Fliess survived until 1928—does something to confirm the view that there was a neurotic aspect to the relationship: it inherited some of Freud's unconscious anger directed against his father, as well as the alternating feelings of love and rivalry experienced toward childhood companions. But the friendship had also a very firm and very realistic basis, and perhaps the

[1] Kris, p. 162.

most comprehensive description of it would be to say that Fliess, unlike the more cautious Breuer, was able to tolerate, indeed to exult in, in some way even to reflect, the soaring quality of Freud's mind. "My first impression," Freud wrote to Fliess, on October 31, 1895, acknowledging a new batch of his scientific papers, "was one of amazement at the existence of someone who was an even greater visionary than I, and that he should be my friend Wilhelm."[2]

Throughout 1895 Freud's thoughts seem to have turned increasingly to the theory of the mind and, in particular, to the relations between the physiological and the psychological levels. The letters to Fliess, whose general scientific knowledge was invaluable to Freud, are full of such references, and then, in early September, on the train back from a "conference" in Berlin, Freud started on an elaborate theoretical work. He wrote at high speed, and the first two parts were completed by September 25; the third part was started on October 5; and the whole, about a hundred pages long, though still unfinished, was sent off to Fliess on October 8. The manuscript, which has come to be known as the "Project for a Scientific Psychology,"[3] remains a torso. Freud, whose feelings about it vacillated, found it ultimately beyond completion. But, even as it stands, it is a work of the utmost boldness, too compressed for ease of reading, let alone for summary.

Freud called the work a "psychology for neurologists,"

[2] Kris, p. 130.
[3] The text of the "Scientific Project" is to be found in Kris, pp. 347–445, and I, 281–387. In this chapter I shall not give detailed page references, for Freud's text must be studied as a whole.

and his phrase at once reveals and conceals its true and complex character. For, on one level, the "Project" is a neurological account of the brain and its functioning. As such it aims at correspondence to the facts of anatomy. On another level, it is a theoretical model of the mind and mental processes, both normal and pathological. When seen in this way, it is to be judged by the success with which it unifies and suggests clinical observations; and the fact that the theoretical terms that it employs (such as "neuron") have a concrete application in neurophysiology can be looked on as a coincidence. However, the two levels on which the "Project" is conceived fit together. For not only was it Freud's conviction, grounded in the materialism that he never abandoned, that psychology must have a physical base, but he also believed that psychological phenomena exhibit many of the same characteristics and characteristic patterns as the neurophysiological phenomena on which they are causally dependent. Hence the occurrence of neurophysiological concepts in psychological theory could be expected to have a corrective or regulative effect: they would ensure the proper shape to the theory. When in 1915 in a paper on "The Unconscious" Freud announced that he had given up all hope of the localization of mental processes—that is to say, of their correlation with specific parts of the brain or nervous system—he also put by, *for the present,* the enterprise of linking psychology and anatomy.[4] But it does not follow, as some critics have hastily assumed, that the neurological model to which the "Project" is committed was not highly useful to Freud, both for the errors from which it saved him and for the speculations which it suggested.

[4] XIV, 175.

The model of the mind presented in the "Project" posits two fundamental types of element and a principle of operation. The elements are, first, the units of structure, or the "material particles" out of which the apparatus is constructed. These are known as "neurons," and they form a complex network. Secondly, there is energy, or quantity, known as Q, whose flow throuh this network is governed by the general laws of motion. The working principle of the model is that of neuronic inertia, or the constancy principle, according to which the apparatus has a tendency to divest itself of energy, or to reduce tension, where tension is identified with the accumulation of energy. From the constancy principle we can, however, immediately infer a difference between sensory neurons, which receive stimulation, and motor neurons, which control movement or action. For energy arises from stimuli and is got rid of, or discharged, through motor activity, of which the preferred form is flight.

At first it might seem that the constancy principle could be stated in terms of the reduction of tension to zero, and that this could be attributed to the mind as its characteristic aim. The mind, in other words, tries to expel all energy as and when it enters the system. But, Freud insisted, this is true of the mind only in what he called its "primary function." A complication arises from the fact that the mind receives stimulation not only from the outside world, as in perception, but also from the inside, from the cells of the body, as in appetite and instinct. It is only if we confine our attention to external stimuli that the simple conception of the mind modeled on the reflex arc of neurophysiology—in which all that is supposed is a sensory or receptor element, a motor element, and discharge that is immediate and total, i.e., equivalent to stimulation—is adequate. The energy that arises from internal or endogenous stimuli and that corresponds to the major human needs of hunger, respiration, and sex cannot be discharged in this way. Relief is achieved only if suitable conditions exist in the external world—food, for instance, where the need is hunger; and in order to bring about these conditions, in order, that is, not to remain at the mercy of the environment, the apparatus must learn to engage in what Freud calls "specific actions."

However, if the mind is to be thought of as able to engage in such actions, it stands in need of two further capacities. In the first place, the apparatus must possess some means of registering experience, so that stimuli and conditions of discharge can be appropriately paired off. Otherwise, there could be no assurance that, when the apparatus is stimulated in a certain way, it will initiate the relevant action, and not some other. The model of the mind must, in other words, find room for a representation of memory. Secondly, the apparatus must be able to tolerate an accumulation of energy, upon which it can draw when it engages in whatever action is called for. In the case of external stimulation, the quantity generated is enough to secure its own discharge —as in the reflex arc. But, with internal stimulation, and the need for securing the right conditions in the world before discharge occurs, there has to be a recruitment of energy, or a booster. This can only be from a store of energy, which the apparatus must not try to divest itself of as it enters the system.

Much of the neatness of the "Project" comes from the way in which Freud hit on one and the same modification of the model to accommodate both these requirements. What he did was to introduce a further distinction within the system of neurons. Sensory neurons—and it is with them that the "Project" is basically concerned —are now subdivided into two classes: ϕ-neurons and ψ-neurons. The two classes do not mix, and so we have, by extension, two neuronic systems: the ϕ-system and the ψ-system. The effective difference between the two classes of neuron is this: that ϕ-neurons are totally permeable, they offer no resistance to the flow of quantity through them, and, consequently, are totally unaffected by it, whereas ψ-neurons are to some degree or other impermeable, they offer some resistance to, and hence retain permanent traces of, quantity as it flows through them. Corresponding to this modification in the actual stuff of the model, there is an amendment to its mode of operation. The apparatus still works according to the constancy principle, but this principle is now taken as crediting the mind with the aim, not of eliminating tension, but of keeping it as low as possible or of maintaining an optimum tension. In using stored energy to get rid of current energy along suitable channels of discharge, the mind is said to enter on its "secondary function."

The question that now arises is, How does the division of neurons into two classes account for those extra attributes which the mind needs in order to deal with endogenous stimuli? To answer this we must understand precisely how Freud thought the differentiation between the two classes was effected. On anatomical grounds, he would not allow that the difference lay in the neurons themselves—say, in the kind of tissue out of which they were formed. Instead, he located it in the protoplasm or foreign substance that lies between neurons and through which the paths of conduction run: in what Freud called the "contact-barriers," or, as they were two years later to be renamed by Foster and Sherrington, who also found further evidence for postulating them, "synapses." ϕ-neurons are, then, identified as those neurons which function as though there were no contact-barriers between them: ψ-neurons are those neurons whose contact-barriers make themselves felt to some degree or other. In other words, when a ψ-neuron is filled with energy—or "cathected," in technical language—some resistance will be put up to the passage of this energy into adjacent neurons. Adjacent neurons, note: for, from any given neuron there are a number of paths of conduction, each leading to a different neuron. And within the ψ-system this last fact is of considerable importance: for, though energy, on seeking to leave a particular ψ-neuron, will encounter resistance along every path of conduction, the degree of resistance will vary between the different paths, or, to put it another way, the different neurons to which the paths lead will be "facilitated" to different degrees. The next question to arise is, On what does the lowering of resistance, or the establishment of a "facilitation" between two ψ-neurons, depend? The answer lies in the passage of quantity. It is quantity, plus the frequency of its recurrence, that serves to break down the contact-barriers, and, as a result, the same quantity of energy tends always to select the same path through the neuronic network. But, of course, frequency of recurrence indicates adequacy of discharge. In other words, if a given quantity recurrently follows one specific path through the ψ-system, then it is safe to assume that this is the path along which relief, for that quantity, is to be found. We can now see how the introduction of contact-barriers, which establish permanent pathways through the system, ultimately allows for the paring off of quantities of stimulation and forms of discharge.

Through facilitations—or, more accurately, through the differential between facilitations, so that one path is easier for energy to follow than another—the apparatus has been invested with a form of memory, which, as we have seen, is essential if it is to cope with internal stimulation.

The other essential, if the secondary function of the mental apparatus is to be performed, is that there should be a store of energy. This too Freud accounted for by invoking the hypothesis of contact-barriers. There are some neurons, he postulated, whose contact-barriers are so high that they retain a constant fund of quantity; they are permanently "cathected." These neurons, which lie, of course, in the ψ-system, form what Freud called "the ego." From this fund, energy is sent out to various parts of the system as and when it is wanted: sometimes to boost the flow of energy, sometimes (as we shall see) to retard or control it. Thus the ego has from the start a directive role assigned to it.

We can now see how Freud felt that he could account for both the capacities that the apparatus requires in order to cope with endogenous stimulation by the postulation of contact-barriers or, what is the same thing, by the distinction between ϕ-neurons and ψ-neurons. By a seemingly simple alteration in the model, the powers and operations of the mind have been considerably extended and enhanced.

So far, however, the model of the mind has been presented in an almost totally abstract fashion, and next to no indication has been given how the model relates to what we think of as the ordinary activities of the mind: perception, desire, thought, and so on.

The first step toward this is to locate the model inside the human frame. Of the two neuronic systems, the ϕ-system is that which is turned outward toward the world. Through the "nerve-ending apparatus," which acts as a kind of protective shield, it receives quantities of a very high order of magnitude. (Indeed, Freud speculated that the difference in permeability between the two classes of neurons might find an explanation within the history of the individual: in, that is, the vastly higher stimulation to which the ϕ-neurons have been exposed from the beginning of life. On this view, ϕ-neurons might be seen as a limiting case of ψ-neurons, or as ψ-neurons that have been battered into total penetrability.) Of the quality received by the ϕ-neurons from the outer world, some will be discharged straightaway through the motor apparatus, which is directly attached to the ϕ-system, and some will filter through into the ψ-system, where it will ultimately leave its trace in the form of memory. The ψ-system, on the other hand, lies on the inside of the mental apparatus. Just as the ϕ-system receives direct stimulation from the outside world (perception), the ψ-system, in addition to the quantities it has transferred to it from the ϕ-system, is directly stimulated from the interior or cells of the body (instinct or need). The internal or endogenous stimuli are received by the nuclear neurons of the ψ-system, whereas those quantities which reach the ψ-system through the ϕ-system are first received by the pallium (or "mantle") neurons. The distinction between the pallium and the nuclear neurons of the ψ-system is something to which we shall have to refer later, since it plays a part in the explanation that Freud gave of a type of breakdown to which the mental apparatus is susceptible.

At this stage it is necessary to remember only how the two parts of the ψ-system are arranged.

One difference between the ways in which the apparatus receives quantity from external and from internal sources is that, though in both cases stimulation is more or less continuous, in the case of internal stimuli the quantities are so small that there is a process of accumulation, or "summation," and it is only when a certain threshold has been reached that the facilitations become operative and the flow of energy through the system toward discharge takes place. This process of summation corresponds to what in directly psychological terms are such facts of experience as that hunger does not make itself felt continuously as it mounts. On the contrary, it becomes exigent, and demands satisfaction, only when it attains a peak.

A somewhat special kind of case, standing outside the normal cycle of stimulation and discharge—indeed, it coincides with a temporary failure of the normal contrivances of the apparatus—arises when there is an excessive irruption of quantity through the ϕ-system and into the ψ-system. This occurs either because the stimulation itself is massive, or because the nerve-ending apparatus, which, as we have seen, is the filter for external stimuli, has been evaded, with the result that all contact-barriers are overwhelmed and the network is inundated with quantity in a way that leaves permanent traces. Because of its subjective counterpart, or the way in which it is experienced, this special kind of case is called "pain." Pain, Freud wrote, falls upon the ψ-system like "a strike of lightning."

We have now a comprehensive if still rudimentary account of the way in which the mental apparatus in its secondary function operates: drawing upon stored energy to discharge energy as it enters the system, with the aim of reducing tension, no longer to zero, but to an optimum. This mode of operation is acquired through a process of "biological learning"—of need followed by satisfaction—and it finds its base or substrate in the pathways imprinted through the neuronic network. I have called this account rudimentary because it depicts this learning process as still at a very early stage. For instance, the concept of "specific action," which is integral to the fully fledged secondary functioning of the apparatus, has not yet acquired application. Freud, indeed, was at pains to point out how complex this concept is, and how many different factors have to be brought into conjunction before it is appropriate: there must be the thought of an object needed; there must be the memory of an experience of satisfaction to which that object gave rise; and there must be the mastery of a physical movement capable of bringing about the conditions under which the experience originally occurred. For Freud, the evolution of the discharge of bodily stimuli from its most primitive form, in some kind of internal change (e.g., screaming, emotional expression), through the experience of satisfaction at the hands of an extraneous helper (e.g., mother, nurse), to the stage of specific action, is momentous in the development of the individual. It provides perhaps the earliest, certainly the most important, example of what is a fundamental principle in mental activity—associative learning—and it is crucial in inaugurating relations with fellow human beings, and thus ushers in the moral life.

We have seen that in both its primary and secondary functions—though in the latter more efficiently than in the former—the apparatus works so as to discharge quantity. That is its mode of operation. However, there is also attached to the apparatus what we might think of as a regulatory mechanism, which ensures that this mode of operation is followed, or that any departure or deviation from it is corrected. Furthermore, this regulatory mechanism acquires an independent significance in our mental life. Freud's name for the mechanism is the "pleasure-unpleasure series," and, when the apparatus is regulated by it, it is said to obey the pleasure principle. However, in order to understand how the mechanism makes itself felt, we must introduce a phenomenon of which, significantly, we have not so far heard: consciousness. Though Freud was well aware that any psychological theory that laid claim to adequacy must at some point deal with consciousness and with the knowledge that consciousness offers us, fragmentary and puzzling though it often is, of psychic phenomena, it is significant that he found no need to introduce the topic until the broad outlines of the mind had already been drawn. In years to come Freud might well have been dissatisfied with the actual account of consciousness that he gave in the "Project." But with the general nature of that account—more specifically, with the attenuated role that it assigned to consciousness in the over-all picture of the mind—it is unlikely that he would have found reason to quarrel.

To accommodate consciousness, the "Project" postulates a third class of neuron. These are ω-neurons. ω-neurons, like ϕ-neurons and ψ-neurons, form a system, and the ω-system is sited so that it abuts only onto the ψ-system. It is now indeed possible to give a rough diagram of the mental apparatus.

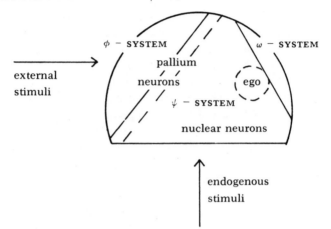

It is distinctive of consciousness that it gives us (to use the most general term possible) "qualities," and so the question must arise, How are these qualities related to the quantity that courses through the system, and in terms of which, to date, all mental activity has been explained? Quantity as such, Freud insisted, never enters the ω-system. But a particular characteristic of the flow of quantity—that is, its frequency, or what Freud calls "periodicity"—is transmitted from the ψ-system to the ω-system, and it is this characteristic that gives rise to the various contents of consciousness.

On more than one occasion, Freud was to compare the ω-system, or consciousness, to perception,[5] and there would seem to be two points of resemblance he had in mind. First, both with consciousness and with perception, there is an object—something of which we are conscious, something that we perceive—and this object

[5] e.g., V, 615–17; XIV, 171; XVIII, 24–29.

is independent of our mental state: though, in both cases, by the spread or fanning outward of attention, we can increase the number or range of objects on which the mental state fastens. Secondly, according to Freud, consciousness, like perception, is exclusive of memory—not, of course, in the sense that we cannot have conscious memories, which we clearly can, but in that the memory traces themselves are unconscious and can produce all their effects without attaining consciousness.

The contents of consciousness fall roughly into two groups. There are, on the one hand, sensory or perceptual contents, plus their derivatives, which, for Freud, include not only memories but also such things as thoughts or wishes, and, on the other hand, there are pleasure and unpleasure. The latter, like the former, are explained by Freud in terms of the flow of quantity, but, in their case, the connection is rather more schematic, in that pleasure corresponds to any drop in the general level of tension in the ψ-system (or to discharge), and unpleasure to any rise.

Now, enough has already been said to make it clear that the mental apparatus in both its primary and secondary functions tends to operate so that pleasure is secured and unpleasure avoided. But, of course, to talk of the mind as obeying—rather than merely conforming to—the pleasure principle, or of the pleasure-unpleasure series as a regulatory mechanism, goes well beyond this, for it places pleasure and unpleasure not simply among the consequences of mental activity, but among its determinants. How does this come about?

Initially, pleasure and unpleasure are experiences that attend upon events, and these events are then thought of as pleasurable or unpleasurable. But, secondarily, pleasure and unpleasure can serve as signals, in that any experience in the pleasure-unpleasure series leaves behind a residue in the form of a new type of mental state. If we take the experiences that lie at either end of the series, the residual state left behind by satisfaction is a wish or a wishful state, and that left behind by pain might be thought of as "apprehension." (Freud had in fact no word for the residue of pain. If, in a couple of passages, he seems to have used the word "affect" for this state, this is highly misleading, since "affect" is generally used, as it will be in the rest of this book, either for instinctual energy or for an emotion or feeling of some complexity.) Now these residual states have two important characteristics. On the one hand, they take as their objects the events that were originally attended with pleasure and unpleasure, and, on the other hand, they involve a heightening of tension and, in this way, press for discharge. The difference, however, is that in the case of those states residual of pleasure, discharge takes the form of attraction toward their object, or the urge to repeat the experience of satisfaction, whereas, in the case of those states residual of unpleasure, discharge takes the form of a fending-off of their object, or the urge to avoid the recurrence of pain. In this way, pleasure and unpleasure, in their role as signals, reinforce the paths of discharge through the system, or the facilitations, to whose establishment they had in the first place contributed in their role as experiences. The facilitations are, of course, a permanent feature of the system, or a true modification of it. By contrast, the signals of pleasure and unpleasure are a temporary superimposition and work in an *ad hoc* fashion. If it is in virtue of the facilitations that the mind by and large conforms to the pleasure principle, it is in virtue of the signal system that we can say that the mind obeys the pleasure principle.

And this brings us directly to a major weakness, or a major source of weakness, in the functioning of the apparatus. This weakness is exhibited most strikingly when the mind operates under the influence of the wish. Accordingly, like Freud, I shall start with this case, and I shall go on to indicate the analogous difficulties that arise when the mind is influenced by the memory of a painful or unpleasurable event or by apprehension.

To understand precisely how the mental apparatus breaks down under the influence of the wish, it is best to begin by looking at the process as it is described in purely theoretical terms. When the mind is in a wishful state, there is a rise of tension, and discharge is sought. Quantity, ultimately originating from an internal source, flows outward, through the ψ-system, toward the ϕ-system, and so ultimately towards the motor part of the apparatus. The path that it follows is identical with that followed on the occasion of the original experience of satisfaction, from which the wishful state derives. Along this path of conduction, in its earlier reaches—that is, as it passes through the ψ-system—are, first, nuclear neurons, and, then, pallium or mantle neurons, and these are successively filled with energy, or cathected. Now, from their positioning in the mental apparatus, Freud concluded that nuclear neurons were peculiarly connected with the representation (not, of course, the consciousness, but the representation) of need in the system, and that pallium neurons were peculiarly connected with representations of the object wished-for and of the various bodily movements necessary to seize it. From this point onward, the outcome depends solely on

SIGMUND FREUD | 48

quantitative issues. For, if the flow of quantity is excessive or, more specifically, if the pallium neurons that lie on the path of conduction are heavily cathected, what will arise is not simply a memory image of the wished-for object but an image invested with all the strength of a perception. If that happens, idea will be mistaken for reality, the wished-for object for an object actually present, and discharge will actually occur. Since, however, the object is not present, is not real, but is imaginary, there will be an absence of satisfaction. Ironically, one of the very features that distinguish the mind in its secondary function, indeed one of those which make this function possible—i.e., the facilitations, or memory—now presents it with a biologically damaging threat.

The phenomenon just described was called by Freud "hallucinatory wish-fulfillment," and it plays a central role in all pathological, as well as in some normal, mental activity. I have talked of it as a breakdown in the functioning of the apparatus, and so, from a biological point of view, it is. Yet it can also be regarded, and Freud himself certainly regarded it, as a part of a primitive but perfectly coherent form of mental functioning, which he called the "primary process." Viewed as part of such a process, the wish is really an embryonic form of desire, marked out by the fact that it seeks satisfaction indifferently in the outer world of reality and in the inner world of phantasy. When the individual wishes, or when he wishes sufficiently strongly, he typically cannot distinguish between the representation that he makes to himself of the object of his wish and that object itself.

To safeguard itself from the dangers that this type of mental functioning involves, the apparatus must take on a yet more complex mode of operation, the requirements for which are already in being. No extra machinery is required, though the use to which existing elements are put is complex.

What has essentially to be achieved is that the apparatus should learn patience, and that discharge should wait upon what Freud called "an indication of reality." The indication, when it comes, will come—or, according to Freud, will probably come—from the ω-system, or from consciousness, but in order to bring about such an indication, two extra stages must be inserted between the wish and the threatened discharge. First, there must be arrest of the flow of energy through the neuronic network, and, secondly, there must be judgment passed on the image, or (to use a later phrase) "reality-testing."

Freud's most important single point about these two stages—on the detail of which he had much of interest to say—was that they are both inhibitory, they both involve at any rate a temporary check upon the shifts of energy in the system. This is obviously true of the first stage, but, to understand why judgment too is inhibitory, we must look at an ingenious hypothesis that Freud held about the nature of thinking. According to this hypothesis, thinking (or practical thinking) is a kind of "trial run": that is to say, it is an internalized reconstruction and rehearsal, with no outward manifestation, of the various possible states of affairs and the various possible courses of action. And this, in terms of the model, means that small flows of quantity are directed through a number of alternate but associated pathways in the ψ-system. On each such flow, the quantity must be adequate to fill successively all the neurons on the various pathways so that the whole of the information that the mind has in store is made available to it, yet the possibility of confusing memory or thought with perception and the consequent danger of premature discharge must be eliminated. Or, if not eliminated, reduced: for it seems to have been Freud's view that the perils to which the mind is exposed as the result of the highly precarious, if biologically necessary, way in which thought comes into being, can never be totally got rid of, that thinking will always retain its provocative character.

Nevertheless, the apparatus clearly asserts a measure of control over the flow of energy. How does it do this? How are the trial runs, in which thinking consists, contrived? To answer this we must consider a feature of the mechanics of the apparatus. Quantity, we have seen, flows toward those contact-barriers which are best facilitated. However, we now learn that quantity is also attracted by quantity in an adjacent neuron. As Freud put it, as far as the passage of quantity is concerned, a contact-barrier that is cathected the far side is equivalent to a contact-barrier that is facilitated. Accordingly, the flow of quantity can be arrested if quantity from some other source is channeled into neurons adjacent or parallel to the pathway it would otherwise follow. This process is called "side-cathexis," and it is the contrivance by which the mental apparatus controls quantity in passage.

How is side-cathexis achieved? The answer must lie with that part of the mental apparatus, or that agency, which has quantity under its control and to deploy. In other words, the ego. The ego, originally postulated to account for specific actions, or the way in which current energy is discharged with the help of stored energy, now has assigned to it the performance of certain prefatory tasks which amount to the arrest of discharge: the aim being that, when the specific actions come to be carried out, they will be in keeping with the real needs of the organism and the actual state of the environment— more succinctly, they will conform to reality.

If, then, the mind is at one and the same time to avoid hallucinated wish-fulfillment and yet to draw upon experience, the ideas or images which are the products of experience must occur in a "tamed" or controlled fashion. They must form part of a train of thought. In the language of the theory, free-flowing quantity must be "bound." The attractions and counter-attractions in the apparatus must be so delicately poised that neurons may remain cathected with energy and yet the threat of discharge be attenuated. In this distinction, so casually made, between free and bound energy, Freud was in later years to find inspiration for numerous ideas about how instinct could be controlled and the ego assert its rule over psychic forces.

And now mention must be made of the analogous dangers that arise when the mind is influenced by ideas of highly unpleasurable events or of objects associated with pain. In these cases the danger is not one of premature discharge, followed by frustration, though it is in some ways an internal analogue to this. The danger is that, when the hostile memory image is so heavily cathected that it becomes indistinguishable from perception, there will be a fresh release of unpleasure equivalent to that which attended the original bad experience. To account for this danger Freud was led to postulate, in a somewhat *ad hoc* way, key or secretory neurons, which act directly upon the cells of the body, which in turn stimulate the ψ-system. However, by a contrivance similar to that used against the wish, the ego is able to deploy the energy at its disposal in such a way as to immobilize the release of unpleasure. The inhibition of unpleasure is called "primary defense."

It is, of course, a precondition of primary defense that there should be stored in the mind some anticipation of the unpleasure that the hostile image will provoke. But there are cases where this unpleasure cannot be anticipated; and this happens when unpleasure has somehow become attached to the image since the original experience. In these cases, there will be what Freud called a "posthumous" reaction to the experience, and, though there is more than one form that this can take, what is certain is that it will be an overreaction and that its effect will be to distort mental functioning. Here, of course, we have the correlate in theoretical terms to the account that Freud was currently prepared to give of pathological defense. In the life of the adult, pathological defense greets the revived image of an early sexual experience, precisely because, with the intervention of puberty, the image has acquired a charge of affect that the original experience did not generate.

At this point it is worth interrupting the sequence of Freud's thought to ask why he came to believe that the operation of the mind in obedience to the pleasure principle was peculiarly susceptible to hallucinatory wish-fulfillment, or (in the case of unhappy recollection) to excessive unpleasure. To reverse the question: Why did Freud believe it was only through a form of biological learning, in which unpleasure was the teacher, that the mind came to distinguish between memory or imagination, on the one hand, and perception, on the other? For it is clear that, though Freud found it very convenient to exhibit the primary process within the theoretical framework of the "Project," he had reasons, quite independent of that theory, for thinking that this was a mode toward which the mind was drawn, and which, indeed, on a certain level, it never abandoned. I think that there are two influences that were at work with him.

The first is a philosophical view to which, as we have seen, Freud subscribed from his student days. According to this view, all mental states—and this would include the states residual from pleasurable and unpleasurable events—have two constituents. One of these constituents, which also determines the object of the mental state, is an idea. Now, an idea is easily conceived of on the model of a visual image, and, once this has been done, it is natural to suppose that it requires a certain sophistication, which can at moments of excitement be lost, to distinguish between mental states that contain a visual image as just one part of them, and mental states that simply consist in a visual image, i.e., perceptions. Secondly, Freud would seem to have run together the very different relations that can hold between recollection or expectation, on the one hand, and pleasurable or unpleasurable events on the other, and to have thought that in each case the character that attaches to an event also attaches to the memory or the anticipation of it. It may, for instance, be plausible to think that recollection of an unpleasurable event generates unpleasure, but it does not follow that expectation of a pleasurable event generates pleasure, let alone to the point of discharge.

This is not to dispute the valuable point that a sense of reality is something that has to be learned. What is at stake is whether the description that Freud gave of our mental condition before the sense of reality has been acquired is an adequate description of that condition, or whether it does not read more like the description of a condition in which the sense of reality, once acquired, has been lost: in which the individual lives in a state, not of ignorance, but of confusion.

The adaptation to which the mental apparatus must submit, if it is to avoid gratuitous frustration or unpleasure, was characterized in the "Project" as the inhibition of the "primary process" in favor of the "secondary process." These same phrases reappear in Chapter VII of *The Interpretation of Dreams*, as part of a somewhat modified (and abbreviated) theory of the mind. Then, in 1911, in a classic but highly compressed paper, "Formulations on the Two Principles of Mental Functioning," Freud restated the distinction and, in a way that had become characteristic of his thinking, he related it to a particular stage in the development of the individual, at which the pleasure principle is abandoned and the reality principle takes its place. Freud went on to connect this stage with a number of recent modifications in mental life: the development of attention, the increased importance of the sense organs, the introduction of a notation for the register of memory, the conversion of mere motor discharge into action, the development of trains of thought, and the linkage of thoughts with words. However, in talking of the individual as abandoning the pleasure principle, Freud did not mean that the individual abandons pleasure as an aim. Pleasure is only ever deferred so that it shall be the more secure. "The substitution of the reality principle for the pleasure principle," Freud wrote,

> implies no deposing of the pleasure principle, but only a safeguarding of it. A momentary pleasure, uncertain

in its results, is given up, but only in order to gain along the new path an assured pleasure at a later time.[6]

And, Freud insisted, there are areas of life over which the writ of the reality principle never runs, where the primary processes survive. These, indeed, were to provide him with the topics of research for the next ten years or more: dreams, errors, symptoms, jokes. It is no small sign of Freud's genius that, having completed the comprehensive map of the mind contained in the "Project," he should, out of the vast area under his survey, have chosen the parts he did to work so thoroughly. In the mid-1890s he could not possibly have foreseen how richly his labors were to be rewarded. For, while the "Project" reveals the narrow line between the primary and the secondary processes, and gives some indication of the mind's tendency to move from one side of this line to the other, it nowhere suggests how frequent and tempestuous these fluctuations are. It was through studying them that Freud came to supplement his account of the mind at the point at which the "Project" is peculiarly thin: namely, the substantive or material form that human instinct, here disguised under the abstract name of "endogenous stimuli," can assume.

It is often said of the "Project" that its effect was wholly baneful: a view most often expressed by saying that the tendency of the "Project" was to blind Freud to the significance of intentions, aims, motives, desires in human nature—something which his clinical experience otherwise forced him to recognize—and to strengthen him in a conception of the mind as a machine subject to causal laws of the utmost simplicity.

[6] XII, 223.

But, first, the "Project" did not equate the mind with a machine. What it did was to use a mechanical model to represent and to explain the workings of the mind. And if it went beyond this, it only did so to insist that there is a physiological substrate to psychological phenomena and this substrate must ultimately be understood.

Secondly, the model that figures in the "Project" is more complex in conception than is often realized. The point can be brought out by considering two labels, one of which is often bestowed on the model—"economic"— while the other—"dynamic"—is denied it. A model would be economic if its working can be explained solely in terms of a certain structure and a given quantity of energy that seeks discharge. Each state of the model would then be correlated with a specific shift of energy from the previous state. Now, on one level, the model that is used in the "Project" is an economic model, but it is worth pointing out that one particular consequence attributed to placing an economic interpretation on the model—that it cannot account for any one form that discharge takes rather than another—does not follow. If the model were unable to account for specific vicissitudes of energy, this would simply reflect the inadequate specifications that the model gave of the internal structure or "plumbing" of the mind. It would have nothing to show about any inherent defect of an economic model. However, the interpretation of the model contained in the "Project" is not rigidly economic. For instance, no regulatory mechanism is postulated to control quantity at any level below the maximum that the apparatus can tolerate. Indeed, in its more complex functioning—for instance, all those contrivances that make the secondary processes possible—the model has to be understood in terms of certain tendencies or tasks that the apparatus takes on and for which it finds the energy, rather than in terms of certain tendencies to which it is driven by the energy.

In fact, it can plausibly be argued that it was through the attempt to construct a model of the mind, and the detailed analysis of mental phenomena in which this involved him, that Freud was led away from any crudely economic conceptions. And here an illuminating contrast may be drawn between Freud and Breuer. In the theoretical chapter that he contributed to the *Studies on Hysteria*, Breuer subscribed to a view of the mind, particularly in its affective processes, to which the crude analogy of the reflex arc, beginning in stimulation and terminating in discharge, seems fully adequate. Yet it is Breuer who was insistent throughout that the mind must be considered uniquely in psychological terms and that any more abstract model was superfluous.

Finally, when commentators on Freud discuss his theory of the mind and consider the inadequacies of the theory interpreted economically, they usually dwell exclusively upon the distortions to which it is supposed to give rise as far as our view of human action is concerned. In other words, they concentrate upon that part of the theory which concerns the discharge of energy or the eruption of it from the system. But there is another part of the theory which they overlook, which concerns shifts or transfers of energy within the system. And it too has its implications. It was, indeed, to this part of his theory that Freud was heavily indebted in his investigation of the details of the primary process and in his analysis of displacement and substitute gratification. Without it, his views on this range of topics might have taken much longer to form.

The "Project" was never explicitly referred to in any of Freud's later writings. However, in *The Interpretation of Dreams* Freud devoted one chapter to the theory of the mind, under the heading "Psychology of the Dream Process," and it is plausible to read this as an informal presentation of the ideas in the now abandoned manuscript. There is one significant change, which had already been announced in a letter to Fliess, dated January 1, 1896: the transfer of the ω-system to a position between the ϕ- and the ψ-system so that it is in direct contact with each, and they have no direct communicaion with each other. This change considerably simplified the workings of the mind, but at the same time, some of the richness of interaction between perception, memory, and consciousness was lost.

Dreams, Errors, Symptoms, and Jokes

• • •
iii

The theory of the mind that Freud put forward in the "Scientific Project" exerted a powerful and probably incalculable influence over his whole thinking. Not merely was most of his greatest work achieved in its shadow, but, over the years, as his ideas took this or that new turn, its influence would suddenly be revived, so that we can perceive in some fresh and bold speculation of his later years the derivative of an idea implicit in the "Project," or barely enunciated there and then put aside. Witness Freud's final account of anxiety, and much of what he was to say concerning the ego.

Apart from its influence on the detail of Freud's thinking, the "Project" was of enduring importance for the encouragement it gave him in resolving one of his largest problems: that of connecting psychopathology with general psychology. Just as mental abnormality can be explained only by reference to an over-all account of psychic functioning, any general account of the mind is incomplete without some indication where the weakness of the system lies and how malfunction can develop. According to the "Project," it is in the inherent inadequacy of the primary process, or, alternatively, in the failure of the individual to engage in the secondary process, that the sources of disturbance lie. More specifically, it is the strength of instinctual impulse and the urgency with which it presses for discharge, irrespective of reality, that makes the life of the mind so vulnerable.

As we saw at the end of Chapter I, it was precisely to some such point as this that Freud's clinical experience had led him by the end of 1897. If we add the insights he was gaining from his self-analysis, we can see that he had every reason to put impulse, the clamor of instinct, in the forefront of his picture of the mind. In this chapter I want to consider four phenomena, taken from normal and abnormal functioning, all studied by Freud to great depth in the decade after 1895. These confirm the general weight Freud attached to instinct, they accord with the picture of its working contained in the "Project," and they furnish us with a mass of information about its content.

I

I shall begin with Freud's study of dreams, which is in many ways the most distinctive and the most remarkable single element in his vast survey of the mind. It is the topic of his most important work, *The Interpretation of Dreams*, which, besides being what its title indicates, is also a work of confession, in that Freud committed to its pages many of the findings of his self-analysis. And Freud continued to feel a special attachment to dream interpretation, both for the exactness of its findings and for the precious evidence it provided for the deeper workings of the mind in normality and abnormality alike. The view expressed in the maxim *"The interpretation of dreams is the royal road to a knowledge of the unconscious activities of the mind"*[1] is one from which he never wavered.

Let us start with the most general statement about dreams, which is repeated with slight variations at several places: *"A dream is a (disguised) fulfilment of a (suppressed or repressed) wish."*[2] One feature of this thesis, which calls for immediate comment, can best be brought out by considering an objection to it, now standard: If the wish that finds fulfillment in a dream is invariably disguised, how can we tell of its existence? Or, How can we tell that there is disguise, unless we know of the existence of the wish and what it is? The point that this objection effectively makes is that the thesis falls into parts—the assignment of a fulfilled wish to each dream, and the predication of disguise or concealment of that wish—and, consequently, it insists that there should be separate evidence for each of the two parts of the theory. I shall respect the objection, or its implicit point, to the extent of expounding the two parts of the thesis successively.

First, then, that dreams are wish-fulfillments. This, we can see, is itself a composite thesis: for it traces dreams to wishes, and it asserts that these wishes belong to the primary process. They belong, that is, to that mode of mental functioning within which, character-

[1] V, 608.
[2] IV, 160.

istically, no distinction is observed between a desire and its satisfaction—indeed, even to use these terms is perhaps anachronistic, in that as yet the difference has not manifested itself. For the wisher the experience is unitary, and, in consequence, dreams cannot be said merely to express a wish, for, wherever the wish belongs to the content of the dream, so also does the fulfillment of the wish. "A dream does not simply give expression to a thought, but represents the wish fulfilled as a hallucinatory experience."[3] And Freud goes on to say that if the wish "I should like to go on the lake" instigates a dream, the dream has for its content "I am going on the lake."

Freud at various stages considered the objection that not all dreams are wish-fulfillments, and that surely some derive from other types of mental state; the most obvious counterexamples being anxiety dreams. But, with minor exceptions, Freud held to the universality of his thesis, and he was at pains to point out that in every case brought against it there is either an inadequate analysis of the dream or an inadequate conception of the wish. It was in development of the second point— the first we shall have to take up at greater length—that Freud was led to make a distinction in Lecture XIV of the *Introductory Lectures*. "No doubt," he wrote,

a wish-fulfilment must bring pleasure; but the question then arises "To whom?" To the person who has the wish, of course. But, as we know, a dreamer's relation to his wishes is a quite peculiar one. He repudiates them and censors them—he has no liking for them, in short.[4]

[3] XV, 129.
[4] XV, 215–16.

Freud then went on to distinguish between two separate people amalgamated in the dreamer, one of whom has the wish whereas the other rejects it, and it is only the former who is satisfied. Freud's distinction could be made, less dramatically, as one not between two different people, but between two different roles—the man insofar as he has the wish, and the man insofar as he rejects it; or, weaker still, we could contrast the satisfaction of the man and the satisfaction of the wish; and the point would hold. A wish can be satisfied, even though the man who has it isn't. Of course, we might press for an explanation why this was so, and the answer in the case of dreams is obviously connected with the deviance of wish or its discrepancy from the man's other wishes. It is no gross anticipation of Freud's argument to say that we are here approaching—though now from the other side, from consideration of its consequences, not its causes—the issue of the "incompatible" idea with which Freud had been struggling since the first drafts for the "Preliminary Communication." For the wish that, when satisfied, leaves the wisher unsatisfied is "incompatible."

Secondly, the wishes expressed in dreams are disguised. Here we come to a central notion of Freud's, that of the dream-work. To understand this notion, we must first understand a distinction upon which it rests and which he claimed was always to some degree or other misconceived by his critics: that between the "manifest content" and the "latent content" of the dream. The manifest content is that which we experience or remember; it constitutes the subject of the dream report. The latent content is that which gives the dream its sense or meaning: it is sometimes called the "dream thoughts," where these are contrasted with the dream content. On the distinction two points are to be observed. First, the dream thoughts are not restricted to the wish that instigates the dream. Rather they include the whole setting or context of the wish. Secondly, the distinction between manifest and latent content is a functional distinction: that is, it refers to the role the thoughts play, so that the possibility is open that the manifest and the latent contents may coincide.

Once this distinction is clear, the dream-work may then be regarded as the process, or piece of mental activity, by which the dream thoughts are converted or transcribed into the dream content. Note "dream thoughts": for it is crucial to Freud's conception of the dream that the latent content of the dream goes piecemeal, element by element, into the manifest content, inside which only a halfhearted attempt is made to mold it into a unity. For this reason a metaphor which it seems natural to invoke in this context, and which Freud himself employed, that of translation from one language to another, is inexact. For the dream lacks that which is most characteristic of a language: grammar, or structure. A more appropriate comparison that Freud makes is to the rebus, or picture puzzle, in which pictorial elements, words, letters of the alphabet appear side by side and it is only by replacing each element with a syllable or word that sense can be made of the whole.

There are four activities in which the dream-work consists: condensation, displacement, representation (or consideration of representability), and secondary revision. On whether the last properly forms part of the dream work Freud was later to have his doubts. Each of these activities is, more or less, explained by its name.

Condensation is exemplified in the fact that "the manifest dream has a smaller content than the latent one,"[5] or, more exactly, that this abbreviation is achieved without omission. Freud lists various results of condensation—such as the preference given to items that occur several times over in the dream thoughts, and the formation of composite or intermediate figures. But condensation is seen at its clearest in the handling of words or names, which makes it, from an expository point of view, peculiarly vulnerable in translation. It is condensation that prevents there being any neat one-one correspondence between the elements of the manifest content and those of the latent content. And it is also condensation that permits a more general feature of the dream: that is, overdetermination, according to which, for any given manifest content, there can be more than one latent content, or any one dream can express several quite separate wishes.

By "displacement"—or "transference" as Freud sometimes called it in the early years, before the word took on its technical sense in psychoanalytic theory—Freud meant two distinct but related processes. One is that whereby the dream is differently "centered" from the dream thoughts, so that it does not reflect the relative importance of those thoughts. The other is that whereby elements in the dream do duty for elements in the dream thoughts, the substitution being in accordance with a chain of association. Displacement is peculiarly connected with the disguise that the dream wears.

The third process, of representation, is the transposition of thoughts into imagery. Freud, in one of his many apt analogies, compared the difficulty under which the dream labors as a representational device to the limita-

[5] XV, 171.

tions that, according to classical aesthetic theory, are inherent in the plastic arts of painting and sculpture in contrast to poetry, and he revealed the ingenuity with which the dream work tries to incorporate the most recalcitrant or abstract material. Freud said—and it may sound surprising—that this third process is "psychologically the most interesting."[6] Possibly what he had in mind is the way in which the plasticity of dreams links them to the prototype of the primary process: the hallucinatory experience of satisfaction.

The processes of condensation and displacement can be economically illustrated from the so-called "Autodidasker" dream from Freud's own experience.[7] One evening Freud's wife, who had been reading some stories which he had given her, by J. J. David, an Austrian writer and a friend of Freud's brother, told him how moved she had been by one of them about a man of great talents who went to the bad: and she then went on, after a discussion of the talents their children might have, to express the wish that a similar fate would not be theirs. Freud reassured her, and talked of the advantages of a good upbringing. That night he had a dream in which two wishes were expressed: one for his son's future, and the other that his still unmarried brother, Alexander, might have a happy domestic life—and both wishes are represented as fulfilled. The dream fell into two distinct parts. The first consisted simply in the made-up word "Autodidasker." The second was the reproduction of a phantasy recently entertained to the effect that the next time Freud saw a colleague of his, Professor N., he would say, "The patient about

[6] XV, 175.
[7] IV, 298–302.

whose condition I consulted you recently is in fact only suffering from a neurosis, just as you suspected."

Let us now see how the dream thoughts that Freud somehow collected are transposed into the dream content by the means we have been considering. As to the dream thoughts Freud enumerated the following: an author; a good upbringing; Breslau, as a place where a friend of Freud's who had married had gone to live; then the names of two men, both of whom lived in Breslau and who had come to a bad end through women —Lasker, who died of syphilis, and Lassalle, killed in a duel; a novel of Zola's, *L'Oeuvre*, in which the author introduces himself, with his name ingeniously altered, as a happily married character; and the desire, pertaining to both wishes, that Freud might be proved wrong in his fears. The last thought is expressed fairly directly in the second part of the dream, where it is shown as fulfilled—for Freud is apologizing. The other thoughts are all crammed into the first or prefatory part of the dream. Author, Lasker, and Lassalle figure fairly evidently inside "Autodidasker." A good upbringing is represented through its opposite, i.e., "autodidact." *L'Oeuvre* appears more obliquely, in that the transformation, in the book, of Zola's name into "Sandoz" exhibits a parallel to that of "Alex(ander)" into "Autodidasker"—in both cases an anagram of the original is buried at the end of the substitute name, which contains a prefix for disguise.

If this dream very well illustrates the processes of condensation and displacement in action—indeed, in joint action—the third element in dream work is present to a degree so peculiarly low as to elicit comment from Freud. To illustrate visual representation, I shall follow

Freud and cite specific details from dreams.[8] So, a man dreams that he is an officer sitting at table opposite the Emperor: and this represents his putting himself in opposition to his father. Or a woman dreams that she is walking with two little girls whose ages differ by fifteen months; and this represents the fact that two traumatic events of childhood, of which she is dreaming, were fifteen months apart.

As to secondary revision, this is the attempt by the mind to order, to revise, to supplement the contents of the dream so as to make an acceptable or intelligible whole. Even in *The Interpretation of Dreams* Freud distinguished this factor from the rest of the dream-work by pointing out that it makes no new contribution to the dream in the way of representing dream thoughts not otherwise included, and he suggested that it should be attributed to the very psychic agency that the dream is otherwise intended to evade. In the encyclopedia article of 1922 entitled "Psycho-analysis," Freud definitely excluded secondary revision from the dream work.[9]

Freud insisted that the dream work is confined to these three (or four) processes. Other activities, which appear to take place in dreams—mathematical calculations, or the making of a speech—are simply to be regarded as items or elements that constitute the content of the dream. In reporting them, we report not what we did, but what we dreamt of. For in a dream we do not do things, we only dream of doing them.

At this stage, I should perhaps introduce a topic mentioned only briefly in the original text of *The Interpretation of Dreams* but which figured increasingly in later editions, and which is widely assumed to be central

[8] V, 409.
[9] XVIII, 241.

to Freud's theory of the dream. I refer to the symbolism according to which there are certain invariants in dream representations so that certain basic thoughts or pre-occupations find a regular form of expression: for instance, the parents are represented by kings and queens; the penis by sticks, tree trunks, umbrellas, nail files, or long, sharp weapons; the womb by boxes, cupboards, ovens, or hollow objects like ships.[10] In one way, such symbolism must be classified with the dream-work, since it provides a transition from the latent to manifest content; yet in another way it must be contrasted to it, precisely because it reduces the element of work on the part of the dreamer. It is a corollary of this last point that, where symbolism is employed, the dreamer is unable to associate to his dream. Furthermore, Freud pointed out that, insofar as dream symbolism is found plausible, it exhibits a capacity of the mind more general than the phenomenon of dreaming. In the *Introductory Lectures* Freud spoke of an "ancient but extinct mode of expression" or "a primal language"[11] which legitimizes the occurrence of symbols in dreams: seemingly an old idea with Freud, which we first catch sight of in a letter to Fliess of 1897, where he talks of a new subject, "psychomythology." But in the massive application of symbolism to dream interpretation it would seem that Freud was heavily influenced by a pupil later to go astray, Wilhelm Stekel.

So much for the nature of the dream work. Two questions now arise, Why is the dream work necessary? and, Are any limits imposed upon its scope?—of which the

[10] e.g., V, 353–60, 683–85; XV, 151–65.
[11] XV, 166, 168.

first is really about the latent content of the dream and the second about the manifest content.

In answer to the first question, Freud said that the dream work is necessary because the wish that finds expression in the dream is invariably a repressed wish. In a footnote added in 1909, Freud said that "the kernel of my theory" lies in the "derivation of dream-distortion from the censorship."[12] Two other characterizations of the dream wish—that it is infantile, and that it is generally (though not always) sexual—are intimately connected with this thesis, but at the time that Freud was writing *The Interpretation of Dreams*, he was not yet in a position to establish the connections.

In answer to the second question, Freud said that the material for the dream comes from varying sources, and in Chapter V of *The Interpretation of Dreams* he classified them: recent and indifferent events, infantile experiences, somatic needs, and the repertoire of what Freud called "typical dreams"—dreams of flying and falling, of being naked, of examinations, of the death of loved ones. But Freud laid particular weight on the first of these sources. Indeed, he committed himself to the thesis that every dream contains "a repetition of a recent impression of the previous day."[13] The impression itself may have been significant or it may have been indifferent—where significance and indifference mean, respectively, belonging or not belonging to the latent content of the dream.

Putting together the answers to these last two questions, we may now follow Freud in reconstructing the immediate history of the dream. There is a persisting repressed wish, which forms the motive behind the

[12] IV, 308*n*.2.
[13] IV, 180.

dream. In the course of the day, this wish comes into contact, or forms an association, with a thought or train of thought. This thought has some energy attached to it, independently of this contact, through not having as yet been "worked over": hence the phrase, the "residues of the day." The upshot is that the thought—or an association to it—is revived in sleep, as the proxy of the wish.

The question that remains to be asked about this alliance is, Why should it assert itself while we are asleep? The answer is not that sleep is peculiarly well-disposed to the alliance, but that it prefers it to any more naked version of the same forces. If the wish did not express itself in the disguise of the dream, it would disturb sleep. And so we come to the over-all function of dreams: they are *"the guardians of sleep."*[14]

I now want to ask, What is the evidence for the Freudian theory of dreams? I have already argued that we require separate evidence for the two parts of the theory—for the ascription of dreams to wishes, and for the characterization of the wishes as disguised.

The first piece of evidence comes to us just because the thesis that the wishes involved are disguised admits of a few exceptions. There are dreams that directly express wishes. Such dreams, which Freud referred to in *The Interpretation of Dreams* for their evidential value and to which he devoted a whole lecture in the *Introductory Lectures*, are commonest among children. Freud cited the story of his daughter, then nineteen months old, who, after an attack of vomiting, had spent the day without food and in her sleep called out, "Anna Fweud, stwawbewwies, wild stwawbewwies, omblet,

14 IV, 233; V, 678; XV, 129.

pudden." At this time the little girl used to use her own name to express the idea of taking possession of something.[15] Undisguised dreams also occur to people subjected to extreme privation, and Freud quoted from the explorer Otto Nordenskjöld, who tells how on an Antarctic expedition his men would dream of food and drink in abundance, of tobacco piled up in mountains, of a ship arriving in full sail, or of a letter delivered after a long delay for which the postman apologized.[16]

Turning to the great majority of dreams which do not overtly express wishes, Freud adduced evidence to show that these dreams are disguises. The evidence is that we can, i.e., we have a capacity to, undisguise them. In the majority of cases, we can produce associations to each element in the dream in turn, and these associations, after running for a certain while, will terminate on a point that seems natural. Here Freud is using as evidence something he had already used in therapy as a method of collecting evidence; for in therapy he had used the associations themselves, here he is using the fact that such associations are forthcoming. This capacity, Freud argues, finds additional support in the thesis of psychic determinism (which, as we have seen, was equivalent for Freud to a commitment to science), and also in the word-association experiments devised by Wundt and taken up in Zurich by Bleuler and Jung, which constituted "the first bridge from experimental psychology to psycho-analysis."[17] Of course, the appeal to association as establishing the existence of a disguised thought instigating the dream is plausible only if we already accept the far more general assumption that

[15] IV, 130.
[16] XV, 132–33.
[17] XV, 109.

a man may know something, or something about himself, without knowing that he knows it: a point which Freud thought was proved beyond doubt by hypnosis and hypnotic suggestion.

That the process of association should sometimes run into difficulty is no argument against its evidential value. For if disguise has been found necessary, should we not expect the process of removing it to be attended with difficulty? Indeed, if no difficulty were encountered, disguise would be inexplicable.

If we now assume that dreams are disguises and that they can be undisguised along paths of association, and we then proceed to undisguise them—or "interpret" them, as the activity is usually called—we find that we are led to a wish whose existence can be independently established. Alternatively, if association is not forthcoming, though there is evidently disguise, and we proceed to interpret the dreams as examples of primal symbolism, we once again find ourselves led to wishes that are independently verifiable. This is the third piece of support that the theory receives. A related argument starts from the character of the wishes that dreams express. Given that they are, as Freud tersely put it, "evil," by which he meant evil in our estimation, it is only to be expected that they should find expression in a disguised form. Neither of these last two arguments, it should be pointed out, offends against the evidential requirement that the two parts of the theory should be confirmed separately, for this is compatible with one part of the theory being used to confirm the other.

Fourthly, the infantile form of dreams—for instance, their plasticity—does much to suggest that they have an infantile content, which means, in Freud's view, that they deal with wishes. Or, to use the terminology of *The*

Interpretation of Dreams, the regression in dreams is both formal and material.

Nevertheless, much of the plausibility of Freud's theory of the dream must derive from a somewhat more general conception of the mind and its engagement in the primary processes. As Freud later, somewhat laconically, put it:

> It was discovered one day that the pathological symptoms of certain neurotic patients have a sense. On this discovery the psycho-analytic method of treatment was founded. It happened in the course of this treatment that patients, instead of bringing forward their symptoms, brought forward dreams. A suspicion thus arose that the dreams too had a sense.[18]

By the time Freud came to write *The Interpretation of Dreams*, not merely had his suspicion hardened to a certainty, but the parallel between dreams and symptoms had allowed his two sets of findings to confirm each other.

Finally, I want to turn to the application of the dream theory, to that remarkable feat of prestidigitation, the interpretation of dreams. The dream I shall select is cited in all three places where Freud talked extensively of dreams—*The Interpretation of Dreams*, the essay "On Dreams," and the second section of the *Introductory Lectures*, in the latter receiving its most elaborate treatment.

A lady, who though still young had been married for many years, had the following dream: *She was at the theater with her husband. One side of the stalls was completely empty. Her husband told her that Elise L.*

18 XV, 83.

and her fiancé had wanted to go too, but had only been able to get bad seats—three for 1 florin 50 kreuzers— and of course they could not take those. She thought it would not really have done any harm if they had.[19]

As a preliminary the dreamer disclosed to Freud that the precipitating cause of the dream appears in its manifest content. That day her husband had told her that her friend Elise L., approximately her contemporary, had just become engaged. She then produced the remaining dream thoughts by association to different elements in the dream. Thus: The week before she had wanted to go to a particular play and had bought tickets early, so early that she had had to pay a booking fee. Then on arrival at the theater, one whole side of the stalls was seen to be empty, and her husband had teased her for her unnecessary haste. The sum of 1 fl. 50 kr. reminded her of another sum, a present of 150 florins (also alluded to during the previous day) which her sister-in-law had been given by her husband, and which she had rushed off to exchange, the silly goose, for a piece of jewelry. In connection with the word "three," introduced in a context where we would expect "two," all the dreamer could think of was that Elise, though ten years her junior in marriage, was only three months younger than she. But to the idea in which the word was embedded—that of getting three tickets for two persons —she could produce no associations.

In reaching an interpretation, Freud was struck by the very large number of references, in the associations to the dream, though, significantly, not in the manifest content of the dream, to things being too early, or done in a hurry, or got overhurriedly, to what might be called

[19] XV, 122. For this dream see also V, 415–16, 669–70, 673; XV, 122–25, 139–40, 178, 224–25.

temporal mismanagement and the absurdity that attaches to this. If we put these thoughts together with the precipitating cause of the dream—the news of her friend's belated engagement to an excellent man—we get the following synthesis or construction: "Really it was *absurd* of me to be in such a hurry to get married. I can see from Elise's example that I could have got a husband *later*." And perhaps, if we take up the ratio between the two sums of money: "And I could have got one a hundred times better with the money, i.e., my dowry." If we pause at this stage, we can observe massive displacement, in that the central dream thoughts, i.e., the preoccupation with time, do not figure in the dream. And there is an ingenious piece of representation in that the important thought "It was absurd (to marry so early)" is indicated simply by a piece of absurdity, i.e., three tickets for two.

But this last element has gone uninterpreted and, since there were no associations to it, Freud invoked the symbolic equivalences of "three" with a man or a husband and "going to the theater" with getting married. So, getting three tickets for 1 fl. 50 kr. and going to the theater too early also express the idea of a marriage regretted: too early, and to a man of low value.

It is to be observed that the link whereby a visit to the theater can symbolize marriage presupposes that marriage is seen in a happy light. For not merely can young wives go to the theater and see all the plays which respectability had hitherto prohibited, but marriage initiates them into an activity which hitherto it had been their secret desire to gaze on: sexual intercourse. (We can see here how a universal symbolism gains its authority from widespread ways of thinking and feeling.) Now this put Freud on the track of another interpretation, showing another wish-fulfillment in the dream, this time relating to an earlier phase in the dreamer's life. For who is not at the theater? Elise, as yet unmarried. So the dream expresses, as fulfilled, an older wish, that she, the dreamer, should see what happens in marriage, and that she should see it before her friend and near-contemporary. In this case, of course, the two dream wishes are not unconnected. Indeed, Freud suggests that the new angry wish could not have instigated a dream without support from the older, more obviously sexual, wish. Within the dreamer's world, "an old triumph was put in the place of her recent defeat."

2

At much the same period as Freud was working on the subject of dreams, we find him investigating another phenomenon that reveals the unruly influence of wish or impulse in the normal mind. The first reference to these investigations occurs in a letter to Fliess of August 26, 1898, in which he discussed his temporary inability to remember the name of the author of *Andreas Hofer*. In the same year, in "The Psychical Mechanism of Forgetting," he considered in some detail another lapse, the forgetting of the name of the painter of the Last Judgment at Orvieto: then in 1901, the year of the publication of *The Interpretation of Dreams*, he collated his investigations in the *Psychopathology of Everyday Life*, a book which, through several editions and the proliferation of evidence, acquired its present shapelessness. Freud always thought of the theory of errors as exhibiting in a clear and accessible form, without use of pathological material, certain elementary principles of psychoanalysis: hence, the placing of it as Part 1 of the *Introductory Lectures*.

The word "error" is too narrow in connotation to catch the scope of this new theory, and "parapraxis" is the English translator's attempt to render Freud's *Fehlleistungen*, which he applied to the forgetting of names, words and intentions, slips of the tongue, slips of the pen, misreadings, bungled, and what are called "symptomatic," actions. It is Freud's thesis that in all these cases, where chance or accident or inattention are thought to reign, there is an operative impulse or intention.

To get the full force of Freud's theory, it is useful to divide its domain of application in two. In the first place, it applies to many "acts" (to use a neutral term) which we do not naturally regard as actions but which, if the circumstances of their occurrence had been different, we might well have done so; they are, in other words, of a kind that includes actions. Take, for instance, Freud's favored example of the President of the Lower House of the Austrian Parliament who, at the beginning of a sitting, declared it closed instead of open.[20] There are many circumstances—indeed, most circumstances—in which his declaration of a sitting closed would be an action. Secondly, the theory applies to acts which could never be thought of as actions, or which are of a kind to which no actions belong: for instance, mislaying a book, or forgetting a name. Some of the radical character of Freud's theory emerges when we realize that it is intended to range over the second as well as the first kind of case.

Nevertheless, in order to understand precisely what

[20] VI, 59; XV, 34–35; XXIII, 284.

the theory says about these acts, or the way in which it attributes to them a motive or intention, it is necessary to look more closely at the internal structure of the parapraxis. In any parapraxis there is what we might think of as a disturbing act and a disturbed act; a piece of commission and a piece of omission. Now, Freud, in investing the parapraxis with meaning, concentrated on the piece of commission; the intention that his theory posits is the intention to do the disturbing act, not the intention not to do the disturbed act. This is extremely important, but often overlooked in, for instance, the popular talk about "Freudian errors." And one reason may be that, over a large number of cases, the two intentions are very closely associated, so that one is the most obvious contrary of, or alternative to, the other—as in the example above, or in the case of the domineering young woman who told Freud that her husband had been advised by his doctor that no special diet was necessary: "He can eat and drink," she said, "what *I* want."[21] Indeed, in some cases, the link between the two intentions is necessary—for instance, between wanting to mislay a book (the act committed) and wanting not to hold on to the book (the act omitted). In such cases, the distinction that I have suggested is central to an understanding of Freud may not seem so significant: except, of course, that it stresses that it is never the feebleness of the disturbed intention, it is always the presence of a "counterintention" or "counterwill"[22] that is operative.

However, the importance of the distinction comes out clearly in the remaining cases: where the disturbing and the disturbed intentions have nothing to do with one

[21] VI, 70; XV, 35.
[22] XV, 72.

another, outside the immediate context of the parapraxis, where the act committed and the act omitted
are only coincidentally related. An example would be
the case, reported by Lichtenberg, of the man who had
read so much Homer that he always read "*Agamemnon*"
for "*angenommen*" ("supposed").[23] In these cases, we
can ask, Why does the disturbing intention manifest
itself exactly at the point at which it does? And the
answer takes the form of a chain of association leading
from the disturbing intention to the act it disturbs. It
does not, however, postulate an intention not to do the
disturbed act. The man had nothing against the word
"*angenommen*" as such.

What sorts of intention emerge as a disturbance to
others? And here we note an immediate contrast between parapraxes and, say, dreams. For parapraxes
need not express a person's repressed and most secret
wishes. In Lecture IV of the *Introductory Lectures* Freud
gave a threefold classification of the wishes or intentions that express themselves in parapraxes: intentions
known to the person and noticed by him just before
their expression; intentions known to the person, but
of which he had no recent awareness; and intentions
not known to the person and which would be vigorously
rejected by him, were the parapraxis interpreted. These
three types of intention can be arranged on a spectrum;
and the common factor is that of having been, to some
degree or other, wittingly or unwittingly, "forced back."
An intention "must itself have been disturbed before it
can become a disturbance."[24] Of course, neither the
disturbance done to it nor the disturbance it makes is

23 VI, 112; XV, 39, 70–71.
24 XV, 66.

totally effective, and so Freud is able to describe parapraxes as "the outcome of a compromise."

It follows from the fact that parapraxes do not always express repressed wishes that elaborate disguise is not required. In the majority of cases the intention reveals itself in a naked form: as when the President declares the sitting of the Lower House closed. But, as the disturbing intention gets closer to the repressed, so to a corresponding degree does it seek disguise. In other words, as we move to one end of the spectrum of intentions, we get a distinction between the manifest and the latent disturbing intention. And here we have a further reason why it is right to emphasize that the significance of the parapraxis lies with the disturbing intention, even when the disturbed and the disturbing intentions are closely linked. For, of course, the link is only between the disturbed intention and the *manifest* disturbing intention. So if we were to regard the disturbed intention as an adequate clue to the understanding of the parapraxis, we might miss the latent disturbing intention, to which the parapraxis is really due.

Finally, as an example of a parapraxis which expresses a deep wish and is therefore in heavy disguise, I want to consider the famous case of "forgetting" with which Freud opens the *Psychopathology of Everyday Life*.[25] In the summer of 1898, Freud was driving, in the company of a stranger, from Ragusa (now Dubrovnik) in Dalmatia to somewhere in Herzegovina, and, as the conversation turned to Italy, he found himself unable to recall the name of the painter of the "Last Judgment" in the cathedral at Orvieto, "the finest I have

[25] Kris, pp. 264–65; III, 290–96; VI, 2–7.

seen." Instead of "Signorelli," he could conjure up only "Botticelli" or "Boltraffio," knowing both to be wrong as he did so.

The background was that, just before, Freud had been telling his companion of a remark, supposed to be typical of the general attitude of life of the Turkish population of Bosnia and Herzegovina, which had been told him by a doctor who had practiced there. When the father of the family is about to die, one of the members will say to the doctor "Sir (*Herr*), what is there to be said? If he could be saved, I know you would have saved him." Close to this remark in Freud's memory was another, told him by the same colleague, and which he suppressed just as he was about to tell it. The second remark was about sexual enjoyment, and it ran, "*Herr*, you must know, that if *that* comes to an end, life is of no value." In other words, the very people who can contemplate death with such resignation are utterly despairing if this source of pleasure seems threatened. Freud's reluctance to retail this second remark to his companion sprang in part from a reticence to discuss the topic of death and sexuality ("the delicate topic" as he called it in all editions prior to 1924) with a stranger. But Freud had a deeper reason. A few weeks before, while staying at Trafoi in the Tyrol, he had heard of the suicide of a patient over whom he had taken much trouble and who suffered from an incurable sexual disorder: the incident darkened the whole of Freud's journey to Herzegovina. Freud, then, wished to banish from his mind thoughts of death and sexuality. The immediate effect of this was that he checked himself in retailing remarks on this topic: the deferred effect was that he forgot the name of the painter of Orvieto. For an association now connected these thoughts, through the word *"Herr"* in the two remarks and the first syllable of Herzegovina, to Signorelli, *"signor"* being the Italian for *"Herr."* And, in confirmation that it is this association that is operative, it is to be noted that the second part of the name ("-elli") fares better than the first, reappearing in "Botticelli." Indeed, the two substitute names confirm the interpretation, for both can be linked with the forgotten name along a series (*Signor, Herr, Bo, Trafoi*) which passes through the latent thoughts as the diagram below, which is Freud's own, reveals:

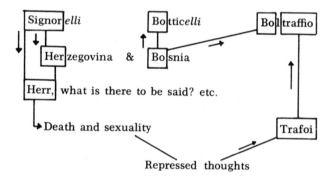

Finally, Freud suggested that we can find a deeper link than mere verbal association between the unwelcome thoughts and the painter's seemingly innocent name, when we reflect on the themes depicted in the Orvieto frescoes: Death, Judgment, Hell, and Heaven.

So we have the stage set for the over-all characterization of the case: In trying to forget one thing intentionally, Freud forgot another against his will. And with this characterization in mind, we can look again at the point that, even in cases where the disturbing and the disturbed intentions are intimately linked, the significance of the parapraxis is grasped through the disturbing intention. The disturbed intention is, presumably, to give the name of the Orvieto painter. But Freud's explanation does not require us to believe that this intention as such encounters any kind of resistance or censorship. It simply marks a point on the surface of conversation at which the wish to forget the name "Signorelli" erupts. Of course the wish to give, and the wish to forget, the name Signorelli seem intimately linked, until we recognize that the latter does duty for another wish.

3

Freud's interest in the symptom was, as we have seen, as old as his interest in psychopathology. It was through studying the symptoms of psychic disorder that he arrived at his views about the causes and character of such disorder. But as these views changed, so also did his view of the nature of the symptom.

The last view we have seen Freud hold was that the symptom is a memory of an earlier traumatic event: a view which he expressed by talking of a symptom as a "mnemic symbol." But, as he came to recognize that what makes an event traumatic is that it contains a wish or an impulse, so he tended to play down the mnemic aspect of the symbol. Instead of linking the symptom to a historical event, which in turn acquires its significance from a contained impulse somewhere within that event, he now directly connected the symptom with the impulse. It was Freud's mature view that the symptom is the expression of a wish or wishful impulse: furthermore, of an unconscious or repressed wish.

The view is, of course, the response to new findings. Nevertheless, it had cast its shadow before. For the authors of the "Preliminary Communication," while analyzing the symptom as primarily a congested or unabreacted memory, insisted that, if the symptom was to be extirpated, it is insufficient for the patient to recall the traumatic event to consciousness: he must recall it along with the original accompanying affect. Why this was so was unexplained.

One obvious consequence of the new view was that it allowed for symptoms whose mnemic content is false, which cluster round what Freud called, after the abandonment of the seduction theory, a "screen-memory," and later a phantasy. But it also permitted a greater insight into the nature of the symptom in those instances where the mnemic content was veridical.

A good illustration of this is provided by a case discussed by Freud in the *Introductory Lectures* which had already been described in "Obsessive Actions and Religious Practices" of 1907.[26] A woman, aged about thirty, who had been separated from her husband for some years, performed the following action (among others) many times a day. She would run out of her own room into another room where there was a large table. She would straighten the tablecloth on it and ring for the housemaid. When the maid came, she would immediately be sent away on some trivial errand. The woman then went back to her own room, and the ritual would be repeated. Now, on the tablecloth there was a stain and the woman always arranged things in such a way

[26] IX, 120–22; XVI, 261–64, 276–78.

that the maid could see the stain when she was summoned. Freud connected this action with events on the woman's wedding night, when her husband proved impotent. The husband had come running into her room throughout the night, without success. The next morning he said that he would feel ashamed before the housemaid, and he picked up some red ink and poured it over the sheet, though not exactly in the right place. Now, if the symptom is regarded as a mnemic symbol, its significance is exhausted by the reference or series of references it makes to a past event. But if it is seen in the new way, it can immediately be connected with something that had been, and still was, operative in the woman's life. For it represents—in a fulfilled form, like a dream—a wish, which can be expressed as, "No, he had no need to feel ashamed in front of the housemaid, he was not impotent." The woman, though separated from her husband, could not bring herself to seek a divorce, and her neurotic illness was an attempt to protect him from gossip and criticism.

As with dreams, Freud went on to connect the repressed wish that the symptom expresses with sexuality. Indeed, though not every dream expresses a sexual wish, every symptom is the expression of a sexual wish. More precisely, since symptoms are overdetermined, there is a sexual wish among the determinants of every symptom.

Freud's view that every symptom expresses a wish asserts two conditions. The first is that the person who manifests the symptom—I shall call him for short "the patient," to show that we are now moving in pathological territory—has a concept of the symptom, or a thought under which it falls, and his possession of this thought or concept is a necessary condition of his manifestation of the symptom. The second is that the symptom should be linked associatively with an unconscious impulse; the concept under which it falls should be the last member of an associative chain which has as its first member the concept or thought identificatory of that impulse.

These two conditions, which had been forming themselves in Freud's mind since his Paris days, are closely related to those which underlie dream interpretation. The first condition is implicitly recognized in the case of the dream in the obvious requirement that a dream must be reported before it can be interpreted. The second condition is evidently common to both dream and symptoms. But the resemblance goes further. For the chains of association that connect wishes to symptoms are identical in character, that is, in the nature of the links they contain, with those which connect wishes to dreams. In other words, they exhibit condensation and displacement. "The mechanism of dream-construction is the model of the manner in which neurotic symptoms arise."[27] And in the *Introductory Lectures* Freud supplemented the comparison of symptoms to dreams with a contrast: the old contrast between the symptoms of the psychoneuroses, which are the relevant ones here, and the symptoms of the actual neuroses.[28] For the symptoms of the actual neuroses are not only bodily in their manifestation (as are the symptoms of at least one psychoneurosis, hysteria) but also bodily in their causal history. In order to explain or understand them, one need not introduce any complex mental mechanism; all that is required is to invoke correlations between their occurrence and some disturbance in the

[27] XV, 183. cf. V, 597; XI, 36.
[28] XVI, 385–89. cf. II, 107; XII, 249.

sexual metabolism. Unlike the symptoms of the psycho-neuroses, the symptoms of the actual neuroses have no sense.

However, the very symmetry between the explanations offered for symptoms and dreams might cast doubt on whether the former is adequate as it stands. For in attributing sense or significance to the symptom, it seems to leave out of account a vital feature of the symptom—namely, that it manifests itself, that it occurs. So far, the account fails to bring out any difference between the patient's merely thinking of the symptom and his manifesting it. And yet except in the limiting case of an obsession, where the symptom may be a thought, there clearly is a difference. Why is the patient not content with the former, and what is he doing when he engages in the latter? (Perhaps the force of this question can best be grasped if we go back for a moment to the dream, for there no such question can arise. Once we have explained a dream, we cannot ask, What was the dreamer doing dreaming that dream?—unless, of course, we are asking about the general function of dreams, on which, as we have seen, Freud has something to say.)

Freud's answer is that, in manifesting the symptom, the patient acts on or expresses the impulse that is the sense of the symptom. Bearing in mind that the most important impulse signified by a symptom is a sexual impulse, we may see this answer in such *dicta* as "The symptoms of the disease are nothing else than *the patient's sexual activity*"[29] or "*The patient's symptoms constitute his sexual activity.*"[30]

To illustrate this I shall draw on a case history which

[29] VII, 115.
[30] VII, 278.

we shall look at in much greater detail later on: that
of the so-called Rat Man. The patient reported that one
summer, while on holiday in the mountains, he suddenly conceived the idea that he was too fat and that
he must lose weight.[31] He put the idea into operation
in the harshest fashion. He would get up from meals
before the pudding came round and run along the roads
in the heat of the August sun, or he would clamber up
a precipitous mountainside until he collapsed in ex-
haustion. The understanding of this symptom was delayed, until one session, a chain of associations was
produced by the Rat Man which led from the word "*dick*"
(fat) to the name of his American cousin, Richard, who
was known as Dick. The Rat Man, it also emerged, was
very jealous of this cousin because of the attentions he
paid to the girl with whom (as we shall see) the Rat
Man was by way of being in love. So the symptom of
getting rid of his fat signified, for the Rat Man, getting
rid of or attacking Richard. And when the Rat Man
embarked on his regime, he would be said to be thereby
attacking Richard.

Perhaps the best way of examining this view would
be to look at certain objections that could be raised
against it (just as the best way of examining Freud's
theory of the dream is, I have suggested, to look at the
evidence for it). But first, a further element must be
introduced. A symptom exhibits a complexity that is
not to be found in the dream. Of course, a dream is,
in its way, a complex formation in that it invariably
expresses more than one wish. This is the phenomenon
of overdetermination, in which, incidentally, the symptom also shares, indeed on a massive scale. But all these
wishes are libidinal or positive, and they occur on the

[31] X, 188–89, 318.

same psychic level. The symptom, however, expresses not only a repressed wish or set of wishes but also the forces of repression. And here we have wishes on different psychic levels—the former are unconscious, the latter preconscious. This phenomenon is called compromise-formation, and, in thinking of symptoms as essentially compromise-formations, Freud partly drew on observational or clinical evidence and partly adduced the more theoretical consideration that the symptom must make concessions to the forces of repression, otherwise it too would be repressed. "Every symptom must therefore in some way comply with the demands of the ego which manipulates the repression; it must offer some advantage, it must admit of some useful application, or it would meet with the same fate as the original instinctual impulse itself which has been fended off."[32] In the case of the dream, no such compliance is required: for the condition under which the dream occurs—that is, sleep—places constraint enough upon the wish.

A fairly schematic example of the symptom as compromise-formation comes from *The Interpretation of Dreams.*[33] A woman patient was given to hysterical vomiting. Her associations showed that this represented an old wish dating from puberty that she might be continuously pregnant and have innumerable children. To this wish was later added another wish, that she might have these children by as many men as possible. In the symptom both these wishes are represented and in the condition familiar to us from dreams, i.e., as fulfilled. However, these wishes had aroused repression, and Freud explained how the defensive force against them

[32] XIV, 53.
[33] V, 570.

is also represented in the symptom. "Since the patient might lose her figure and her good looks as a result of vomiting, and so might cease to be attractive to anyone, the symptom was acceptable to the punitive train of thought as well; and since it was permitted by both sides it could become a reality."

The first objection that might be raised against Freud's extended view of the symptom is that it presupposes a degree of confusion on the part of the patient about what he is doing that surely cannot be present. But in characterizing, say, the Rat Man's behavior as he does, Freud was not saying that the Rat Man thought of himself as attacking Richard as opposed to thinking of himself as slimming. On the contrary, Freud's analysis required that the Rat Man thought of himself as slimming, for otherwise the Rat Man's association from "getting rid of his *dick*" to "getting rid of Dick" would be irrelevant.

However, it might now be objected that Freud's view does presuppose a massive misconception on the part of the patient, if not about what he is doing, then, at any rate, about what he can achieve by what he is doing. The Rat Man hopelessly misconceives the efficacy of slimming as a form of murder. But this objection in turn presupposes that the Rat Man can distinguish between the expression of a certain desire and its satisfaction, whereas the desires expressed in symptoms (and in dreams) are of a form to which this distinction does not apply. In the symptom not merely is the desire acted upon but it thereby finds its fulfillment. For this aspect of the symptom Freud coined the description "substitute satisfaction"; we have already seen this at work in the case of the woman who wanted a large number of children and vomited a great deal.

Finally, it might be objected that Freud's view of the symptom requires us to believe that many involuntary acts are really actions that we undertake. This is an objection that has already arisen over the parapraxis, but it might seem that the implausibility is much greater here, in the case, say, of tics or attacks of vomiting than it was with forgetting names or bungling actions. Against this Freud had three lines of defense. First, that he was not overlooking a distinction, he was challenging it: and in support of this he could cite the large number of analogies and similarities that unify human behavior, as well as the difficulties traditionally encountered by philosophers when they have tried to define action. Secondly, that, though a particular piece of behavior might be out of our control, we can use it most evidently to express a feeling—as when we put feeling into a twitch or a grimace that we do not initiate—and, less evidently, but arguably, to express a desire. Thirdly, that in the case of many symptoms it may be that the behavior is out of the patient's control just because he does not realize its sense or significance, i.e., just because it is a symptom. For, as we saw from Freud's earliest work, once the sense is realized or the wish becomes conscious, the symptom vanishes.

There is one important respect in which Freud's view of the symptom, as we have it, might seem too narrow. And if we now try to make good this deficiency, we shall be following Freud's own historical development. For I have talked, as Freud wrote, of a symptom as the expression, and the satisfaction, of a desire. But there cannot be a direct link between a desire and an action, for the appropriateness of an action to the desire always depends on the circumstances: or, to put the matter from the agent's point of view, an action will be judged appropriate to the satisfaction of a certain desire only against the background of certain beliefs. In many cases, particularly with the most fundamental desires, this proviso may prove nugatory, for the relevant beliefs are obvious and universal: it is hard to see when putting food in one's mouth would not be adjudged appropriate to hunger. Nevertheless, as Freud shifted from thinking that memories are crucial to thinking that desires or wishes were, he initially went too far in discounting or depreciating the background that the desire or wish requires in order to find expression.

However, Freud soon found a corrective in a notion that had been with him for a long time but which, in the first years of the century, comes to the forefront: that of "phantasy." Originally, it would seem, Freud used the word to designate mental constructs that purported to be memories but were not, though they might be composed out of scraps of visual and, above all, auditory recollection; the function of such constructs was to protect real memories; they were "defensive fictions."[34] Gradually, however, Freud liberated the concept of phantasy from that of memory, both as far as its function is concerned, and also in its content. A phantasy was now the portrayal or representation of a desire come true, that is, of a desire realized in certain circumstances or against the background of certain beliefs. Accordingly, it marked an increasing recogni-

[34] Kris, p. 196.

tion on Freud's part of the importance of belief along-side desire when he came to connect symptoms with phantasies.

An example from the "Fragment of an Analysis of a Case of Hysteria" illustrates the change.[35] The patient, Dora, developed a hysterical attack of appendicitis. Through her associations Freud equated this with a hysterical pregnancy—in other words, the appendicitis expressed her love, unconscious and repressed, for K., the friend of her father and the husband of his mistress. But, of course, pregnancy could be an expression of her love for K. only if she had made love with him—which in point of fact she had not. So the symptom includes, as the background to her love for K., the belief, unconsciously held, that she had been deflowered. And this belief ran counter to truth, though in accord with her wishes.

So far I have considered symptoms as expressions of impulses or, on a more extended view, of phantasies. In other words, I have looked at symptoms from a positive point of view—though some of the impulses that symptoms express are in themselves negative, i.e., prohibitory or ascetic. However, we have to consider not only what the symptom achieves but also what it avoids. If it is a poor or substitute form of satisfaction for the impulse, it is vastly preferable to denying or renouncing the impulse altogether. For, if the impulse is denied, anxiety ensues. "The symptom," Freud put it, "has been constructed in order to avoid an outbreak of anxiety"[36] and he gives the example of a neurotic who is unable to cross the street alone—force him to do what he be-

35 VII, 22, 101–105.
36 V, 581.

lieves himself incapable of doing, and the consequence will be an attack of anxiety. A form of therapy that concentrated simply on the removal of symptoms would presumably deny this consequence.

This last point will have to be taken up again when we come to consider that of which the symptom is really only a part or constituent; the neurosis. However, the point bears on an issue several times raised in this chapter: the resemblances and differences between the symptom and the dream. Following Freud, I said that the symptom differs from the dream in being a compromise between an unconscious and a preconscious wish. To this it might be retorted that so is the dream, in that it brings together an unconscious impulse and a preconscious wish—namely, the wish to sleep. Yet, though sometimes Freud seems, surprisingly, to concur with this formulation, the parallel it suggests is misleading: for the wish to sleep is not a determinant of the content of the dream in the way in which the repressing force determines the content of the symptom. I now want to suggest that there is a parallel that can be fruitfully drawn between the wish to sleep and a feature of the symptom: but this feature is not the representation of the repressing force, but the avoidance of anxiety, or what Freud comes to call "the gain," that the patient derives from the symptom or, more generally, from the neurosis.

Finally, I want to take one example of a symptom and look in detail at the interpretation Freud gave of it. The example comes from the Dora case, to which I have already referred. Dora was an eighteen-year-old girl, closely linked to her father through common interests and through a history of shared illness, and correspondingly alienated from her mother, who seemed entirely immured in domestic concerns. Recently Dora had become estranged from her father, she had begun to behave in an antisocial way, and, as the immediate cause of her coming for treatment, she had threatened suicide. Part of the explanation for this change lay with a couple, with whom Dora's family had been on close terms, introduced as K. and Frau K. Frau K. had formed a deep attachment to Dora's father, who no longer had any emotional or sexual relations with his wife. K. in turn had developed strong feelings for Dora. Two years previously there had been a walk by the lakeside during which, according to Dora, K. had made advances to her, and two years before that he had kissed her. Dora, who was much involved with the young K. children, was convinced that her father encouraged K.'s attachment to her so that his own friendship with the young and beautiful Frau K. might flourish.

In the course of the analysis, Freud unearthed four different layers of emotion in Dora. There was her love for K., barely disguised: there was her love for her father, which had once been so strong: there was homosexual love, which Freud discovered only at the end of the analysis, and which seemed somewhat diffused over her mother, Frau K., and her last governess with whom she had discussed sexual topics and whom she had had dismissed: and there was a fourth love, to be of immense importance in the history of psychoanalysis, but of no great relevance here, that for Freud himself. Now, most of the case history is taken up with the analysis of two long dreams, but there is one interesting symptom, which seems to enter into all these relations, and thus displays a high degree of overdetermination.[37]

[37] VII, 39, 41, 47–48, 51–53, 83.

The symptom was a cough which came on in bouts, each attack starting with a catarrh, lasting for about three to five weeks, and generally producing a loss of voice in the last stages.

The first interpretation was given in the course of a session during which Dora complained that her father used his illness for his own purposes, and made much the same accusation against Frau K., her purpose being to avoid her conjugal duties with K; Dora then went on to talk of her own illness, which, it turned out, invariably lasted as long as K. was away. Freud inferred that Dora's reproach of others concealed a self-reproach, in that she too used her illness for her own purposes—to demonstrate her love for K., just as Frau K.'s illness was used to demonstrate her aversion to K. It fitted in with this interpretation that the cough led to her losing her voice, which she had no need for while K. was away, and that when this happened, writing, which was the only form of communication for which she now had a use, became especially easy for her.

The second interpretation of the cough arose directly out of another reproach. Dora had been insisting that Frau K. was involved with her father only because he was *ein vermögender Mann* (a man of means). From the specific way in which Dora produced this phrase, Freud suspected that behind it there lurked its opposite, *ein unvermögender Mann*, which can mean not only a poor man but an impotent man. Dora confirmed this. The question then arose, If Dora believed that her father was engaged in a love affair with Frau K. and also that he was impotent, how did she conceive that sexual intercourse took place between them? Dora revealed that she knew of the varieties of sexual intercourse, and Freud then felt able to say that she must be thinking of intercourse through that part of the body which in her case was in a state of irritation: namely, the mouth. When she coughed, she represented oral intercourse between the two people who so preoccupied her thoughts —save that, in exhibiting the symptom, she took the place of one of them.

These two interpretations converge on the cough, but it is to be noted that one focuses on the consequences and periodicity of the cough, the other on the organ that it inflames. A third interpretation, which remained fragmentary, suggested a link between her cough and her father's venereal disease, which Dora knew of. The link passed through certain physical similarities—both complaints affected the lungs and involved a mucous discharge. In displaying the symptom under this interpretation Dora at once identified herself with her father (she shared his cough) and also expressed her anger against him for infecting her—where the infection was to be understood very broadly not just as a specific disease that she had inherited, but, more generally, as sexuality. And in these two attitudes toward her father—wishing to be him and to revenge herself upon him—lay the roots of Dora's homosexuality. Insofar as the cough proclaimed these attitudes, it expressed her love for women. So, as Freud put it, "the organically determined irritation of the throat . . . acted like the grain of sand around which an oyster forms its pearl."

4

It involves a leap across a vast intervening stretch of mental life, to move from the symptom, with its roots in the pathogenic and the unruly, to the joke. Yet there are similarities between the two phenomena, and these are best approached by considering what each has in common with the dream. In *Jokes and Their Relations to the Unconscious*, published in 1905, Freud gave as his "subjective reason" for taking up the new problem the fact that, if a dream interpretation is placed in the hands of "an uninformed or unaccustomed person," he will react to it as though it were "in the nature of a joke."[38] This reaction is correct, Freud argued (repeating a point he had originally made to Fliess, who had reacted in just this way on reading the proofs of *The Interpretation of Dreams*), so long as it is recognized that it is the dreamer, not the dream-interpreter, who is responsible for the impression. In other words, the techniques of jokes in many ways replicates the dream-work. And along with similarity of technique goes similarity of content. The joke, like the dream and, to some degree, the parapraxis, expresses a repressed or unconscious wish.

The conformity of the joke techniques with those which constitute the dream-work is most clearly exhibited in the three broad categories under which Freud subsumed them—condensation, displacement, and indirect representation. "So far-reaching an agreement," Freud felt able to observe, "can scarcely be a matter of chance."[39] But the suspicion must arise that agreement had been reached solely through the initial choice of categories, that the new categories had been selected with an eye to the old and had then been forcibly imposed on the material. It was precisely to avoid this imputation that Freud gave *Jokes and Their Relation to the Unconscious* the form that it has, beginning with

[38] VII, 173.
[39] VIII, 89.

a review of a very large number of jokes and then an attempt to extract inductively the techniques according to which they have been constructed.

There are, however, objections that can still be raised to Freud's procedure. The first is that his review is possibly incomplete, and there may very well be important techniques that have been overlooked. In principle Freud concurred, but he believed that he was entitled to a reasonable certainty that the material he had considered exemplified "the commonest, most important and most characteristic methods of joking."[40] Secondly, it might be objected that, even granted the adequacy of the material, there is no reason to suppose that the various techniques have been elicited from it rather than read into it. Against such a charge Freud depended on the operation he called "reduction," which consisted in spelling out the total meaning of the joke, at the price of its ceasing to be a joke. So an acerbic comment by the often quoted Herr N., "Yes, vanity is one of his four Achilles heels" can be "reduced" to "Apart from his vanity, Y. is an eminent man; all the same I don't like him—he's an ass rather than a man."[41] Reduction according to Freud, confirmed the similarly between joke technique and dream-work.

There are also dissimilarities. Some of these simply reflect the constraints that the joke has to accept as the result of the position it occupies in conscious, indeed in social, life. Others arise from the difference in medium between jokes and dreams. In jokes the regression of thoughts to perception is absent, and there is a corresponding preoccupation with linguistic rather than plastic representation. Of course, Freud did not think

[40] VII, 167.
[41] VIII, 25.

that every joke was a play on words. On the contrary, he divided jokes (as opposed to joke techniques) into two categories, the verbal and the conceptual, and he connected these with different joke techniques, the verbal with condensation and the conceptual with displacement and indirect representation. But the essence of the joke, he insisted, lay in its expression, in the envelope, as he put it, and, accordingly, we should expect a correlate to the fact that the joke, unlike the dream, is invariably folded into a linguistic envelope.

But it is when we turn to the second feature of the joke that we notice a marked dissimilarity from the dream. For on one level, at any rate, not all jokes have a purpose. There are "tendentious" jokes, and there are abstract or, as Freud prefers it, "innocent" jokes. Innocent jokes must not be confused with jokes of no substance or jokes that have nothing of value to assert. Freud classified as innocent the epigrams of Lichtenberg, so admired by Goethe and later by Wittgenstein (e.g., "He wondered how it was that cats have two holes cut in their skin precisely where their eyes are," "It is almost impossible to carry the torch of truth through a crowd without singeing someone's beard"), for though they have considerable intellectual content, the thought behind the joke, or its "substance," is independent of the joke, is not of its essence. Tendentious jokes serve two purposes: either they are obscene jokes, serving the purpose of exposure, or they are hostile gibes.

In one sense, tendentious jokes take priority over innocent jokes. They generate greater pleasure—"a slight smile," Freud suggests, "is all we can ordinarily look for from an innocent joke"[42]—and they belong to a more

[42] VIII, 96.

evolved activity, they represent "the highest stage of
jokes."[43] For just this reason, innocent jokes, being less
complex, provide the better starting point. Furthermore,
though they do have fewer elements to their make-up,
they possess in a reduced way much the same structure
as the tendentious joke. (Indeed, ultimately, Freud was
led to the view that, "strictly speaking," no jokes are
nontendentious.)

As a first step, Freud suggested that jokes can be
ordered on an extended scale of free human activity,
on which they will occupy the higher positions. In de-
scending order, the scale runs: tendentious jokes, innocent jokes, jests, play. Play appears in children at an
early stage, when they are learning to acquire or make
use of their verbal skills. It consists in the mouthing of
sounds or in the absurd combination of thoughts, put
together without reference to meaning or coherence,
and the pleasures of play derive from repetition or the
rediscovery of what is familiar. Gradually, however,
with the strengthening of the critical faculty, play is
condemned as meaningless or absurd, and its pursuit
becomes impossible. Nevertheless, the individual is left
with a yearning for these old sources of pleasure, and
he directs his energies toward finding a way of engag-
ing in play which can withstand criticism. There is only
one possibility open to him, and that is that the concatenations of words and thoughts, in which play de-
lights, should also have a meaning. It is not necessary
that the meaning should be valuable, or new, or interesting: it is enough, for the silencing of criticism, that
it should exist. Hence the jest, the jest being distinguished from the joke by the fact that it aims solely at
meeting this elementary or basic requirement. So it is

[43] VIII, 173.

a jest when Rokitansky, the famous anatomist, on being asked the professions of his sons—two were doctors and two were singers—should reply, "Two *heilen* [heal] and two *heulen* [howl]."[44] But, as this example suggests, even to satisfy the very modest demands of the jest, the complex apparatus of the joke-work, with all its resources of invention and ingenuity, has already been called into being.

The transition from the jest to the innocent joke, next above it in the scale of development, is not clear-cut, consisting as it does in the substitution of a thought of some substance or value for one that claims no more than mere intelligibility. So it was already a joke and not a jest when a member of the short-lived "Bürger" ministry in Austria (1867-1869) had answered a question about the cabinet's solidarity by "How can we *einstehen* [stand up] for one another, when we can't *ausstehen* [stand] one another?"[45] By this substitution the pleasure that derives from the reactivation of play receives more adequate protection from criticism: and this protection is reinforced by the way in which the joke always makes "a *total* impression of enjoyment on us,"[46] so that we cannot decide how much of the pleasure arises from the joke and how much we would anyhow derive from the thought. It is this confusion about the sources of pleasure, which is intrinsic to the joke, that makes possible its secondary role. For, not merely does the joke, like the jest, safeguard pleasures of play by a screen of rationality, it also protects and promotes the thought by linking it with so evident a source of pleasure. We are less ready to find fault with a thought

[44] VIII, 129–30.
[45] VIII, 131–32n.
[46] VIII, 132.

if it has made us laugh: though, strictly speaking, it is not the thought but the form in which it has been cast that is responsible for our mood. It is this secondary aspect of the joke that is responsible for the emergence of the tendentious joke proper.

But before going on to the tendentious joke, I want to raise two queries about what the jest and the innocent joke have in common: that is, the aim of obtaining a yield of pleasure from play with words or from the liberation of nonsense, and of safeguarding this pleasure from the objections of reason. Now in the first place it might be asked how we can deliberately set out to retrieve the pleasures of play, when it might seem that these can only arise spontaneously. Certainly, in none of the other circumstances when processes like condensation or displacement have been in evidence, has there been any suggestion that they were invoked or exploited. On this point, Freud was not fully explicit. He never claimed that the processes can be under our control: he pointed out that we do not make a joke in the sense in which we make a judgment or an objection: the thought that is the substance of the joke is *"given over for a moment to unconscious revision,"*[47] and we then perceive, and presumably accept or reject, the result. However, the use or exploitation of unconscious activities by conscious agency was something on which Freud at this stage did not or perhaps could not have a reasoned position. He left it that the view that certain processes arise automatically and the view that they can be used to yield pleasure are "not contradictory." Again, a problem arises concerning the relation between the two parts of the aim and the way in which they both find satisfaction.

[47] VIII, 166.

Freud was insistent that the jest or the joke, unlike the symptom, is not a compromise formation. From one point of view the joke is, and remains, nonsense, and from another point of view it is, and remains, sense. "Nothing," Freud observes, "distinguishes jokes more clearly from all other psychical structures than this double-sidedness and this duplicity in speech."[48] It is precisely this that accounts for "the principle of confusion of sources of pleasure,"[49] which we have already observed in operation, and which is to be of greater use in the tendentious joke itself.

A tendentious joke has a purpose, and this purpose is generally one whose free expression would encounter opposition. The opposition can be an external constraint, but the more interesting and the more fundamental case is where the inhibition is internal. So whereas the jest has to overcome one kind of inhibition, the tendentious joke has most often to overcome two kinds of inhibition—"those opposed to the joke itself and those opposed to its purpose."[50]

To understand its mechanism, we must see how these two tasks are dovetailed, how the pleasure released through the overcoming of one kind of inhibition is then harnessed to the overcoming of the other. The pleasure that serves to initiate the larger release of pleasure Freud calls "forepleasure," and the principle by which the two tasks are linked is called "the forepleasure principle."[51] So, just as in the jest a thought is used to protect play from criticism, in the tendentious joke the pleasure that arises from play is used to

[48] VIII, 172.
[49] VIII, 137.
[50] VIII, 173.
[51] VIII, 137.

free from inhibition a purpose that would otherwise be suppressed.

On the question how in a tendentious joke the fore-pleasure derived from the free use of words or thoughts is of the right strength to secure the lifting of an inhibition (a point which touches on the internal regulation of unconscious processes), Freud found himself with little to offer. He pointed out that the aptitude for making jokes is not universal; and if we inquire into its subjective determinants it is interesting to observe, though the observation will not sustain any hypothesis, how often these determinants seem to be fulfilled among neurotic people.

Nevertheless, if the question suggests that the redistribution of psychic energies upon which the joke depends for its efficacy can be achieved by the individual unaided, then it is misleading and points to an inadequacy in the account so far given. For it is intrinsic to Freud's argument that the joke is essentially a social activity: it is "the most social of all the mental functions that aim at a yield of pleasure."[52] Now, what Freud means is not simply that the hearer of a joke benefits from the skill of the person who made it, but also that the person who makes the joke is dependent on the hearer. "A joke," Freud says, "*must* be told to someone else"[53]—and here he is contrasting the joke with some rather broader category of the comic. For just this reason the joke must submit to demands unrecognized by the dream or the symptom.

To explain the requirement that a joke must be shared, Freud invokes another fact of experience: that we cannot laugh at a joke that we have made ourselves.

[52] VIII, 179.
[53] VIII, 143.

Freud then links these two conditions by suggesting that "we are compelled to tell our joke to someone else because we are unable to laugh at it ourselves."[54] The laughter of others convinces us that we have constructed a good joke; it adds to our pleasure; and, above all, it allows us to discharge the pleasure that has been generated, something which we otherwise seem unable to achieve. To arrive at a proper understanding of this last point, which is the most important, we need to turn to Freud's theoretical account of the joke: that is to say, his account in terms of the theory of the mind.

One factor that accounts for the peculiar difficulty, and peculiar neglect, of *Jokes and Their Relation to the Unconscious* is the constant shifts that take place in it between theory and psychological observation or generalization. This is confusing, because the reader can sometimes be uncertain on which level the argument is moving, but also, more radically, because Freud himself was sometimes confused, that is to say, he sometimes treated propositions about energy and its liberation as though they were descriptions of observable or even introspectible phenomena. But it is not hard to understand why Freud found it necessary, in discussing this topic, to refer so heavily to theoretical considerations. For it is one thing to see in general terms how jokes might serve to produce pleasure and to lift inhibitions, and another thing to assess the likelihood of such processes; for this latter purpose a quantitative account must be given of the redistribution of energies involved, and how they balance out. This can be done only on a theoretical level.

In translating his account into theoretical terms, Freud stressed a distinction between two different situ-

[54] VIII, 155.

ations in the economy of the mental apparatus: one where energy has been released or where there has been a saving of energy, and the other where the energy that has been liberated is available for discharge and is not put to some further psychic purpose. Freud argued that play, or the processes of the joke work, invariably result in an economy of energy. But the individual cannot by himself—perhaps because of the degree of attention required for the making of the joke—use this energy for discharge. It is the hearer, taken unawares by the joke, who can readily and immediately divest himself of the energy that accrues to him from it. It is only when he laughs that, by a process resembling infection, the person who has made the joke can laugh too.

There are two final points worth making about Freud's treatment of the joke. In his only other, and much later, contribution to the subject, Freud described *Jokes and Their Relation to the Unconscious* as written "only from the economic point of view."[55] This is not strictly true. Though the discussion is in terms of the saving and expenditure of energy, the idea is explicitly abandoned that economies are to be measured in terms of absolute quota of energy: otherwise, as Freud pointed out, we might observe a tendency, in the pursuit of pleasure, toward "the greatest possible restriction in the use of words and in the establishment of chains of thought."[56] And we find no such thing. The economies involved in jokes are in the first place very small and, secondly, their importance is relative to anticipated or accustomed expenditures. "The factor of the expendi-

[55] XXI, 161.
[56] VIII, 156.

ture's being one that was expected and prepared for moves unmistakably into the foreground."[57]

The second point is this: I have already referred to the orthodox view according to which the influence of theory or of a model of a mind upon Freud was to lead him into a mechanistic view and a denial of the role of human intention and motive. It is interesting to observe that the highly theoretical discussions that figure so large in *Jokes and Their Relation to the Unconscious* concern a mental phenomenon that is much closer to action, much further away from mere reflex, than, say, dreams or errors. In fact, Freud's treatment of the joke became in many ways the prototype for what he was to say about the processes and activities of the ego, as they came to be defined.

5

Dreams, errors, symptoms, jokes—all exhibit to varying degrees the fundamental role played by impulse in our psychic life. Furthermore, all four stand in some relation or other to what Freud in the "Scientific Project" had postulated as the most primitive, as well as the most vulnerable, way in which impulse seeks discharge: that is, by stimulating a mnemic image of the object it seeks and then, without establishing whether there is a "real" or merely a "perceptual" identity between image and object, instantly spending itself. Dreams seem to be straightforward examples of "the wish," as impulse is called when it seeks satisfaction in this immediate or hallucinatory way: symptoms, being compromise forma-

[57] VIII, 157.

tions, are impure examples, but do not lie far behind: and errors and jokes are related more obliquely to the wish.

This suggests one ordering of these phenomena, in which dreams will appear as the most impulsive or the most instinctual, jokes the least so. However, this is not the only possible ordering, and other orderings will bring out features that this conceals. For instance, if we look at the joke, we observe that an impulse that is ordinarily controlled and, indeed, does not even seem to be particularly clamorous for discharge, is deliberately afforded release: it is, as it were, momentarily dipped into the unconscious. Of course, it is precisely because the activity is and will remain so well under control that it is permitted at all. Nevertheless, the joke presents us with a case where there is an undoing, if a deliberate undoing, of the processes of repression and of the binding of energy. A moment's mobility is granted to the mind. By contrast, both the dream and the symptom, while indubitably expressive of impulse, can also be seen as attempts to deal with it and master or tame it. For, in these cases, the impulse is clamorous for discharge, and, though discharge is secured, at least in part, the price that the impulse pays is to lose some of its mobility. Both in the dream and in the symptom, energy is bound, if in some ultimately unsatisfactory way: in the case of the symptom, unsatisfactory because of the manifest element of conflict, and in the case of the dream, unsatisfactory because the binding is so evidently temporary, for the duration, that is, of the dreamer's sleep. Looked at from this point of view, the dream and the symptom, though predominantly unruly elements in our life, are also tentative beginnings toward the imposition of rule.

This theme will be taken up much later in this book, as it was taken up much later by Freud, under the heading of the ego and its activities. Indeed, outside a notion of ego activity, it is hard to give a coherent account of the taming of impulse. Nevertheless, it is worth indicating another area of psychic life where Freud, even at this stage, held the taming of impulse to occur. I refer to the way in which impulse or instinct can be bound in the form of emotion, where this includes love, fear, hate, anxiety, etc. Freud assumed a developmental continuity between an impulse and an emotional state, and the latter is treated as a kind of reservoir into which the former drains when it cannot find an outlet. This metaphor, though not Freud's, is indeed peculiarly appropriate to Freud's way of thinking. For he would appear to have conceived of the conversion or reduction of impulse into emotion as itself a kind of discharge: an internal discharge, which, in its lesser way, did duty for the external discharge that was denied it.

Sexuality

●

IV

In the last chapter we have seen how Freud brought together four mental phenomena, none of them from out of the upper reaches of the human mind—dreams, jokes, errors, and symptoms of the psychoneuroses—and attributed to them a depth or significance that went beyond anything that ordinary opinion would credit them with. In the majority of cases, the significance turned out to be sexual. Freud first identified the phenomenon with the expression of a wish or impulse; then, the repressed impulse with a sexual impulse. With such powerful evidence for the importance that Freud by now attached to sexuality, we might come to think of Freud as attaching a unique importance to sexuality or as identifying our impulses exclusively with the sexual. And so the idea of a Freudian pansexualism arises.

Or by another route, also discernible to us by now, we might reach the same conclusion. In the last chapter but one, we saw how Freud conceived of the mind as a system primarily engaged in ridding itself of any excessive accretions of quantity, or Q. Dreams, jokes, errors, and symptoms, being expressions of wish or impulse, are therefore special instances or variants of the mind in discharge; and, since in the majority of cases, it is a sexual impulse that they discharge, it seems plausible to identify quantity—or rather quantity insofar as it arises from an endogenous source—with sexuality. And so we are back at pansexualism.

It cannot, however, be too often insisted that, though Freud heavily emphasized the element of sexuality in human nature, he utterly rejected pansexualism, which he regarded as a travesty of his theory; and on many occasions he explicitly and energetically denied the equation of all instinctual life with sexuality. In a letter of early 1921 written to Professor Edouard Claparède, of Geneva, Freud wrote:

> From me you borrow the sexual nature of the libido and from Jung its generalized meaning. And it is thus that there is created in the imagination of the critics a pan-sexualism which exists neither in my views nor in Jung's. . . . The wider public, however, are ignorant of this; it is kept hidden from them.[1]

Indeed one of the most significant reasons why Freud did lay such emphasis on sexuality—that is, its importance as a causal factor in neurosis—required him to postulate another group of instincts over and against sexuality. The explanatory value of the concept of sexuality in mental disorder depended on its not enjoying

[1] XI, 214–15n.

a monopoly in the domain of the instincts. It was a dark moment in Freud's theory, comparable to the shock it sustained in 1897 on the abandonment of the seduction theory, when, in 1914, it looked as though all instinctual energy might have to be subsumed under libido or sexuality. For this would have meant that the pathogenic role of sexuality would be unsubstantiated. Sexuality would still have been of great significance to normal psychology but of only marginal interest to abnormal psychology.

Freud's major work on sexuality is the *Three Essays in the Theory of Sexuality*, published in 1905, and then substantially expanded and amended through six editions over the subsequent twenty years. The work has a richness, complexity, and elegance which popularization has obscured.

The privileges or liberties in which Freud confirmed sexuality, and which have so often been contested by his more pious or respectable critics, derive from two distinct sources. On the one hand, there is an extended inquiry into the history of sexuality, which traces it to a time before that at which it is ordinarily found: on the other hand, there is an extension of the concept of sexuality, which stretches it beyond the sense in which it is ordinarily defined. Often only one or other of these two projects is attributed to Freud—and then both it and the account as a whole are distorted: so we are told that Freud's insistence on sexuality is of no more than peripheral interest (some perverse histories have been unmasked), or quite arbitrary (a word has been redefined). However, not merely are these two projects present in Freud: not merely do both have the effect of subsuming under sexuality phenomena that are not ordinarily identified as, or recognized to be, such: but the two projects are themselves linked in an interesting and illuminating way. To appreciate the boldness of Freud's theory of sexuality, we must note the link.

Let us consider the following passage, to which parallels can be found elsewhere in Freud:

> Popular opinion has quite definite ideas about the nature and characteristics of the sexual instinct. It is generally understood to be absent in childhood, to set in at the time of puberty in connection with the process of coming to maturity and to be revealed in the manifestations of an irresistible attraction exercised by one sex upon the other; while its aim is presumed to be sexual union, or at all events actions leading in that direction.[2]

Now the first two points on which, according to this passage, popular opinion takes its stand—those concerning sexuality in childhood and at adolescence—might well seem straightforwardly empirical: while the second two points—about heterosexuality, and the centrality of sexual intercourse—are conceptual or analytic. But note that when Freud came to challenge popular opinion, his challenge was all of a piece, though articulated into parts. First, he brought out the absurd narrowness of the conventional definition of sexuality; then he showed sexuality to have a complex and lengthy history; and finally, in the light of this history, an emended definition of sexuality was made to look far from arbitrary.

To bring out the inadequacy of the conventional distinction, Freud introduced a distinction between the *sexual object*, i.e., the person from whom attraction proceeds, and the *sexual aim*, i.e., the act toward which the

[2] VII, 135.

instinct tends. He then went on to point out that there are many forms of behavior deviating from the norm in object, or in aim, or both, and yet which we could not but think of as sexual. As deviations in object (or inversions), Freud cited homosexuality and attraction to those who are sexually immature or of another species. As deviations in aim (or perversions), he cited practices involving an extension of interest, anatomically, from the genitals to other parts of the body, such as the mucous membrane of the lips or the anus, or an insurmountable attachment to a preparatory or intermediate activity, such as looking, or touching, or the exchange of pain.

None of this material, as Freud made clear, was new. It could be found in the various encyclopedic works of Krafft-Ebing, Havelock Ellis, or Magnus Hirschfeld, which are still sought after by amateurs of sexuality. Nor did Freud suppose that these varieties of behavior were ever held to be anything but sexual. But he did think that the discrepancy between the way in which the notion of sexuality was ordinarily defined and the way in which it was in fact employed was well worth pointing out, for, if ordinary usage was more liberal than it professed to be, it was also more wayward or unthinking than it should be.

However, the interest of Freud's treatment of this material lies in the way in which he used it to effect a systematic extension of the concept of sexuality. Here the perversions proved more rewarding than the inversions. For the inversions present us with a "connected series," or a range of adjacent cases running from the normal to the deviant. With the perversions the situation is more complex, for the normal and the deviant cannot be arranged on a single scale. What relates them is the overlap, or shared possession, of certain "components"—the preference for this or that bodily activity, the attachment to this or that anatomical zone—some of which will be common to several forms of behavior but none common to all. More specifically, each deviant form of behavior emphasizes one or more components of that "amalgamation" of instincts which we call normality. Now, if with Freud we reject any explanation of sexual deviation in such nineteenth-century terms as disease or the taint of degeneracy, then we are likely to think of the varieties of sexual behavior as corresponding to earlier stages in a common development or to exaggerations of these stages. The string of intermediate forms in the case of the inversions and, more strikingly, the recurrent components in the case of the perversions suggest that the phenomena collected under the common concept of sexuality could also be hung on the branches of a common family tree of sexual development. Thus we find implicit in the extension of the concept of sexuality pointers to the hypothesis of infantile sexuality.

Before turning to the detail of Freud's developmental account, I want briefly to survey the types of evidence upon which Freud relied. They are diverse, and, though Freud did not make the point, it may very well be that their diversity, given their consistency, was taken by him as an indication of strength of support for his theory.

The first type of evidence is that provided, profusely, by the psychoneuroses. For the neuroses are "based on sexual instinctual forces."[3] This hypothesis, Freud argued, is itself well supported by evidence. If we now combine this with the further hypothesis, also taken to be well grounded, that the neuroses reveal, or make

[3] VII, 163.

reference to, infantile impulses, then we have strong evidence, though indirect, for infantile sexuality.

However, we might now wonder why, since we have all been infants once, we do not also have strong direct evidence, through memory, for infantile sexuality? And, since we clearly don't have such evidence, why is this not strong direct evidence against infantile sexuality? To this, Freud first pointed out that, while we don't have any memories about infantile sexuality, neither do we in general have many memories about infancy: for most, though not all, of us, the earliest years, up to the sixth or eighth, are buried in amnesia. Freud now argued that this phenomenon itself needs explanation, and, if we look for a parallel, the closest is to be found in the amnesia of hysterics, where the unavailability of memory can be traced directly to the repression of sexual impulses. In other words, the fact that we cannot obtain direct evidence for infantile sexuality along a path where we might naturally expect to find it is taken by Freud as further indirect evidence for the phenomenon. This, then, is the second type of evidence.

The third type of evidence, which is the most obviously direct in kind, did not come Freud's way till later: the evidence from child analysis. In a paper of 1909 entitled "The Analysis of a Phobia in a Five-Year-Old Boy" (the case of "Little Hans"), Freud expressed "the wish for a more direct and less roundabout proof of these fundamental theorems,"[4] but he himself very rarely took on children as patients. In a note to the *Three Essays*, added in 1910, he wrote, "It is gratifying to be able to report that direct observation has fully confirmed the conclusions arrived at by psycho-analysis,"[5]

[4] X, 6.
[5] VII, 193–94n.

and much the same result was reported in the *Introductory Lectures*. However, it would seem that much the most significant piece of evidence that Freud himself extracted from the direct observation of children is, oddly enough, itself indirect as to infantile sexuality. I refer to the powerful and in many ways terrifying sexual theories of children,[6] which, overtly about their parents' practices, about birth and copulation, are taken by Freud, surely rightly, as "reflections of their own sexual constitution"—or, perhaps more accurately, indices of their own sexual development.

A final type of evidence, to which we shall return in considering therapy and Freud's changing conception of it, is provided by the phenomenon of transference.

The most general feature of infantile sexual development, as recounted by Freud, is that it is periodic or oscillatory, the oscillations being explained partly in terms of the waning and reinforcement of the sexual impulse, partly in terms of the building up of mental forces opposed to sexuality, i.e., disgust, shame, and the moral and aesthetic ideals. I shall consider this developmental account, first, under the heading of sexual aim, then under the heading of sexual object. Freud has very much more to say under the first heading than under the second: and this disproportion will itself receive an explanation.

Central to Freud's developmental account in terms of sexual aim is the concept of an erotogenic zone of the body. To grasp this concept we need to see how an erotogenic zone becomes established. Any such zone is, in the first instance, bound up with a vital somatic function: the labial zone with feeding, or the anal zone with

6 VII, 194–97; IX, 131–39, 209–26; X, 5–149.

defecation. When this somatic function is complete, a pleasurable sensation is experienced in the zone. The next thing is that a need arises for repeating this pleasurable sensation, independently of the somatic function which introduced it. This need is experienced as a general state of tension but also, more locally, as an itching or stimulation of the zone in question. And so the aim arises of having the zone so played on or manipulated by an external stimulus that the itching will be removed and a pleasurable sensation ensue: a development facilitated by the fact that each zone is not merely an identifiable expanse of the body, but an expanse with a characteristic use or employment. By now we have not merely an application for the concept of an erotogenic zone, but also something which can be considered as an impulse directed upon this zone and which is later to be a component instinct of sexuality.

This account of how an erotogenic zone comes to be established is, basically, an account of how one instinct is acquired or learned on the basis of another, and certain features deserve comment. Starting off, as it does, from the pleasure experienced in the satisfaction of an original or vital instinct, it retains the pleasure connected with this original instinct as somehow primary or exemplary. "Sucking at the mother's breast," he was to write, "is the starting point of the whole sexual life, the unmatched prototype of every later sexual satisfaction, to which phantasy often recurs in times of need."[7] Secondly, though any instinct can be satisfied only through an external agency or stimulus, this agency initially in no way enters into the internal representation of the instinct or the concept under which the instinct is brought. (As an empirical corollary of this, Freud em-

[7] XVI, 314.

phasized the role of masturbation in the acquisition or reinforcement of the component instincts of sexuality.) And, thirdly, the object of an instinct being a later accretion which is "soldered" onto the instinct, the instinct itself is identified through the zone or somatic source with which it is linked. In point of fact, the whole account of erotogenic zones and their emergence clearly exemplifies the general theory Freud enunciated in the "Scientific Project" about impulses and the experience of satisfaction: and it is worth pointing out that many later psychoanalytic writers would not follow Freud in his relegation of the object to such a secondary place.

The other component instincts that have to be fitted into the total account of sexuality fall into pairs, each with an active and a passive member: looking and being looked at; touching and being touched; inflicting, and enduring, pain. These are, Freud said, distinct in the first instance from erotogenic sexual activity, and, indeed, of the cruel instinct he says that it "develops in childhood even more independently of the sexual activities that are attached to erotogenic zones."[8] So the question arises, How do these instincts get united with sexuality? The answer must lie in the instrumental role that the paired instincts play vis-à-vis the erotogenic instincts. For instance, there is a direct instrumental link between any erotogenic instinct and looking; or a more indirect link starting from the erotogenic instincts, passing through curiosity, and leading to mastery or cruelty. This last example is peculiarly interesting: because it brings out clearly, in the step from curiosity to mastery, the very primitive way in which these links are conceived, and how powerful, in the forging of them, are the influences of analogy and assimilation.

[8] VII, 192.

In the 1915 revision of the *Three Essays*, Freud introduced a new concept, which had been slowly forming, that of an "organization of the libido," in terms of which he was able to reassemble and coordinate a number of ideas about infantile sexuality. In the first place, each organization of the libido is identified by reference to an erotogenic zone which enjoys primacy within it: hence the oral organization, the anal organization, and the genital organization. All of these were recognized by 1915. Eight years later, in "The Infantile Genital Organization: An Interpolation into the Theory of Sexuality," Freud added to this list a further organization, which he called the phallic organization to indicate that, at this stage, though the genitals are paramount, only one type of genitals is recognized: the penis in boys, and, derivatively, the clitoris in girls. Secondly, the new concept suggested that any fitting together of the various component instincts of sexuality is always relative to, and under the aegis of, a dominant erotogenic zone. Freud suggested two general ways in which this fit can come about. There can be certain pervasive phantasies, originating from the erotogenic zone and its specific employment, which emphasize, or modify, certain non-erotogenic instincts: so, for instance, inside both the oral and the anal organizations, the over-all sexual aim can become identified with an attack—in the one case, of a cannibalistic, in the other case, of a poisoning or incendiary, nature. Alternatively, the nonerotogenic instincts may come to service the erotogenic instincts by providing what Freud called "forepleasure": pleasure which is not merely prior to, but somehow anticipatory of, the fundamental pleasure to be experienced in the erotogenic zone. Incidentally, it is forepleasure that gives rise to a most important mechanism in sexual development: for it is by becoming the source of fore-pleasure that one erotogenic zone gives way to its successor, or that one organization of the libido can become absorbed by, and transcended in, the next. This brings us to the third and best-known use to which Freud puts this new concept. The development of sexuality is now neatly characterized as a linear progression moving through the various pregenital organizations of the libido—the oral, the anal, the phallic, in that order—and culminating in the genital organization. For any reader with a general acquaintance with Freud, it must come as something of a shock to learn how late it was that Freud came to weld together the two themes which had been with him for many years—the complex history of human sexuality, and the erotogenic zones—into a unity so that the former could be divided up into stages by reference to the latter. Only in 1915 did he state the fully evolutionary thesis; and no sooner had he done so than he felt it necessary to issue warnings that the schema must not be taken too literally, that the various stages overlap, and that each stage leaves permanent and ineradicable traces.

Of the various transitions that are implicit in the oral-anal-phallic-genital story, it is notoriously the last that exhibits the greatest complexity and that most exercised Freud.[9] But before looking at this I shall, for reasons that will readily emerge, take up what Freud has to say about sexual development under the heading of sexual object. For so far I have been almost exclusively con-

[9] A tradition that begins with Abraham and issues in Melanie Klein has concentrated on the earlier transitions. According to this tradition, the later transitions cannot be fully understood except in the light of the earlier ones.

cerned with sexuality in relation to its aim. (I say "almost" advisedly. For it will be observed that the non-erotogenic instincts involve from the very beginning an object upon which they are directed. But this by itself does not justify talking of a sexual object: for that to be appropriate the two types of component instinct must exhibit a measure of unification.)

Sexuality in its earliest phase does not, Freud contended, possess an object. It consists in sexual aims which the infant endeavors to fulfill through its own body, and for this reason Freud applied to the whole period the term "autoerotism": a term invented, and also (according to Freud) "spoilt," by Havelock Ellis. Freud then went on to account for the introduction of an object by what he calls the "attachment" or "anaclitic" route. That is to say, just as sexuality—at any rate in its erotogenic aspect—derives from the infant's vital somatic functions, so the earliest object of sexuality derives from the person or persons who satisfy these functions, who feed or nurse him. The first objects of sexual longing, like sexuality itself, supervene on the infant's dependence on the mother as the source of food and comfort. The mother, Freud writes, is "the first *love*-object."[10]

It is, of course, the history of this ill-fated passion that runs across the last two stages in the development of the libido, and it might now look as though we were ready to return to this theme. However, before doing so, we need to take account of some of Freud's later views concerning object choice and its origins.

Around 1909,[11] Freud began to work on the idea that

[10] XVI, 329.
[11] VII, 145n.; XI, 100; XII, 60–62. See, for earliest reference, *Minutes of the Vienna Psychoanalytic Society*, November 10, 1909.

an intermediate phase needs to be inserted between early autoerotism and object choice proper. In this phase there is already a sexual object, but the object is the infant's own body or person; in consequence, the phase is called "narcissism." The question immediately arises, How does narcissism differ from autoerotism? Or, to put the matter more sharply, How can Freud distinguish the two phases when both reveal that feature which led Freud to posit autoerotism as primary, i.e., the absence of any external object that exercises sexual attraction over the infant? Freud's explicit treatment of this question, in his famous paper "On Narcissism," was highly perfunctory. Nevertheless, it is possible to reconstruct an answer, which would fall into two parts. For narcissism, like other key Freudian notions, such as projection, rests on two criteria for its application, one to do with the possession by the person involved of a specific concept, the other to do with consequences. Narcissism differs from autoerotism in that it involves a concept of the infant's own person or ego: the infant loves himself *as himself*. Secondly, narcissism can give rise to a primitive or inchoate form of object choice, called "identification," in which the infant (or the adult who inherits the infant's sexual immaturity) seeks an object conceived of in his own image, and therefore loved as he loves himself. These two criteria—which are themselves linked, in that the concept referred to in the first criterion reappears in the second criterion, since the concept of one's own person is involved in identification —would seem to justify the distinction between autoerotism and narcissism: even if they also call for a revision of the arguments that Freud used in favor of autoerotism. Furthermore, this account of narcissism already allows us to glimpse what is to be another of the great

evolutionary themes—the link between sexual development and the development of the ego. The history of
object choice is, not surprisingly, the nodal point in
Freud's account of the emergence of the individual.

Freud is sometimes charged with being dangerously
ambiguous in his formulation of narcissism, since he
conceives of it sometimes as an attraction to one's own
person, sometimes as an attraction to one's own body.
There is an ambiguity here, but I think that Freud would
have claimed that the ambiguity lies in the situation
itself, not in his conception of it. For, as we shall see, the
concept that is integral to the situation—the ego—is
itself ambiguously a mental and a corporeal concept.

After narcissism, there is object choice proper. We
have already seen how, according to Freud, object choice
can be established only when sexuality has undergone
various vicissitudes in respect of its aim. In the *New
Introductory Lectures*, Freud asserted more specifically
that "consideration for the object"[12] makes its first appearance midway through the anal phase. However, with
the oncoming of object choice, another set of component
instincts is brought into the orbit of sexuality, and their
relations with the other instincts are of special significance in the sexual life of the adult, or in "the psychology of love." These constitute the "affectionate
current." Unlike the erotogenic component of sexuality,
affection is directed upon an object from the beginning,
and difficulties arise when this object does not, indeed
refuses to, coincide with the object of the rest of sexuality. From this a distinctive set of adult miseries and
degradations of adult life derive: and these form the
themes of Freud's three essays on the "psychology of
love," written between 1910 and 1917.

[12] XXII, 99.

It should at this stage be pointed out that, though affection is a necessary condition of love, it is not identical with it. Love (and hate) are concepts that "cannot be made use of for the relations of *instincts* to their objects, but are reserved for the relations of the *total ego* to objects."[13]

It is now time to return to Freud's account of the later stages of infantile sexuality, before, that is, it undergoes, around the age of six or seven, a massive repression and the period of latency sets in. The theme is provided by the infant's first, incestuous object choice and its unhappy history: the famous Oedipus complex. This is first mentioned in a letter of Fliess of October 15, 1897,[14] first written of in *The Interpretation of Dreams* (along with a reference to the deep and perennial appeal of *Oedipus Rex* and *Hamlet* for touching upon this theme), and first named in an essay in 1910 entitled "A Special Type of Object-Choice."

I shall for the sake of simplicity (perhaps of plausibility also) confine myself to this theme as it is worked out for the male infant. Freud originally thought that there was a total symmetry between the courses pursued by the two sexes, so that, as the boy falls in love with his mother, the girl falls in love with her father, and so on. Gradually, however, Freud abandoned this, and substituted, in the case of the girl, a much more hazardous and complex path, which initially coincides with that of the boy and then branches off.

Of course, when I talk of boys and girls and their differing sexual development, an element of abstraction has been introduced. For it is a central tenet of Freud's,

[13] XIV, 137.
[14] Kris, p. 223.

originally owing much to Fliess but confirmed in clinical experience, that human nature is inherently bisexual. In any given individual one sexual character will prevail, but it never enjoys monopoly. In a letter to Fliess, Freud had written that he was accustoming himself "to the idea of regarding every sexual act as a process in which four persons are involved."[15] That was in early 1899.

The child's original object choice is, then, his mother. He wants his mother and, moreover, wants her exclusively to himself; and this brings him into direct conflict with his father. On account of the loving wish for the mother and the hostile wish against the father, the child feels threatened by the father, and this threat is represented in his mind as the threat of castration. The child, however, also loves his father; and so along with fear of the father goes some measure of fear for the father— fear, that is, for the father on account of his, the child's, hostility. In consequence of these two fears the child's sexuality comes to grief and is altogether suppressed and the so-called latency period sets in. Years later[16] Freud constructed, by the side of this "positive" Oedipus complex, a "negative" version, stemming from the child's bisexual constitution, but which incurs the same fate. The child—and the process was well represented by the Wolf Man—has also an erotic attachment to the father and wishes to be loved by him. But his passive tender feelings seem to require the loss of his genitals, and so, again, sexuality is suppressed under the fear of castration.

The latency period lasts from the abrupt end imposed upon infantile sexuality up till the onset of puberty. With the revival of sexuality the adolescent is presented

[15] Kris, p. 289.
[16] XIX, 31–34; XX, 106–108.

with the problem of object choice at the very point at which it was broken off nine or ten years previously: with this difference, that now he is in command of "the sexual products," which gives a physical urgency to his situation. The task with which the male adolescent is confronted is threefold: he must detach his libidinal wishes from his mother, he must reconcile himself to his father, and he must try to find a love object similar to, but not identical with, his mother. "These tasks," Freud wrote, "are set to everyone: and it is remarkable how seldom they are dealt with in an ideal manner."[17] We must believe that, by the time that Freud came to write these words, in 1916, when he had already placed "the infantile neurosis" at the center of most psychological problems, he did not believe this upshot at all remarkable.

Two items in the Oedipus complex deserve closer attention. One is the famous "castration threat."[18] On the earliest view it originated in memories of actual threats of castration, originally uttered by parents or nurses against the child and stored in its infantile mind. In the Little Hans case Freud was pleased to come across the record of such a threat.[19] Gradually, however— though long after the notion of phantasy might have inclined him to adopt a less literal or historical view of the matter—Freud conceded that "children construct this danger for themselves out of the slightest hints." There were also in existence various other ideas which could be collected into a composite picture of how this phantasy was maintained—for instance, the "falsified

[17] XVI, 337.
[18] V, 619; IX, 217–18; XIII, 130–31.
[19] X, 8*n*.

perception"[20] that girls too have a penis which could be, and then is, castrated. It was only, however, when Freud had totally reconstructed his views on anxiety that he could produce an over-all account of the castration threat which amalgamated the elements of history and phantasy. But the interest of the castration threat is not exhausted by its role in the Oedipus complex. In fact, the castration complex is an excellent example of a symptom overdetermined: for it also plays a part in another subplot of the nuclear family drama. One of the two great intellectual concerns of the infant is, as we have seen, the differentiation of the sexes. An answer to this is that girls have lost a penis. So the male infant sees the castration threat as actually realized, and this accordingly reinforces the threat.

The other item in the Oedipus complex is the envious relations that arise between siblings as they vainly compete for the favors of the parent they love. In *The Interpretation of Dreams* the topic is placed in the center of the family drama,[21] and Freud talks of "a child's death-wishes against his brothers and sisters." Years later Freud returned to these internecine conflicts as offering a secondary route to homosexuality: the boy's loving feelings for his own sex are a compensation for, or a reaction formation against, initial murderous impulses he felt toward his rivals in his mother's love.[22] (The primary route, expounded in the Leonardo essay, is where the child defends himself against his excessive love for his mother and disappointment in it by identifying him-

[20] IX, 216–18; X, 11–12n; XI, 95–96; XVIII, 273–74; XXI, 153–55.
[21] IV, 250–55.
[22] XVIII, 231–32.

self with her and loving boys in his own image as she loved him.)[23]

By now we have seen how Freud redefined the concept of sexuality and how he rewrote the history of sexual development. These two projects, I have argued, are interconnected. While his redefinition of sexuality is initially based on the temptation we feel to designate a wide variety of behavior "sexual," this temptation is provided with a rationale when we see how these various forms of behavior fit together in a genetic account. Conversely, the genetic account which gives us the successive phases of infantile sexuality is confirmed by the fact that there is, in existence, such a variety of behavior, which corresponds to those phases and which we can think of as sexual. Freud brings the two projects together in the following words:

In psycho-analysis the concept of what is sexual . . . goes lower and also higher than its popular sense. This extension is justified genetically.[24]

However, a residual question arises, often ignored, but only to the detriment of our understanding of Freud's views. Why did Freud attach such importance to sexuality? We have seen how he uncovered its hidden variety, how he demonstrated its utter pervasiveness: yet, in principle at least, could there not be a phenomenon as varied, as pervasive as sexuality, and yet not fundamental? But Freud did think sexuality fundamental, and it is worth asking why. The answer seems to be distributed between four very general and interrelated

[23] XI, 98–100; XVIII, 108, 230–31.
[24] XI, 222.

properties that Freud predicated of the sexual in human nature: its antiquity, its imperiousness, its plasticity, and its proneness to maldevelopment or fixation.

From the fact that sexuality begins so early, there must be a very strong likelihood that it will have a powerful influence on our life. We would make the same inference, and would be amazed if anyone were to deny it, in the case of, say, training an animal or tending a plant: and it is an often ignored strength of Freud's argument that he bases himself upon an intuitive principle of such obviousness. Freud further strengthened this inference by accepting some general principle, true of the history of both the individual and the species, that in his infancy man lives in the moment and it is only as he grows older that memory becomes dominant over present impression.

Secondly, there is the strength or imperiousness of sexuality, the fact that in sexual matters we do not readily tolerate frustration. Once again it is the very simplicity of the point that allows us to overlook it, but also gives a theory built on it such weight.

Thirdly, there is the plasticity of sexuality, which means that many aspects of our life—far more than we ordinarily have occasion to realize—can become sexualized: that is to say, can become attached to a sexual impulse along a line of association. Two examples, studied by Freud in some detail, may bring this out: the sexualization of thinking, and of vision.

In the essay on Leonardo, written in 1910, Freud dealt most closely with the relation of thinking and sexuality.[25] Curiosity, Freud asserted, is first aroused in trying to answer the two great sexual questions with which the infant struggles, How are babies born? (where this in-

[25] XI, 77–81.

cludes the problem of sexual intercourse) and, What differentiates the sexes? And this inquiry in turn is felt as a quasi-physical investigation of the parents' bodies. Thought, we may say, becomes sexualized not merely in its object but in its aim; in confirmation of this, thinking falls victim to the repression to which infantile sexuality succumbs. There are then three possible outcomes. The first is that "research shares the fate of sexuality; thenceforward curiosity remains inhibited and the free activity of intelligence may be limited for the whole of the subject's lifetime"—especially, Freud added, as, shortly after this, the powerful inhibition of thought by religion is brought into play. The second possibility is that intelligence is stronger, is not altogether suppressed, but cannot free itself from sexuality. Not merely is all thinking still, unconsciously, directed into sexual research, but investigation "becomes a sexual activity, often the exclusive one, and the feeling that comes from settling things in one's mind and explaining them replaces sexual satisfaction." But this process, like the infantile researches that it continues, is interminable: the outcome is compulsive brooding, and "the brooding never ends." Thirdly, thinking may to some extent liberate itself from its sexual past. It is still in part a sexual activity, but no longer has imprinted on it "the complexes of infantile sexual research" which it is compelled to repeat in all essentials. To this outcome Freud attached a word: *sublimation.*

In a paper, also of 1910, entitled "The Psycho-Analytic View of Psychogenic Disturbance of Vision" Freud considered how vision may undergo the same fate as thinking.[26] Here, the initial connection is closer. For the eye is a bodily organ, intrinsically at the service of both

[26] XI, 215–18.

vital and sexual functions. It perceives changes in the external world which are important for survival, but it also observes and enjoys the charms that arouse sexual pleasure. Psychogenic disturbance in vision can occur when the sexual component which makes use of looking —Freud uses the technical term "scopophilia"—becomes so assertive that it suffers repression; but the repression is not total, and the repressed instincts reassert themselves and incapacitate the ego in its normal function. Or perhaps the same result can be achieved along a simpler route: in repressing scopophilia, the ego goes too far in its demands and blots out vision. The eye behaves, as Freud put it, amusingly if not altogether accurately, "like a maid-servant who refuses to go on cooking because her master has started a love-affair with her."[27] And what is true of the eye can go for any other organ that has these dual loyalties. Later, Freud suggested that the plasticity of sexuality is deep-rooted in the zonal confusions that seem an inherent part of our thinking or feeling about the body. The vagina is taken "on lease from the rectum":[28] the faeces is the child's first gift: the young girl's desire for a penis becomes a wish for a baby.

More generally, Freud made the point that a man's sexual position tends to influence everything else in his life because of the way in which sexuality can serve as an exemplar for all his other feelings and thoughts. "A man's attitude in sexual things has the force of a model to which the rest of his reactions tend to conform."[29] So, for instance, indecision, or uncertainty, in sexual matters induces indecision elsewhere, and so leads to a

[27] XX, 89–90.
[28] XXII, 101; the phrase is Lou Andreas-Salomé's.
[29] X, 241.

skeptical coloring of the mind. "A man who doubts his own love," Freud wrote, finely, "may or rather *must*, doubt every lesser thing."[30]

And, finally, Freud, in his view of the importance of sexuality, was influenced by its proneness to maldevelopment. Any evolutionary process that is long and complex is peculiarly open to distortion and in the case of sexual development, its diphasic course, or its interruption by the latency period, significantly increases the hazards to which it is exposed. In the *Three Essays* Freud made use of a notion which was to be a great influence in bringing together the ideas of sexual development and sexual aberration—that of a fixation point. A fixation point is a point on the evolutionary path which we have crossed, without, as it were, all our sexual forces at our disposal; some have lagged behind; and when we encounter further difficulties in life, we return, or regress, to this point. In the *Introductory Lectures* Freud compared the evolution of our instincts to a primitive people in migration. At each stopping point detachments are left behind, so that, if the advance party comes up against opposition, it will have a place of security to which it can retreat. But the more numerous the detachments left behind, the greater will be the changes of defeat at the hands of the enemy.

As Freud's sexual chronology becomes more specific, so the fixation points are plotted with greater determinacy. We shall hear more of this in the next chapter.

[30] X, 241.

The Neurosis: Its Nature, Cause, and Cure

V

Psychoanalysis, both the word and the movement, came into the world obscurely. The first
recorded use of the word is in a paper on
"Heredity and the Aetiology of the Neurosis"
prepared by Freud for a French neurological review in early 1896. "I owe my results," Freud
wrote there, "to a new method of psycho-analysis."[1] Five or six years later, and Freud was
beginning to collect around him a group of men
of like interests, attracted by his ideas and prepared to work within this general method. Stekel,
Kahane, Reitler, and Adler had arrived by 1902,
Federn in 1903, Hitschmann in 1905, Otto Rank
and Isidor Sadger in 1906, in 1908 Ferenczi and
Oskar Rie, and already by this date there had
been interested visitors from abroad, such as
Max Eitingon, Jung, Binswanger, Karl Abraham,
A. A. Brill, and Ernest Jones. And as the move-

[1] III, 151.

ment developed, it seemed most natural to its members that they should call themselves after the method that they practiced. They were psychoanalysts. In April 1908, the informal Wednesday evening meetings, at which they came together to discuss their ideas and the progress of cases, became known as the Vienna Psychoanalytical Society. In the same year the first International Psychoanalytical Congress was held at Salzburg.

Already history was repeating itself. For, once again, that part of the teaching which seemed the most secure —indeed, so much so as to give its name to the rest— had been called in doubt by Freud himself. In a number of passages, all of this period, Freud referred to a revolution, to a fundamental transformation, that had occurred in his therapeutic technique since the publication of the *Studies on Hysteria* and the adoption of the cathartic method. The earliest of these references is to be found in the Dora case history, which, though not published till 1905, was complete, except for a few minor alterations, by 1901. In 1910 Freud was telling the Second Psychoanalytical Congress that the transformation in technique still awaited "final settlement."[2]

The issue is set out in the Dora case history. "At that time," Freud wrote, referring to the period 1893–1895,

the work of analysis started out from the symptoms, and aimed at clearing them up one after the other. Since then I have abandoned the technique.[3]

And he gave as his reason for abandoning it that it had shown itself inadequate to what he calls "the finer structure of a neurosis," its "intimate structure,"[4] or its

[2] XI, 144.
[3] VII, 12.
[4] VII, 13.

"complicated texture."5 Accordingly, he had evolved a technique which, instead of concentrating on the symptoms one by one, ranged over them more freely: in which "everything that has to do with the clearing up of a particular symptom emerges piecemeal, woven into various contexts, and distributed over widely separated periods of time."6

The newly discovered characteristic of the neurosis that led Freud to revise his technique consisted in two phenomena, occurring on somewhat different levels. First, there was the overdetermination of symptoms. From the early days Freud had acknowledged this phenomenon, but it was the scale on which it operated, the degree to which the mind was conservative, for which he was quite unprepared, and which eventually won from him such recognition that he suggested that, if once one could lay hold of "the main symptom," then "the whole analysis" might be needed to explain it.7

The second phenomenon was what I shall call the residual character of the neurosis: what remains to the neurosis over and above the symptoms. In the *Studies on Hysteria*, a cosmetic attitude to neurosis prevails. Patients are presented, suffering from various blemishes —tics, phobias, visual disturbances, gastric pains—and the task assigned to the consulting room is the removal of these blemishes and the consequent restoration of the patient to health. But this attitude could not long survive experience—although experience, unchecked against theory, might lead to quite wild and unacceptable views about what there was to the neurosis over and above the symptoms. Several years later, in the

5 X, 156.
6 VII, 12.
7 XII, 93.

Introductory Lectures, Freud explicitly addressed himself to this question. "For a layman," he wrote,

> the symptoms constitute the essence of a disease and
> its cure consists in the removal of the symptoms.
> Physicians attach importance to distinguishing the
> symptoms from the disease and declare that getting
> rid of the symptoms does not amount to curing the
> disease. But the only tangible thing left of the disease
> after the symptoms have been got rid of is the
> capacity to form new symptoms. For that reason we
> will for the moment adopt the layman's position and
> assume that to unravel the symptoms means the same
> thing as to understand the disease.[8]

It is hard not to think of Freud as being somewhat dis-
ingenuous in this passage. For, in the first place, to
admit the capacity to form new symptoms is already to
dispute the identity of neurosis and symptoms. It is,
in Freud's terms, to align oneself with the physicians, so
that the next step is to ask what this capacity consists
in. The only way of avoiding this implication would be
to assert another identity: between the capacity to form
new symptoms and their actual formation under the
appropriate conditions. But not merely would such a
highly reductive approach be alien to Freud on general
grounds, but, in the particular case of the neurosis, it
looked as though there was experience that ran counter
to it. For to adopt this approach would imply that the
formation of new symptoms on the part of the patient
would simply be the reiteration of old symptoms or
patterns of symptoms, and hence uninstructive for the
analyst. Yet, as we shall see by the end of this chapter,
Freud was constantly learning that the formation of new
symptoms during the course of an analysis provided in-

[8] XVI, 358.

valuable insight into the nature of the neurosis. Secondly, when Freud says that he will for the moment "side with the layman" in assuming "that to unravel the symptoms means the same thing as to understand the disease," he is compounding his disingenuity. The layman, as defined by Freud, identifies symptoms and disease. Here Freud identifies the unraveling of symptoms and the understanding of disease. Whether this is to side with the layman depends on what is thought necessary for the unraveling of symptoms. If, for instance, it were thought possible to explain symptoms exclusively in terms of other symptoms or of events lying outside the neurosis, then Freud's and the layman's positions coincide. But Freud thought no such thing. Indeed, if we look at the elements which Freud did think necessary for the unraveling of symptoms— desires and beliefs, or, in the language of psychoanalysis, impulses, phantasies, and amnesias—we can see not merely that he accepted the residual character of the neurosis, but also what he considered this residue to consist in.

In this chapter, I shall illustrate Freud's conception of the neurosis by reference to one case history which for various reasons is peculiarly suitable for exposition. Nevertheless, difficulties arise. The case is one of obsessional neurosis, and dangers inhere in generalization from one type of neurosis to all others.

I

On October 1, 1907, a man of twenty-nine came to see Freud, suffering from certain fears relating to people he loved—specifically, his father and someone referred to throughout as "his lady"; certain compulsive impulses, e.g., suddenly to cut his throat with a razor; and certain prohibitions, which were often so related as to make compliance with them all impossible. Treatment began immediately, and Freud gave a number of reports on its progress to the Wednesday evening circle. Then, in April 1908, while the case was still continuing, Freud delivered a much longer report, lasting four hours, to the First International Psychoanalytical Congress. In the summer of 1909, the case was written up and published as "Notes upon a Case of Obsessional Neurosis." In the Standard Edition, the original notes that Freud kept, session by session, have been appended to the text, which consists in an account of the case taken from the notes but not strictly chronological, along with some observations upon obsessional neurosis, generally and in particular. The whole thus provides a brilliant and fascinating insight into Freud's therapeutic work.

The direct occasion of the patient's consultation with Freud was the lingering shock he had experienced on being told by a fellow officer on summer maneuvers of a Chinese torture in which a pot was strapped onto the criminal's buttocks, filled with rats, and the rats then bored their way into his anus. The patient was overwhelmed with this story, and immediately found himself imagining the torture applied to "a person who was very dear to him," i.e., "his lady"—indeed, as it turned out, to the two people dear to him—and the next few days were consumed by his trying at once to carry out, and to evade, certain very complex and ultimately incoherent instructions which he imposed upon himself as a "sanction," i.e., as a means of averting the fulfillment of the thought or phantasy. It is because of this story, and its hold over the patient, that his case is known as that of the Rat Man. However, I shall pass over the central theme of the analysis, largely because of the vast degree of condensation that it involves—some of which, indeed, is not fully reconstituted by Freud—and, instead rely on more manageable detail to bring out the structure that Freud assigns to the neurosis.

In Freud's over-all diagnosis, the Rat Man can be seen as the victim of two very general conflicts: the first between his father, or his father's wishes, and his lady; the second between love and hatred—a conflict which qualified his relations with both the major figures of his life. However, the two conflicts readily associate themselves, in that (supremely) the hatred of the father couples itself with love for the lady. Now, it is evident how love for his lady might well have coupled itself with fear of the father. But why with hatred? The answer, gleaned from the material of the analysis, was twofold. First, the Rat Man's hatred of his father was in origin tied to the belief, or better the phantasy, of his father as an interferer in his sensual desires: a phantasy which found its epitome in the occasion when as a child he had been beaten by the father. (Significantly, Freud was no longer concerned—as he would have been years earlier— whether what the child had been beaten for was actually something sexual: it was enough that this is how the Rat Man conceived of it. "In constructing phantasies about his childhood," Freud wrote, "the individual *sexualizes his memories*.")[9] All later forms of sexual desire, by reactivating this phantasy, put him in such direct antagonism to his father that the appropriate reaction seemed hatred, not fear. Secondly, there was the Rat Man's own violence of character, which invariably led him from awareness of his father's anger (which might

[9] X, 207n.

have been the object of his fear) to anger or hatred on his own part in response to his father's. For these two reasons, then, the fear of his father that the Rat Man might naturally have experienced when his desires turned toward his lady became associated with, or transformed into, hatred. And so the two over-all conflicts find a point of union.

I now want to look at some of the detail of the case, with the aim of exhibiting how certain recurrent elements in the life of this gifted and unfortunate young man so fit together that we can ascribe not merely a neurosis to him but also a structure to his neurosis. Indeed, the neurosis lies as much in the structure as in the elements that it contains. The structure exhibits itself in three different areas.

First, there are the relations between the internal constituents of the neurosis, between, that is, belief (or amnesia) and desire. Ordinarily, belief may be related to desire in one or other of two ways. The first, or presuppositional relation, is when the belief gives rise to, or conditions, the object of the desire: as when the desire is to avenge one's father's death, and the belief is that one's father has been foully killed. The second, or instrumental relation, is when the belief determines how, or whether, the desire may be satisfied: as when the desire is to eat, and the belief is that there are apples in the orchard, or, that all the food around is poisoned. Inside the neurosis, however, we find a third relation between desire and belief which is superimposed upon whichever of these two happens to hold.

Consider the following routine that the Rat Man established for himself when he was studying for an examination: The Rat Man used to arrange his day so that he should be working up till the hour between midnight and one, when he thought that his father might appear. He would then interrupt his reading, to which he could only with great difficulty apply himself, and get up and open the door as if to let his father in. Then, returning to the hall, he would turn on all the lights, undress, and examine his penis in the looking glass. In the first part of this routine, the Rat Man expressed his desire to impress his father with his habits of work: in the second part, which is a thinly disguised form of masturbation, he expressed defiance of his father. "Thus," as Freud puts it, "in a single unintelligible obsessional act, he gave expression to the two sides of his relation with his father."[10]

It must now be explained that—a point on which Freud himself was not enlightened for some time—by the beginning of the treatment, the Rat Man's father had been dead for nine years. So how could the Rat Man's nocturnal ritual, or, indeed, any act of his, express any desire vis-à-vis his father—unless, perhaps, he believed that his father was in some sense alive? And, in the course of the analysis, it emerged that, about a year and a half after his father's death, the Rat Man, contrary to the rationalistic tenor of his mind, had indeed developed a belief in the afterlife, and it was at this moment that his self-reproaches concerning his father began to dominate his mind. The belief that the Rat Man's father lived stands in a presuppositional relation to the Rat Man's desire to impress, equally to his desire to defy, his father: and this manifests itself in the fact that it was only when the Rat Man held the belief that he had either desire. But this is not all there is to it.

If a desire presupposes a belief, then that belief re-

10 X, 204.

ceives support from the desire. However, though one might reasonably argue—as Freud did in the case of the Rat Man—from what someone else desires to what he believed, it would, for a number of reasons, be absurd to do so in one's own case. Yet this is very much what the Rat Man did. One way of putting it would be that the point of the Rat Man's desires vis-à-vis his father—that is, the point for him of his retaining them long after they would normally have expired—was just to reinforce the false belief in which they shared. And we see this most dramatically in the case of his self-reproaches about not attending his father's deathbed: for, at the very point at which he came closest to admitting his father's death, he proved himself most strenuous in denying it. Desire immured him in belief.

In this example the new relation between desire and belief is superimposed on the presuppositional relation. This superimposition can also occur when the initial relation is instrumental: though, in this case, we must take into account a feature of the desire familiar to us in a general way, but irrelevant to the Rat Man's nocturnal ritual—that the desire occurs in the mode of the wish, or is experienced as fulfilled. An example of this is provided by a symptom referred to in Chapter III: Dora's hysterical appendicitis, which simulated a pregnancy, and which thus expressed both her love for K. and her desire to be a mother. Now, it would evidently be impossible for Dora to satisfy either of these desires unless she had had sexual intercourse (with K.); sexual intercourse was instrumental to their satisfaction. Yet Dora's desires are expressed as if satisfied: from which Freud inferred that she must have believed that she had had sexual intercourse with K., and he then found confirmatory evidence for this. But, once again, superimposed on this relation we find the new relation running in the other direction, in that the point of Dora's desires is to reinforce the belief that would have to be true if the desires were to be—not, in this case, entertained, but—satisfied.

Of course, in each of the two cases the belief that is so ingeniously protected—that the Rat Man's father was still alive, that Dora had had sexual intercourse with K.—are themselves the objects, and the products, of desire; of, that is, further and more fundamental desires.

A second area in which we can consider the structure of neurosis concerns the relation between its internal constituents and its outer manifestations: between desire and belief (or amnesia), on the one hand, and the symptom on the other hand. Ordinarily, belief, desire, and action are related so that (very roughly) given the belief and the desire, the appropriate action is determined; or, conversely, that a given action can be explained by reference to the concomitant belief and desire. Consider, for instance, the desire to save a child's life, the belief that oxygen will save it, and administering oxygen. However, inside the neurosis a number of complexities arise, two of which we have already looked at.

The first is that there is overdetermination, so that various desires, or various sets of desire and belief, express themselves in the same symptom. The second is that the symptom is a compromise formation, so that various conflicting desires, or various sets of desire and counter-desire, express themselves in the same symptom. And the third is that a given set of desire and belief express themselves as they do only in virtue of a wider context of desire. Restrict this context: pair off action,

on the one hand, and desire and belief, on the other—
and the action, far from being explained, is likely to
seem incomprehensible.

To appreciate this last point, consider the following
behavior that the Rat Man exhibited when his lady was
about to leave him:

> On the day of her departure he knocked his foot
> against a stone lying in the road, and was *obliged* to
> put it out of the way by the side of the road, because
> the idea struck him that her carriage might be driving
> along the same road in a few hours' time and might
> come to grief against this stone. But a few minutes
> later it occurred to him that this was absurd, and he
> was *obliged* to go back and replace the stone in its
> original position in the middle of the road.[11]

Now, in the first of these actions the Rat Man, it might
be thought, expressed his desire to protect his lady,
given the belief that the stone might be dangerous; in
the second, he asserted his desire to be rational, given
the belief that it was absurd to think of the stone as
dangerous. But, taking the first action first, Why should
the Rat Man have been so concerned to move the stone,
if all he believed was that the stone might be dangerous?
To account for his action we have also to ascribe to him
a readiness to see in any action that could conceivably
harm his lady something like an attempt to harm her
that had been checked or momentarily arrested. And
this would be related to, and must derive from, a desire
on his part to harm her. Accordingly, the first action
makes sense only against the background of this desire
too. If we now turn to the second action, Why, if all the
Rat Man wanted to do was to disown his earlier action,
did he replace the stone? And once again we need to

[11] X, 190.

invoke the desire to harm his lady. For the action is comprehensible if we see it not merely as a repudiation of the irrationality of the first action but also as an undoing of it. In reversing his action the Rat Man was also reversing his desire to protect her, just as, in protecting his lady, he was also protecting her from his desire to harm her. And hanging over both these actions, is another, more pervasive desire: the desire to question and to doubt, to doubt whether she loves him and whether he loves her, which presses upon and distorts the expression of all his other desires.

Finally, there is relation of the neurosis as a whole to reality. The central idea here is that, inside the neurosis, desire, belief, and action are so concatenated that there is no interaction between the neurosis and reality: in that none of the outer manifestations of the neurosis are directed upon reality, nor are any of its internal constituents ever tested against reality.

Freud's earliest characterization of the neurosis was contained in the maxim of the "Preliminary Communication": "Hysterics suffer mainly from reminiscences." Experience, as we have seen, showed this maxim to be inadequate, since it omitted all reference to impulse or desire. Years later, Freud worked round to a new formulation, which, while still recognizing the dynamic aspect of the neurosis, fully restored its backward-looking character on which the earliest formulation had rightly seized. But the relation of the neurosis to the past is no longer secured by just a single tie, that of a memory to its object. Desire, belief, the forces of repression—these are all fitted together into the structure of the neurosis, and then the neurosis as a whole is seen as orientated toward the past. For neurosis is repetition. And repetition, so far from being a synonym for reminiscence or memory, is now explicitly contrasted with it. The neurotic "repeats instead of remembering."[12]

The view of the neurosis as repetition built itself up slowly in Freud's mind by a process of successive generalization. Initially, in a short note of 1908, repetition was introduced as the explanation or characterization of the hysterical attack. Then, in a paper on technique of 1914, Freud extended it to describe the behavior of the patient in analysis. He re-enacts what he cannot recall; he "acts out." But since the behavior of the patient in analysis was, according to Freud, simply his life pattern writ large, it seemed only natural to make the last step and think of all neurotic behavior, as Freud did in the *Introductory Lectures*, as essentially repetition. What is repeated may be an historical event, but it need not be. There may be, that is, a sincere attachment of the mind to some earlier condition which it is unable to forgo: Alternatively, the central theme of the neurosis may never have been adequately exposed to reality—as, for instance, with the Rat Man's relations with his father— so that some imaginary version of it is endlessly, and quite inconclusively, reiterated. Again, if it is an historical event that forms the core of the neurosis, the neurotic may have forgotten it, as is generally the case in obsessional neurosis. But, even if the event itself is not forgotten, its significance has been lost, and thus its connection with the present is severed. For this reason the neurotic cannot remember it, and repetition replaces recollection.[13]

In his last phase, Freud developed and deepened his view of the neurosis as a form of repetition. Originally,

[12] XII, 151.
[13] XVI, 273–76, 282–84.

everything could be put down to the "adhesiveness" of the libido. But, as Freud came to explore the forces of repression with the thoroughness he had given to the study of the repressed, he recognized that there was a conservatism not merely in the demands of impulse but also in the habits of defense and control.

> The adult's ego, with its increased strength, continues to defend itself against dangers which no longer exist in reality: indeed, it finds itself compelled to seek out those situations in reality which serve as an approximate substitute for the original danger, so as to be able to justify, in relation to them, its maintaining its habitual modes of reaction. Thus we can easily understand how the defensive mechanisms, by bringing about an ever more extensive alienation from the external world and a permanent weakening of the ego, pave the way for, and encourage, the outbreak of neurosis.[14]

2

I now want to turn from what Freud has to say about the nature of the neurosis to what he has to say about its cause. From his first involvement with psychopathology, Freud had always been deeply concerned with the etiological issue: both in the general sense of the cause of neurosis and in the specific sense of the cause of this neurosis rather than that, or, as he called it, "the choice of neurosis." If, at different stages in his career, Freud weighed differently the explanatory against the therapeutic claims of psychoanalysis, he never believed that the problem of cure could be solved without a solution to the problem of cause.

[14] XXIII, 238.

Freud's earliest etiological formulation consisted, we have seen, in picking out a traumatic event, which would be the precipitating cause of the neurosis, either with or without a predisposing cause in the background, in the form of a constitutional or hereditary state. Gradually, however, as the traumatic event was increasingly identified with a sexual happening, it was divided into two, and the earlier part was moved back further and further in time. The result was the seduction theory, which then collapsed under the impact of experience. The next stage was to abandon the search for an event as the cause of the neurosis, and, instead, to look for its determinants in some state of the "sexual constitution," where this was the product of hereditary, infantile, and extraneous factors. This is roughly the position Freud took in the *Three Essays* and in the contemporary "My Views of the Part Played by Sexuality in the Aetiology of the Neuroses." If, in the previous phase, predisposition had been either ignored or swallowed up in the extended trauma, now, with predisposition to the fore, the precipitating cause was almost totally neglected. The balance was not restored until a paper of 1912, "Types of Onset of Neurosis," in which Freud undertook a detailed examination of the various forms that "frustration," as the precipitating cause was now called, might take. The shift in terminology is significant, for Freud returned to this problem only when, as we shall see, he was convinced that the precipitating cause need no longer be looked on as something purely external, as the earlier term "privation" suggested, but was internally connected with the deeper or predisposing factors. More generally, Freud thought that any etiology of mental disorder must satisfy three criteria: the causal factors that it introduces should be suitable in character as determinants, they should have the necessary degree of force, and, as far as possible, they should not be fortuitous or external. The seduction theory, as we have seen, satisfied the first two criteria, but not the third. By 1914 Freud had evolved an etiological theory which, if incomplete, broadly satisfied the three criteria.

However, in his more popular exposition of the account—in the *Introductory Lectures*—Freud fails to bring out its internal connections. He sacrifices these to ease of presentation. I shall follow Freud to the extent of first presenting his account in its simplest form, in which the different factors stand out clearly and then going back over it, showing its underpinning.

Neurosis, the account runs, depends causally on a triad of factors: frustration, fixation of the libido, and the tendency to conflict. Frustration occurs when the individual is unable to secure satisfaction in the mode in which he desires it. Various alternatives are then open to him. He can simply endure frustration. Or he can divert his desires into a social form genetically connected with their existing form: that is, he can sublimate them. But there are limits set to the mobility of the libido and to the capacity to tolerate dissatisfaction. Accordingly, another outcome is that the individual will regress, or move backward down the path of the libidinal development, and then seek satisfaction in a form suitable to an earlier stage. The precise point at which regression comes to a halt and satisfaction is sought has been already fixed in the course of the libido's forward development. The fixation point may occur in the register of either the sexual aim or the sexual object—or both. However, when regression has occurred, there are, once again, alternatives. For frustration and the fixation of the libido by themselves account only for perversion;

that is, the individual might secure satisfaction in the more primitive mode in which he now seeks it. To obtain neurosis, we must assume that the individual forbids himself, or that a part of his personality forbids him, fulfillment at the very point to which the libido has regressed. If this happens, the libidinal impulses can find expression only in symptoms, and thus the neurosis is formed. The requirement on which Freud was here insisting, that a tendency to conflict must be added to the other two factors to complete the etiology of the neurosis—is intimately connected with two theses of major importance in Freudian psychology. The first is that the neuroses are "the *negative* of perversions."[15] And the second, more fundamental still, is that there must be instinctual forces other than the sexual.

In this account we can recognize certain items that Freud had for years thought of as responsible for psychic disturbance: the heritage of infancy, sexuality, and repression. Since the *Three Essays* the first two had been conjoined as infantile sexuality, which had then been gradually elaborated in terms of libidinal development. Now infantile sexuality (or, rather, inhibition of it) and repression are assigned the role of predisposing cause, and a third factor introduced to serve as the precipitating cause and thus credited with the power to reactivate one or both of the predisposing causes in certain circumstances. The merit of the account is its lucidity. Its demerit is that it suggests that the convergence of the three causal factors, when this occurs, is quite coincidental, as we can see from the way in which it leaves open at each stage various alternatives to the path of neurosis. Furthermore, at one point, the account seems to rely not just on coincidence but on implausibility.

[15] VII, 50, 165, 277; XII, 209.

For why should there be regression to a certain developmental point in the interests of libidinal satisfaction, when conflict at that point makes satisfaction impossible?

If we now turn to some other papers that Freud wrote around this period—that on the Schreber case (1911) and the two metapsychological papers of 1915, "Repression" and "The Unconscious"—we can see how the different factors are interconnected and in this way arrive at an account richer in both content and explanatory value. However, in presenting this I shall shift my point of view. Instead of following the individual as he falls back into neurosis, I shall trace how the potential neurotic is formed. Accordingly, I shall start with repression.

Repression has now been redefined so as to absorb the whole of the predisposing cause. In a letter to Ferenczi dated December 6, 1910, Freud suggested that repression is best conceived of as falling into three conceptually distinct phases,[16] and this suggestion reappears in an elaborate form in the Schreber case history, and in "Repression." The first phase, which occurs in infancy, is primal repression, and it consists in the establishment of a fixation—which means that an instinct or an instinctual component is at once denied entry to consciousness and also cut off from normal development. Fixation is, Freud said, "the precursor and necessary condition of every 'repression.' "[17] The second phase is repression proper, which is directed against mental derivatives of the repressed instinct or against trains of thought that have come into associative connection with it. The dependence of this second phase

16 Jones, II, 499.
17 XII, 67.

on the first is not, however, confined to this ideational link between what is repressed in the two phases. For the attraction exercised upon the newly repressed ideas by those which were primally repressed contributes as much to their repression as the repulsion which comes from the side of consciousness: the two trends make up what Freud calls "after-pressure." The third phase, which completes repression as a pathogenic factor, is the return of the repressed. This marks the failure of repression: the repressed irrupts, and the irruption occurs at the point of fixation, to which the libido now regresses.

This account requires an explanation of *why* repression fails, and for this we need the precipitating cause. I have already said that when Freud, in reviving this part of the etiology, called it "frustration" rather than "privation," this corresponded to a new view of how it fitted into the whole. Let us look at this.

From the time when Freud first recognized the importance of sexuality in human life, he tended to think of psychic disturbance as the sequel, or the potential sequel, to any large-scale sexual abstinence; this is seen most strikingly in the actual neuroses. In "Types of Onset of Neurosis" Freud enumerated, alongside frustration in the real world, three other precipitating causes, identified, rather unclearly, as failure to adapt to the demands of reality, inhibition in development, and a quantitative increase in libido: and to these, he later added success (in certain special circumstances), as when he wrote of "those wrecked by success,"[18] and narcissistic frustration. However, Freud's concern was not simply to extend the list of precipitating causes. To understand his thinking, we must take seriously his insistence that, for an external frustration to become

[18] XIV, 316–31; XVII, 118.

pathogenic, an internal frustration must be added. In the *Introductory Lectures*[19] he seems simply to mean by this that there must be both frustration in the real world and psychical conflict at the point to which the individual regresses, but when the same phrase appears in the delicate essay on Lady Macbeth and Ibsen's Rebecca West, his meaning is more interesting: namely, that there must be an essential link between the two types of frustration. What makes "success" pathogenic for those two heroines is that it forces upon them something which, for reasons going back into their history, they cannot allow themselves to possess. Frustration, in depriving the patient of satisfaction, thereby implicates him in the psychic conflict that lies dormant. To be a precipitating cause, frustration must reactivate the primal repression.

A very lucid example is provided by the Schreber case. Senatspräsident Schreber, a judge of appeal and local politician of some eminence in the affairs of Saxony, fell ill of a disorder culminating in paranoid delusions and religious mania, when, after several years of marriage, in all other ways happy, it became clear to him that he would have no children. Freud diagnosed Schreber's illness as a regression to a passive homosexuality, and he saw in his dominant religious delusion—namely, that, through the operation of the sun's rays, he was being transformed by God into a woman from whom a new race of men would spring—a wishful expression of an impulse of this kind toward his father. On this interpretation, it is not hard to see how Schreber's childlessness connects with his neurotic predisposition in such a way as to justify our thinking of it as a precipitating cause. On the one hand, it deprived him of a son, on

[19] XVI, 350.

whom he could have drained off his unsatisfied homo-sexual affections, and, on the other hand, it drove him back into feminine phantasies of how fruitfully he would have served his father with his body.

Frustration, then, looks back to repression. Similarly, inside the extended phenomenon of repression, all later conflict looks back to fixation. This last point not merely accounts for the implausibility that attached to the earlier etiological account provided by the *Introductory Lectures*, it also plants the neurosis firmly in infantile experiences—from which Adler and, above all, Jung had been trying to uproot it. It might, however, be felt that this extended account, by placing such heavy emphasis on the first phase of repression, removed one implausibility only at the expense of another. If primal repression is the ultimate determinant of neurosis, then the task assigned to regression of reactivating such distant conflicts seems singularly arduous. Freud's response was to postulate a half-way house between the earliest conflicts and later neurosis. "I am ready to assert," he wrote, "that every neurosis in an adult is built upon a neurosis which has occurred in his childhood but has not invariably been severe enough to strike the eye and be recognized as such."[20] Within the etiology of the "infantile neurosis," the path of regression would be correspondingly shortened.

With this new etiological account before us, two large questions still arise: the one prior, the other posterior, to the account. Why is there repression? or, Why should an impulse be repressed? And, Given neurosis, why does it take this form rather than that? Freud was being true to his medical education when he tried to bring the

[20] XVII, 99.

answer to the second question under that to the first: when he tried, that is, to find the cause of a specific variant of a disorder in a specific variant of the cause of that disorder. It cannot be said that Freud was totally successful in bringing the two answers together. Nor, for that matter, did he ever succeed in answering the first question altogether to his satisfaction.

The origin of repression had been raised in the *Studies on Hysteria*. There, as we have seen, Freud relied on the notion of incompatibility. It is an "incompatible idea" that is fended off in repression. However, as the phenomenon of impulse, and, more ominously, of sexual impulse, came to dominate the scene of psychic conflict, the notion of incompatibility gave rise to two questions: Incompatible with what? and, What happens to the incompatible? As long as what is repressed is a mere idea or memory, a kind of quasi-aesthetic answer—as though it were natural for the mind to discard, like an artist, any element that does not fit in—seemed good enough. But, when what is at stake is an impulse, which offers gratification if satisfied, and which presses for discharge, the questions, what gets repressed, and how, become urgent. Both the motive and the mechanism for repression required definition.

Freud's first account of incompatibility was made on the assumption that there was no such thing as infantile sexuality. Indeed, it was the discrepancy in tone between a sexual experience undergone in childhood and the memory of that experience entertained after puberty that accounted for a pathological warding-off of the memory, or repression. The discovery of infantile sexuality plus the formulation of libidinal development suggested a fresh account. What is repressed is now a component instinct that lags behind the main body of sexuality in its forward march. To the question, Incompatible with what?, the answer is, Incompatible with the prevailing organization of the libido.

There is a suggestion of circularity to this answer, which may have accounted for some of Freud's apparent dissatisfaction with it. For libidinal development itself seems to depend upon repression, in that each phase is ushered in by the repression of its predecessor. But there is no vicious circularity. For, once the objection has been registered, the still substantive thesis remains that it is whatever has evaded normal repression that incurs pathological repression. There was, indeed, in Freud's thinking a "hidden" thesis, which surfaced at intervals of years, and which gave a unified account of libidinal development and the origins of neurosis in quasi-biological terms. The thesis, which first appeared in letters to Fliess, reappeared in a footnote to the Rat Man case, and was then given extended treatment in *Civilization and Its Discontents*, postulates an "organic repression," derived from man's adoption of the upright posture and his consequent devaluation of olfactory stimuli and the replacement of smell by sight as the dominant sense.[21] Anal eroticism, and, later, by association with the excretory zone, genital sexuality fall victims to civilized man's increasing distaste for bodily odors.

Two further observations on the motive for repression: First, it must be pointed out that Freud at this stage was quite unable to make use of a factor that later figured largely in his and subsequent psychoanalytic accounts of the origins of repression: anxiety. For up till 1926 Freud believed that anxiety resulted from repression: anxiety, in other words, was transformed

[21] Kris, pp. 231–34; X, 247–48; XI, 189; XXI, 99–100n., 105–107n.

libido, the transformation occurring upon repression. Secondly, Freud never ceased to respect the constitutional factor, which carried the implication that one individual might fail to tolerate, or to find compatible, what another could readily accommodate.[22]

However, even when those impulses which incur repression have been singled out, the problem remains how repression is effected. Freud was convinced (though the conviction is never explicitly stated) that an instinct can be repressed only through the agency of another instinct. Hence the postulation of nonsexual instincts, which play or can play an antisexual role. For another conviction in which Freud persisted was that repression must not be "sexualized":[23] that is to say, repression must not be directly attributed to sexuality —for instance, to the triumph of the masculine factor over the feminine. It seems fairly clear that Freud's stand on this point is one of the issues that brought him into conflict with Fliess—as well as later with Adler— and it is interesting that when, towards the very end of his life, Freud returned to a point of view reminiscent of Fliess in that he suggested that an ineliminable tendency to neurosis existed in the survival of feminine elements in male psychology (passive homosexuality), and of male elements in female psychology (envy of the penis), he still refused to look within the warring sexual instincts for the agency by which repression was brought to bear against one set of them.[24] Freud, however, said next to nothing about the nonsexual instincts, until, in his paper on the psychogenic disturbance of vision,

[22] e.g. XII, 99n., 237–38, 317; XVI, 431–32, 457; XX, 242; XXII, 153–54.
[23] Kris, p. 234; XVII, 110–11, 200–204.
[24] XXIII, 250–53.

written in 1910, four years after the *Three Essays*, he introduced the notion of ego-instincts, and he firmly linked these instincts to repression.

Nevertheless, it is not clear from what Freud wrote whether the ego-instincts are intended solely to provide the mechanism of repression or whether, as he sometimes suggests, they are to account for its motive as well: whether, that is to say, the impulses that one repressed are repressed just because they come into conflict with the ego-instincts. "A quite specially important part," he writes, "is played by the undeniable opposition between the instincts which subserve sexuality, the attainment of sexual pleasure, and those other instincts which have as their aim the self-preservation of the individual—the ego-instincts."[25] And much the same is said in the *Introductory Lectures*.

The precise role of the ego-instincts in repression is complicated by two inadequacies in Freud's treatment. In the first place, in talking of the role, Freud did not make it clear whether he had in mind primal repression or repression proper. Much of what he says seems to indicate that it is repression proper; but it is only if it is primal repression that the difference between the motive and the mechanism involved in repression is relevant. For in after-pressure, there is no distinct motive, or the motive is merely that the impulse concerned has already undergone repression. Secondly, having introduced the ego-instincts, Freud said little about their character; so little, indeed, that it is hard to determine what role they can, let alone are supposed to, play. Freud's silence on this point seems in part due to his insufficiently developed concept of an instinct. Of the three criteria that he used to identify an instinct—

[25] XI, 214.

source, aim, and object[26]—the first had dominated his earlier thinking. However, this criterion seems barely applicable to the ego-instincts, except for hunger and thirst—with the consequence that, when Freud professed to be talking quite generally of ego-instincts, it seems to be these two that he had specifically in mind. But in part, the fact is that, for most of this period, Freud's interests continued to lie with the other class of instinct, the potential victims of repression, the sexual. By the time his interests shifted, his whole classification of the instincts was under revision. And this in turn called for a new account of the mechanism, if not of the motive, of repression.

Before we leave the etiology of neurosis, something must be said about forms of defense other than repression. The issue is greatly confused, first, by the careless way in which in the 1890s the notion of defense was swallowed up in that of repression: and, secondly, by the overschematic way in which, thirty years later, in *Inhibitions, Symptoms and Anxiety*, the notion of defense was reinstated and repression then defined as a species of defense. In point of fact, it is difficult to extract from Freud's writings any very precise delimitation of the notion of repression such that we can then contrast repressive and nonrepressive forms of defense. Roughly, Freud seems to have used the term "repression" to cover forms of defense in which the impulse is fended off through control or modification of the constituent idea. This definition leaves room both for more primitive, and also for more sophisticated, forms of defense.[27] As an example of the former, Freud cited reversal, and the turning round upon the subject, of an impulse: as when

[26] VII, 168; XIV, 122–23.
[27] XIV, 126.

love is transformed into hate, or sadism into masochism.[28] The impulse is fended off, but there is no
distortion of the idea. As an example of the latter, he
cited sublimation[29] and condemnation,[30] where the impulse is not fenced off, but it is modified in character, or
its strength reduced.

If we now turn to the other end of the scale and consider the specific etiology of the psychoneuroses, we need
to investigate a space or area of mental life that was
considered in Chapter I but not since: that is, what
happens to an impulse after repression, or more generally, after defense, and before symptom formation.
For it is here that the differential of the neuroses are to
be found.

In each case, the vicissitudes of affect and idea can be
separately studied. As far as affect is concerned, the vital
issue, after 1909, was whether the affect flows back
onto the ego, reactivating early narcissism, or whether
some other fate overtakes it—this, up to 1926, being
largely identified with transformation into anxiety. As
far as the idea is concerned, a complexity must be introduced which was missing from the account of symptom formation in Chapter III, where the discussion was
implicitly dominated, as Freud's discussion in the *Introductory Lectures* was explicitly dominated, by a consideration of hysteria. In hysteria there is an associative
chain running from the repressed idea and terminating
in a bodily conversion, which is the symptom. However,
to clarify the situation with the other neuroses, it is
requisite to introduce an intermediary stage, which

[28] XIV, 127–33, 147.
[29] VII, 238–39; XIV, 94–95.
[30] XIV, 146; XXII, 245–46.

Freud in his metapsychological papers called (though not consistently) "substitutive formation," in which a conscious or preconscious idea is substituted for the repressed idea, and it is this idea that is expressed in the symptoms and that forms the core of the neurosis. In obsessional neurosis, the substitution takes the form of reaction formation, in which an idea opposed to the original idea is intensified: in paranoia, it takes the form of projection, in which the original idea is referred away and treated as a perception of the external world: in anxiety hysteria, it takes the form of displacement, from which the phobias derive: in schizophrenia, it passes through a system of symbolic equations, which Freud called "organ speech."[31]

The problem of "choice of neurosis" can now be re-expressed as that of the determinants of the vicissitudes of affect, on the one hand, and of idea on the other. Are these determinants directly linked to the fixation points, or the moment of primal repression, so that libidinal development uniquely determines the choice of neurosis? Freud was clearly troubled by this problem, and was convinced that the choice of neurosis was settled not simply by the phase of libidinal development but also by that of ego development.[32] However, he realized that this conviction meant little so long as our knowledge of ego development was itself so meager. Perhaps the real difficulty was that the two forms of development seemed quite unrelated. No progress could be made with the origins of a specific neurosis until the state of the ego, the phase of libidinal development, in respect both of aim and of object and the mechanism peculiar to that neurosis, could be brought together into a coherent and

31 XIV, 154–57, 179, 196–204.
32 XII, 324–25; cf. Jones, II, 499.

intelligible whole. Freud's first triumph in this area occurred when he managed to exhibit, in the elaborate reconstruction of the Schreber case, how in an emergent ego, narcissism, passive homosexuality, and projection fit together to form the clinical picture of paranoia. And in "Mourning and Melancholia" he did much the same for melancholia.

3

Psychoanalysis originated in therapy. If it hadn't, the therapy would have come out of the theory, for the relation of therapy to theory in psychoanalysis is just a special instance of the way in which every empirical science permits of a practical application. However, this special instance also presents special difficulties. For, ordinarily, a science gives rise, on the one hand, to explanations, and, on the other hand, to maxims or operational instructions, and it is the latter that are directly invoked in the application of the science. Psychoanalysis gives rise to explanations; and the application of psychoanalysis, or psychoanalytic therapy, consists, essentially, in the handing on by the analyst to the patient of these explanations. So the question arises, How can the giving, or the taking, of an explanation be a piece of practice? How can a mere exchange of beliefs be a form of therapy?

We already possess the beginnings of an answer. For symptoms and, by extension, neuroses are the pathological expression of certain wishes or impulses, the expression being pathological if the wishes or impulses are, and remain, unconscious. Accordingly, the practical efficacy of psychoanalytic explanations might be thought to come from the fact that they make conscious wishes or impulses that have hitherto been unconscious.

In essentials this answer is correct. But the phrase "making what is unconscious conscious" is deceptive. Merely to tell a man of his unconscious wishes is not necessarily to make those wishes conscious. The original wishes might remain unconscious—if, that is, repression persisted, now manifesting itself in the form of resistance. Time after time, the behavior of patients in analysis showed Freud that this was not just a theoretical possibility. "If knowledge about the unconscious," Freud wrote,

> were as important for the patient as people inexperienced in psycho-analysis imagine, listening to lectures or reading books would be enough to cure him. Such measures, however, have as much influence on the symptoms of nervous illness as a distribution of menu-cards in a time of famine has upon hunger.[33]

There are, in effect, two distinct problems here. There is the theoretical problem, how we are to characterize the relations that hold between the mind and the wish or, more generally, the idea that is, or might be, simultaneously conscious and unconscious. And there is the practical problem, how analysis is to proceed, given these complications.

The first of these problems I shall discuss in the next chapter. In solving the second problem Freud made ingenious use of a phenomenon, at first sight singularly unpromising, which he had known of since 1895, though without appreciating its full significance.

At the very end of the chapter on psychotherapy in the *Studies on Hysteria*, Freud identified three circumstances in which the patient's flow of reminiscence

[33] XI, 225.

might dry up. There might be nothing more to say, in which case the patient would look calm: resistance might be encountered, in which case the patient would look tense: or the patient's relation to the analyst might be disturbed, and one way in which this would occur would be if the patient had transferred onto the analyst "distressing," i.e., sexual, feelings. By this time Freud had discovered the strange circumstances in which Anna O.'s treatment had been terminated, thirteen years earlier.[34] Anna O. had always struck Breuer as a quite asexual being, until, one evening, she urgently summoned him to the house and revealed herself to be in the throes of a hysterical pregnancy: moreover, by him. Breuer was appalled, and his reaction was to leave Vienna the next day with his wife for a second honeymoon. Freud, however, from the beginning saw that this "untoward event," as we have seen him call it, demanded a deeper understanding; and in the postscript to the Dora case, he was already able to describe transference —as this puzzling and unexpected relation of patient to analyst was called—as, on the surface, "the greatest obstacle to psychoanalysis," and yet potentially "its most powerful ally."[35]

Freud's interest in transference—so that, by 1914, he regarded it as definitive of psychoanalysis that it accepts "the facts of transference and of resistance"[36]—is the result of two converging lines of thought.[37]

On the first view, the value of the transference, which

[34] XIV, 11–12; XX, 26; Jones, I, 246–47.
[35] VII, 117.
[36] XIV, 16.
[37] II, 301–304; VII, 116–20; XI, 51–52; XII, 99–108, 154–56, 159–71; XVI, 439–47, 451–56; XVIII, 21–23; XX, 224–28; XXIII, 174–77, 231–33.

is equated with a straightforward libidinal attachment of the patient to the analyst, is that it guarantees the analyst a fund of erotic feeling on which he can draw in overcoming the resistances as they are encountered. But, regarded in this way, the transference is fairly undependable. Not merely can the patient's love for the analyst easily become a means of hindering, indeed of halting, the progress of the analysis, but the patient's hostile feelings are likely to follow his loving feelings in their attachment to the analyst: there is room for a negative as well as a positive transference.

On the second view of the transference, the displacement of hostile feelings does not necessarily impugn its therapeutic value: indeed, it enhances it. For the transference is now seen as the construction of a miniature or "artificial" neurosis, inside which the patient reactivates and re-enacts his most fundamental conflicts, this time around the person of the analyst. It is because of this that, initially, everything that occurs in the analysis is repetition, and everything that the patient does is "acting out." However, by a series of interpretations, directed no longer upon distant or confused events but upon a drama in which the patient is immediately involved, the analyst is enabled to intervene directly in the process of repetition and to convert it into one of remembrance. Conversely, the patient instead of acting out unconscious impulses, has the opportunity of "working through" the resistances to the impulses, and in this way—for only in this way can it be done—making what is unconscious conscious. An example is provided by the Rat Man case.[38] At one point in the analysis, the patient, having identified Freud with

[38] X, 207–209, 283–85.

his father, since Freud too seemed to be interfering with his sexual life, began heaping abuse on Freud, session after session, and, as he did so, would walk up and down the room. At first he gave out that this was due to delicacy of feeling, in that he could not bear to lie in comfort while Freud was being abused, but later he admitted that it was done in order to avoid a beating in retaliation. Thus in a single sequence of behavior the Rat Man repeated his hostility toward his father, the projection of this hostility upon his father, and the consequent fear in which he held his father, and, in doing all this, he permitted the possibility of interpretation, and, therefore, of remembrance.

Freud also put transference to another use, already mentioned: as evidence. Transference, Freud claimed, provided a high degree of evidence, which was therefore not available outside the practice of analysis, for two important psychoanalytic tenets. First, it provided evidence for infantile sexuality, since, in repeating infantile attitudes, it invariably exhibits them permeated with sexuality. Secondly, the nonoccurrence of transference in certain forms of neurosis was taken as showing something very significant about the infantile attitudes revived within these neuroses: that they lack attachment to an object. From the behavior of a certain type of patient in analysis—that is, one suffering from a "narcissistic neurosis"—Freud confirmed the existence of primary narcissism.

All that has been said so far about therapy assumes that, though the patient's motive to get well may prove weak against the deeply entrenched positions occupied by the resistances, nevertheless he has no other, or no conflicting, motive. Experience showed this too to be false. Already, in connection with the Dora case,[39] Freud had suggested that there could be a motive for illness in that a patient who had fallen ill reluctantly might then find that there was a "secondary function" to which he could put his illness, and he might accordingly be determined to protract it. Freud compared the neurotic to a bricklayer, who, having been crippled by a fall, finds that he can earn a much easier living as a beggar, and then one day is offered a sudden and total return to health by a miracle-worker. Freud distinguished here between the internal gain to be derived from the continuation of the illness—such as the desire for self-punishment—and some external gain—such as, in Dora's case, the wish "to touch her father's heart and to detach him from Frau K."—and he said that the first type of case was less serious than the second. However, as his ideas evolved, Freud came to realize that he had considerably underestimated the depth of the forces working against therapy. It was, initially, the experience of the war neuroses[40] that brought home to him the importance of the "primary gain" to be derived from illness: that is, that it might be induced, as opposed to protracted, in order to escape a danger. When, after the war, Freud reclassified the instincts and began to study aggression and its derivative, self-punishment, he realized how inadequately he had treated the problem in the Dora case. In 1923 he added a footnote to the case history in which he stressed the primary as well as secondary gain, and also the importance of internal alongside external factors in the process of falling ill. To follow out the implications of this view of the matter, as Freud did in *Inhibitions, Symptoms and Anxiety*, was to see

[39] VII, 43–46.
[40] XVII, 207–10.

how deeply compromised from the outset the ego, or repressing agency, is in the process of neurosis formation.

4

This would be a good moment at which to pause and consider what sort of explanation of human behavior and development psychoanalytic theory has to offer. On the one hand, there is what can broadly be thought of as "interpretation." This consists in attaching significance to, say, a dream, or a symptom, by showing that, contrary to appearances, it expresses a thought: moreover, a thought that is the residue or the representative of an instinctual impulse, once repressed yet ineffectively, so that it is active though unconscious. Such interpretations, successively given, can be used to reconstruct a complex of desires and beliefs, which are concatenated in a striking and seemingly indissoluble fashion. On the other hand, there is what can broadly be thought of as "etiology." This consists in assigning a cause, or set of causes, to such a complex of beliefs and desires, by showing how they incurred repression at an early age and thus acquired pathogenic force. This causal account makes use of the fact that such beliefs and desires are typical of a certain stage of development, and also that they are typically found incompatible, or ripe for repression, at that stage.

The two forms of explanation obviously supplement one another, in that one can account for the expression of a particular neurosis of which the other can provide the cause or origin. A line can thus be traced from certain adult or adolescent activities to certain infantile experiences. However, the multiplicity of factors, and, as Freud was later to add, the comparative autonomy of ego development, as well as the importance of quantitative considerations, make any move in the reverse direction impossible, at any rate in practice. Explanation is possible, but prediction is not.

The Unconscious and the Ego

VI

The concept of the unconscious is generally taken as central to Freud's account of the mind, and it is precisely in the importance that it assigns to unconscious mental processes that the characteristic difference between the psychoanalytic and other psychological theories is thought to lie. To poets and thinkers, Freud was in the habit of saying,[1] the existence of the unconscious had long been a known fact, but it had been left to him to see that scientific recognition was afforded it in the field of psychology. "The concept of the unconscious," Freud wrote in one of his very last works, "Some Elementary Lessons in Psycho-analysis,"

> has long been knocking at the gates of psychology and asking to be let in. Philosophy and literature have often toyed with it, but science could find no use for it.[2]

[1] e.g., IX, 8–9, 43–44; XI, 165; XIV, 301–302.
[2] XXIII, 286.

If it seems strange that little attention has been paid to the concept so far in this study, this in part reflects the casual or informal way in which it makes its appearance in Freud's own writings. It was not until 1912 that Freud, in response to an invitation from the London Society of Psychical Research for a contribution to its *Proceedings*, presented his first systematic statement of the hypothesis of unconscious mental processes and the grounds upon which it rested. In 1915 Freud expanded this statement in the more ambitious, though also more fragmentary, metapsychological paper entitled "The Unconscious." But, of course, the hypothesis itself goes back much earlier.

The concept of the unconscious was first introduced in connection with repression or defense, as a way of characterizing the fate that overtakes ideas which incur repression. As Freud was explicitly to put it, "We obtain our concept of the unconscious from the theory of repression."[3] A cycle of the following kind was postulated: An idea, for some reason or other, is repressed; it remains in the mind, at once removed from consciousness and yet operative; and, then, in certain favored circumstances, it may reappear in consciousness.

It is worth emphasizing that the evidence upon which this cycle was initially postulated related entirely to that phase of the cycle which might superficially seem least accessible to confirmation—its middle phase. The investigation of traumatic hysteria clearly revealed cases where a patient's behavior could not be explained, indeed could not be identified, without reference to certain ideas or thoughts of which he had no awareness. Conversely, such behavior could be artificially induced by hypnosis;

[3] XIX, 15.

that is to say, by the insertion of ideas into the subject's mind. These two facts, put together, strongly suggested that ideas were operative in the original behavior, even though the subject knew nothing of them. For both Breuer and Freud, the hypothesis that hysterical manifestations were ideogenic in character was not merely clearly warranted, but treated as something more or less given in observation. Consequently, disagreement between them arose only when, as they saw it, they came to give a causal explanation of the data, Breuer favoring the hypothesis of hypnoid states, Freud postulating a mechanism of defense. Indeed, when we consider how, on the observational level, there was such a close correspondence between hysteria and the results of hypnosis, Breuer's hypothesis must seem the more plausible. It is only by adding in the later discovery of resistance that the balance alters and Freud's hypothesis gains the lead.

I have emphasized the point at which the proposed cycle of unconscious mental processes, or (which is the same thing) the original hypothesis of the unconscious, received its initial evidential support, because when, in the 1912 and the 1915 papers, Freud set out to distinguish between his conception of the unconscious and preanalytic conceptions, it was precisely at this point, in the postulation of ideas that are at once latent and operative, that he found the specific difference. In other words, Freud's conception of the unconscious could claim to be most securely based just where it was most innovatory. Let us look at this in greater detail.

It had long been observed (Freud argued) that there were mental phenomena that, on the face of it, imply quite inexplicable discontinuities in our mental life—an idea is in our mind one moment, out of it the next, and

then, the following moment, reappears there quite un-
changed—and in these cases it might seem reasonable
to make some such assumption as that, all the while,
the idea was "present in the mind" though "latent in
consciousness."[4] To the objection that this would be
merely to introduce a convention or to make a verbal
point, Freud argued that to reject the assumption is also
to rest one's case on a convention. For it is no less a
convention, though a far less expedient one, to equate
mind with consciousness, or to insist that everything
that is mental is conscious. The common-sense convention—which is what this is—"disrupts psychical con-
tinuities, plunges us into the insoluble difficulties of
psycho-physical parallelism, is open to the reproach that
for no obvious reason it over-estimates the part played
by consciousness, and that it forces us prematurely to
abandon the field of psychological research without
being able to offer us any compensation from other
fields."[5]

However, if we relinquish the equation of the mental
with the conscious and interpolate mental events into
the gaps of consciousness in such a way as to get rid of
the discontinuities of mental life, we still have only a
descriptive conception of the unconscious. To get beyond
this, we must look afield and consider the evidence provided by hysterical symptoms and by actions carried
out under hypnotic suggestion. For, in both cases,
we find reason to believe in unconscious mental events
that not merely fill up the otherwise incomprehensible
breaks in consciousness but also manifest themselves in
behavior. "The mind of the hysterical patient," Freud
wrote,

[4] XII, 260.
[5] XIV, 168.

is full of active yet unconscious ideas; all her symptoms proceed from such ideas. It is in fact the most striking character of the hysterical mind to be ruled by them.[6]

And of the post-hypnotic subject who performs a certain action without remembering that he was ordered to do so, he wrote,

The real stimulus to the action being the order of the physician, it is hard not to concede that the idea of the physician's order became active too. Yet this last idea did not reveal itself to consciousness, as did its outcome, the idea of the action; it remained unconscious, and so it was *active and unconscious* at the same time.[7]

In other words, we are led by a consideration of these phenomena to a different kind of unconscious mental event, and this in turn leads us to a different—that is, a *dynamic*, as opposed to a merely descriptive—conception of the unconscious.

We can now see that, not merely does the dynamic unconscious go beyond the descriptive unconscious and have a higher evidential status, but these two facts are linked. For they are both grounded in the further fact that dynamically unconscious events are required in the explanation, not simply in the redescription, of certain forms of behavior. As Freud never tired of insisting, whatever might be the case with the unconscious descriptively conceived, there could be no justification whatsoever for regarding the unconscious dynamically conceived as a convention, or (in the phrase that irritated him so much) a mere *façon de parler*. Its

[6] XII, 262.
[7] XII, 261.

postulation was an addition to our knowledge, not just to our vocabulary.

Along with the introduction of the dynamic conception of the unconscious goes another distinction. For it would be plausible, indeed irresistible, to think of conscious ideas and ideas that are unconscious solely in the descriptive sense as lying upon a single scale calculated in terms of strength or weakness; an unconscious idea would differ from a conscious idea in being that much weaker. However, when we introduce ideas that are unconscious in the dynamic sense, such a view is clearly untenable. The very cases that led to the introduction of the new conception provide us with examples of ideas that are unconscious and yet very strong. Accordingly, another explanation must be given why these ideas are unconscious, and for this purpose the notion of "inadmissibility to consciousness" is invoked: spelled out, this notion means that ideas that are unconscious in the dynamic sense have, in the first place, been repressed, and, secondly, been kept from consciousness by a continuing pressure. From this it follows that there is a distinction within unconscious ideas between those which are capable of becoming conscious, and those which, as things stand, are denied access to consciousness. The former, to which attention had been paid long before Freud, are called "preconscious"; the latter are called unconscious; and the frontier between them, Freud insists, is sharp, and the difference not one that can be expressed in terms of gradations of awareness or degrees of psychic clarity.[8]

So far we have a descriptive and a dynamic conception of the unconscious. More distinctions lie ahead, but,

[8] XIX, 16*n*.

to consolidate the ground we have covered, three questions need answering. The first is, How does repression stand in relation to consciousness or unconsciousness—which is it? As we have seen, Freud originally allowed that repression might be conscious, at least in the sense that it could originate in a conscious effort to forget a certain idea although the subsequent stages of repression might very well be inaccessible to, or unregulated by, consciousness. However, by 1896, when he wrote his second paper on the neuropsychoses of defense, Freud was writing of "the psychical mechanism of (unconscious) defence"[9] and the use of parentheses suggests that the word enclosed is pleonastic. Of course, if repression is relegated to the unconscious, it would not be possible to account for the unconscious solely in terms of repression. This is one of the two horns of the dilemma on which Sartre in *Being and Nothingness* seeks to impale the unconscious, but, as we shall see, the view that is under attack there is not Freud's.

The second question is, What is repressed? In earlier chapters I have written of impulses, desires, and ideas as being repressed, but in this chapter I have suggested that it is exclusively ideas that are repressed. In part, this discrepancy can be accounted for by a shift within Freud's concept of repression. Earlier discussions were concerned with what undergoes, or attracts to itself, repression, whereas now the issue is what, having undergone repression, sufficiently preserves its identity to be recognizable as a content of the unconscious. Now, as we have seen, for Freud all mental states are either ideas or else ideas plus some charge of affect. If a mental state is of the latter kind, or complex, like, say, an emotion, then there are two different criteria by reference to

[9] III, 162.

which it can be identified: through the idea that is a constituent of it, or through the manner of discharge that it seeks. Now, in any mental state that undergoes repression, it is the constituent idea that draws down upon it the forces of repression, though it is only insofar as the idea is charged with affect that repression is necessary. Accordingly, the first thing that happens in repression is that idea and affect are severed. The affect then experiences one or other of three fates: it can be inhibited, it can remain in consciousness but attached to another idea, or it can undergo transformation, notably into anxiety. In any eventuality, the connection between the two constituents has been sufficiently loosened for the first criterion to be inapplicable: and since, after repression, discharge has been precluded, the second criterion is also inapplicable. Accordingly, to talk of, say, emotions that have attracted repression as unconscious in the sense of surviving in the unconscious can only mean that the idea and affect can be reconstituted. Whether this is a real or merely a theoretical possibility, whether the work of repression can be totally undone, is an issue to which, as we shall see, Freud returned. Meanwhile, he concluded that "strictly speaking . . . there are no unconscious affects as there are unconscious ideas." At most there are "affective structures" which might, in favorable circumstances, be re-animated. A so-called unconscious emotion is "a potential beginning which is prevented from developing."

Thirdly, Is there anything to the unconscious except the repressed? If, initially, under the influence of his discovery of defense, Freud tended to think of defense and the unconscious as strictly correlative, he soon came round to another view, which he expressed by saying that, though everything that was repressed was unconscious, this proposition could not be converted.[10] Indeed, it is Freud's mature view that in the life history of the individual, everything was originally unconscious, and it is only under the continual influence of the external world that some of the mind's contents become preconscious and so, should the occasion arise, conscious. And, while this process goes on, the unconscious is replenished by fresh contents that are taken in, found unsuitable, and put down: so that ultimately the unconscious falls into two parts, that which was "innately present originally" and that which "was acquired in the course of the ego's development."[11]

The answers that have been given to the last two questions lead us on to a third conception of the unconscious: the *systematic* conception. For it may be said of both the descriptive and the dynamic conceptions that they present the unconscious rather too much from the point of view of consciousness: that is to say, unconscious contents are those which are required to fill in the gaps of consciousness, or they are those which have been expelled from consciousness, or they are those which exercise a direct influence upon the course of consciousness. However, if it is true that some unconscious contents have never entered consciousness and that others have undergone considerable vicissitudes since they were expelled from it, it then looks as though a shift in our attitude toward the unconscious is called for, and that we need a conception in which the indigenous life of the unconscious—that is to say, its characteristic processes and modes of operation—is placed in the foreground.

[10] e.g., IX, 48; XIV, 166; XIX, 18; XXIII, 95–96.
[11] XXIII, 165.

Freud had, of course, already employed such a conception in talking, as he did in the "Project" and in Chapter VII of *The Interpretation of Dreams*, of the primary process.

But Freud's thinking at this stage was not free from uncertainty. The uncertainty is best brought out by considering condensation and displacement, and the way Freud treats them. For, on the one hand, they can be regarded as methods of distortion, which the censor has at its disposal, and which are imposed on thoughts or wishes as the condition of their entry to consciousness. And this is certainly how Freud expressed himself in writing on the detail of dream-work. On the other hand, condensation and displacement can be regarded as inherent characteristics of unconscious mental activity, and this is very much how they seem to be treated in the more theoretical parts of *The Interpretation of Dreams* and in *Jokes and Their Relation to the Unconscious*. Indeed, some such view is a prerequisite to thinking of the joke as a thought dipped momentarily in the unconscious: if condensation and displacement are regarded merely as methods of censorship, it is hard to make much sense of the mechanism that Freud attributes to the making of the joke. However, there is, on the face of it, a difficulty in putting these two views together. For how can condensation and displacement be imposed on unconscious mental processes by the censor if such processes inherently exhibit these characteristics? And, if they do, what need can there be for censorship? And there seems to be an admission of this point when Freud writes,

> It is not even correct to suppose that repression withholds from the conscious *all* the derivatives of what was primally repressed. If these derivatives have

become sufficiently far removed from the repressed representative, whether owing to the adoption of distortions or by reason of the number of intermediate links inserted, they have free access to the conscious.[12]

However, the dilemma here—that of condensation and displacement as methods of censorship or as characteristics of the unconscious—though it indubitably embarrassed Freud, is more formal than real. It comes from considering too narrow a picture of the phenomena, and even from the last quotation we can get some indication how this may be filled out.

In the first place, given that repression is not an operation performed once and for all, but also requires a continuing pressure, the distinction between distortions imposed by the censor on unconscious processes and general characteristics possessed by unconscious processes is largely a matter of the point of view from which we regard the unconscious. So long as we are primarily interested in the unconscious as it impinges upon consciousness, we shall think of condensation and displacement as the work of the censor; once our interests turn to the unconscious as the seat of ongoing processes, which comprise its life, we shall tend to think of condensation and displacement as characteristics of these processes. In other words, it is a matter of whether we are concerned with unconscious contents solely at the moment of irruption into consciousness or as they were before. As Freud pointed out, the study of dreams and of the psychoneuroses tends to reinforce the former approach.

However, there is more to it than this. For—and here we have the second point—though condensation and displacement invariably produce distortion, the distor-

[12] XIV, 149.

tions to which they give rise are not necessarily more acceptable than the original material. Neurotic phantasies most evidently confirm this. Accordingly, in discussing dreams, symptoms, and to some degree parapraxes, Freud was concerned with a narrower issue than condensation and displacement as such. He was concerned with these mechanisms insofar as they lead to an outcome that is found unobjectionable, or comparatively so. In other words, Freud was considering a more complex process involving on the one hand condensation and displacement, and on the other hand evasion of repression, and it would be natural to characterize this process in an over-all way as distortion by the censor.

Finally, it should be pointed out that, at least in connection with dreams, not all the ideas that undergo distortion are, prior to doing so, repressed or unconscious. Dream thoughts invariably include thoughts which have been drawn into the orbit of the repressed solely for the purpose of the dream. Accordingly, the distortion that these thoughts undergo must be explained in terms of the pressures that may be brought to bear upon mental processes when they seek expression, rather than of any inherent characteristics that an unconscious process possesses.

It is only in the 1915 paper that Freud gave a comprehensive account of unconscious mental activity, or, as he puts it in a side heading, "the special characteristics of the system *Ucs.*" Freud lists, as characteristics found nowhere else in mental life: *"exemption from mutual contradiction, primary process* (mobility of cathexes), *timelessness, and replacement of external by internal reality."* Freud, it must be emphasized, held not merely that contradictory elements, e.g., beliefs, impulses, can coexist in the unconscious, but that they exist there without contradiction. This view had to be revised when the existence of the unconscious ego was recognized, but—except perhaps at the very end of his life[13]—Freud seems to have continued in his denial of unconscious instinctual conflict.

However, the conception of the system *Ucs.* is not exhausted by, though it draws a lot of its sense from, the attribution to the unconscious of inherent or internal characteristics. For there is also the question how the system as a whole is related to other systems. From the very beginning[14] Freud had been opposed to the idea, which was openly espoused by the French neurologist Pierre Janet, and to which Breuer was inclined, of thinking of the unconscious as a second consciousness. There are only, Freud argued, unconscious mental states, and though these states may form a system, they remain states of a person whose other mental states will be conscious or preconscious. Basically what Freud had against the idea of a second consciousness was—in addition to its near incomprehensibility—the way in which it conceived the division between the conscious and the unconscious as a kind of natural or brute fact resembling a fissure in some geologically weak section, and, in consequence, its utter inability to do justice to the dynamic factors involved in "inadmissibility to consciousness."

There was one issue about the relations between the unconscious and other systems that Freud was ready to take seriously, and this he posed as that of the topographical versus the functional hypothesis. (These two

[13] XXIII, 243–45.
[14] III, 45–51; XII, 263; XIV, 170–71.

hypotheses indicate alternatives within the systematic conception of the unconscious; they are incorrectly thought of as further conceptions of the unconscious.) The word "topographical" has been the subject of a great deal of criticism and misunderstanding—the former generally based on the latter—since it has been assumed that Freud in introducing it committed himself to a view of the mind as physically spatial; despite the fact that, on its first use in *The Interpretation of Dreams*, he had explicitly warned the reader against such an error, against mistaking, as he put it, "the scaffolding" for "the building."[15] The topographical hypothesis is, it must be emphasized, a hypothesis about the relations between the various psychic systems, not a hypothesis about the nature of any of them: and it asserts that, when an idea is transposed from the system *Ucs.* to the system *Cs.* or *Pcs.*, a fresh record or second registration is required in the new system, alongside of which the old record in the original system may persist. Freud recognized that this hypothesis bears upon, or is borne upon by, the nature of the physiological or anatomical substrate of the different systems; but, by 1915, as we have already seen, Freud had abandoned hope of any early aid from this quarter. "Our psychical topography has *for the present* nothing to do with anatomy."[16] As against the topographical hypothesis, there is the functional hypothesis, according to which the transposition of an idea from one system to another consists simply in a change in the state of the idea: that is to say, its abandonment of those characteristics peculiar to the old system and its adoption of those peculiar to the new.

The crucial empirical issue on which the decision

[15] V, 536, 610.
[16] XIV, 175.

between these two hypotheses should rest is one that we have already seen to be central in clinical experience: namely, that the analyst may, in the course of a session, present the patient with an idea which he had evidently repressed, and this initially may make no difference. Above all, it does not count as the undoing of the repression, though what was once unconscious is (it seems) now conscious. The repression is not lifted until the resistances have been overcome and the unconscious idea and the unconscious memory trace have been brought both into consciousness and then into connection. "On superficial consideration," Freud said, such observations seem to favor the topographical hypothesis. However, on reflection, it is evident that the idea given to the patient is not identical with that which he had repressed: precisely because the context provided by memory is not included. So, the clinical observations do not, after all, confirm the thesis of separate registrations, and the evidence requires a deeper analysis before it can be used to resolve the issue between the two hypotheses.

That was how Freud left the matter at the end of the second section of "The Unconscious," and in doing so he was virtually recapitulating, though in a more heavily theoretical context, the argument as he had presented it in his paper on technique, "On Beginning the Treatment," written two years earlier. However, when he returned to the issue in the last section of "The Unconscious" he introduced a third hypothesis, much bolder than either of the original two and of much greater intuitive appeal, which, in a way typical of Freud, makes its first appearance with some very specific material attached to it. The material derived from a source that was still comparatively new, and from which psychoanalytic theory was to draw a great deal of fresh in-spiration over the subsequent years: the study of the so-called "narcissistic" (as opposed to "transference") psychoneuroses.

For our immediate purpose, there are two significant facts about these disorders. The first. which gives them their name, is that they are characterized by a regres-sion to a point before any object cathexis, or attachment to an object, is formed. The second is that in one of these disorders, schizophrenia, an extreme importance is attached to words, to similarities of phrasing and to verbal contortions: one encounters what Freud calls "organ-speech." As an example of this phenomenon, Freud cited a schizophrenic patient whose anxieties totally centered round the condition of the skin on his face and the habit he had developed of remorselessly squeezing at his blackheads until their content spurted out. This nervous activity Freud interpreted without difficulty as representing in the first instance masturba-tion, and secondly castration where this is consequential upon masturbation. Accordingly, the blackhead repre-sents the penis, and the squeezed-out cavity represents the vagina in the sense of that which is left when the penis has been lopped off. Freud now argued that this particular symbolism had been formed by following ex-clusively verbal indications: the resemblance between the symbol and what it symbolizes is tenuous until we consider the various descriptions which can serve as a bridge—"squeeze out," "hole," etc. (This last point is, of course, one that cannot be assessed without consider-ing, on a large scale and with a wide variety of cases to compare, the central place played by language in the formation of schizophrenic symptoms and substitutes.)

If we now turn from the evidence to the hypothesis

that Freud invoked to explain it, we are immediately struck by the extent to which the hypothesis transcends the evidence or, alternatively, by the low degree to which the evidence in any simple inductive fashion suggests the hypothesis. We are entering that phase of Freud's thinking which is marked by bold and wide-ranging speculation. Freud's hypothesis can be unfolded in stages. First, we must suppose that our ordinary capacity to entertain ideas about some given object involves two components. On the one hand, there is the presentation of the thing, which has been built up out of mnemic residues. Memory traces of the thing, or remoter traces dependent on these, have been invested with interest, and woven into an inner representation. On the other hand, there is the presentation of the word, which has similarly been built up out of mnemic residues, but, this time, residues of seeing, and, above all, of hearing, the word. Freud now asserted, first, that thing-presentations cannot become conscious until they have become linked with residues from perceptions of words, and, secondly, that the word-presentations belong to the preconscious, not to the unconscious—indeed they are one of the prime agents in giving that stability and cohesiveness to our mental life which characteristically differentiate the secondary from the primary process.

This notion of an idea—or perhaps better, of our capacity to have and use an idea, or to think about something—as an essentially complex phenomenon, in that it consists in the linking of two combinations of auditory, visual, kinesthetic, and other residues, one of which is closed (the word-presentation) while the other (the thing-presentation) is open-ended, is not new in Freud's thinking. We find it fully worked out in one of his pre-analytic writings, the monograph on aphasia of 1891, and references to it occur in the Fliess correspondence and the "Project," in the theoretical chapter of *The Interpretation of Dreams*, and in "The Two Principles of Mental Functioning." However, the notion is now put to a new use (one that had been foreseen, it is true, in a letter to Fliess of December 6, 1896,[17] and then passed over) in that it furnishes the criterion in terms of which conscious and unconscious states of mind can be distinguished. An unconscious mental states involves a thing-presentation that is without links to the corresponding word-presentation. For the state to become conscious, such intermediate links should be laid down. "The question 'How does a thing become conscious?'" Freud writes in Chapter II of *The Ego and the Id*, where the topic receives its fullest treatment,

> would thus be more advantageously stated: "How does a thing become preconscious?". And the answer would be: "Through becoming connected with the word-presentations corresponding to it."[18]

If we now ask why this is enough—and it is enough only in that the thing now *can* become conscious, not that it *will*—the answer is that, once the links have been formed and the connection made, the idea will thereby have attracted to itself sufficient sensory quality to become the object of an "internal perception." For, at this same time, Freud was reviving another idea: that of consciousness as a form of perception, the perception of quality, which can be directed either outward onto the external world, or inward onto mental processes.

It might seem that this new hypothesis about the difference between conscious and unconscious states, so

[17] Kris, pp. 173–75.
[18] XIX, 20.

far from explaining the facts from which it originates, is not even compatible with them, in that the schizophrenic would appear to hold on to the word-presentation and to abandon the thing-presentation, which is surely the reverse of what the hypothesis suggests. Freud was aware that such an inference might be drawn, and he tried to put the matter straight, first, by reminding us that it is a peculiarity of schizophrenia, as a narcissistic neurosis, that it consists in the abandonment of object cathexes, and, then, by plotting the over-all course of the illness, which falls into three phases. The first phase, common to all the neuroses, is that, under the impact of repression, the word-presentation is given up. The second, common to all the narcissistic neuroses, is that regression occurs to a point earlier than object choice, and, consequently, the thing-representation is given up. And the third phase, which is a phase of recovery or cure, is that the schizophrenic endeavors to regain or restore the lost object, but, in his confusion, reanimates the word-presentation which he takes for, and treats as, the thing-presentation. It is only if we telescope the different phases, and, above all, if we fail to observe the nature of the third phase, that we might think there is an incompatibility between the actual progress of schizophrenia and the new hypothesis.

Finally, we must compare the new hypothesis with the two hypotheses it was supposed to supersede. The functional hypothesis is at fault in that it gives no indication of any concomitant change that an idea undergoes when it loses the characteristics of one system and acquires those of another: and the topographical hypothesis is at fault in that, while it does recognize the existence of such a change, it equates it, overliterally, with mere change of locality. Neither hypothesis indicates that a conscious or preconscious idea differs from an unconscious idea in the complexity of the machinery by means of which it presents, or represents, that which it is an idea of. This insight is found only in the new hypothesis; and the suggestion that a conscious or preconscious idea requires a dual presentation of its object is independent of what might seem to some the farfetched reason that Freud gives for it—namely, it is only through a high sensory content or a heavy saturation in quality that an idea can attract to itself consciousness.

In comparing the descriptive and the dynamic conceptions of the unconscious, I suggested that the shift from the former to the latter represented a rise in evidential value for psychoanalytic theory. It might now seem that, in the further shift from the dynamic to the systematic conception, there has been a corresponding fall. For what evidential check can there be on mental processes that exhibit the characteristics listed by Freud as distinctive of the system *Ucs.*—exemption from mutual contradiction, primary process, timelessness, and replacement of external by internal reality—and that are also inaccessible to consciousness? It is important to see that the problem that is often raised about unconscious mental processes is intensified by the conjunction of, or the interaction between, these two general sets of characteristics—what we might think of as their internal and external characteristics. For the fact that a certain mental process is not, throughout its history, accessible to consciousness might not matter from an evidential point of view, if we could observe it as it emerged into, or as it influenced, consciousness. But observation of an idea, direct or indirect, in turn depends upon our capacity to recognize or reidentify that idea: and it is precisely this capacity that seems put in doubt if the idea undergoes the transformations or takes on the characteristics peculiar to the contents of the system *Ucs.* Alternatively, we might be able to trace an idea through these transformations, as it takes in these characteristics, if we could keep it under continuous observation; if, that is, it remained permanently accessible to consciousness.

What is certainly true is that the evidential status of processes that belong to the system *Ucs.* is highly complex. That is to say, they find their evidential support distributed over a very wide range of phenomena. The nearest approach to direct evidence is provided by dreams and symptoms. "Unconscious processes only become cognizable by us under the conditions of dreaming and neurosis."[19] All the rest of the evidence is obviously indirect. There is, however, one type of evidence whose value Freud increasingly esteemed because of the minute and successive observations it permitted of the modifications of consciousness by unconscious processes. These observations, on the one hand, so closely approximated to continuity, and, on the other hand, were so fully backed up by associations, that to the trained analyst it seemed a sure inference from them to the unconscious processes at work and the characteristic transformations that these processes were undergoing. I am referring to the evidence provided by the transference and transference interpretations.

In addition, Freud relied on two heuristic principles that guided him in the postulation of unconscious mental processes. The first was a conviction of the meaningfulness or significance of human action. "A

[19] XIV, 187.

gain in meaning is a perfectly justifiable ground for going beyond the limits of direct experience."[20] Secondly, Freud respected any postulation that resulted in an increase in generality; and he was suspicious of any supposition to the extent to which it seemed *ad hoc* or to result in a loss of generality.

At this stage, a paradox has often been remarked in Freud's thinking. For, it is said, at the very moment when the conception of the unconscious was being refined into its ultimate form, it was, almost without warning, demoted from the central position it had occupied in Freud's psychological theory. "The attribute of being conscious," he wrote in "The Unconscious," "which is the only characteristic of psychical processes that is directly presented to us, is in no way suited to serve as a criterion for the differentiation of systems."[21] And, eight years later: "The characteristic of being unconscious begins to lose significance for us."[22]

These remarks announce the final phase of Freud's thinking, in which the so-called "structural" theory of the mind was developed, notably in *The Ego and the Id*: and to see the transition to this phase in perspective, we must bear in mind three general points.

The first is this: Freud had always been insistent that the existence of unconscious mental processes should receive recognition. That there were such processes was for him an important fact which the scientific study of the mind denied or ignored to its serious loss. But it does not follow from this that the fact that a certain mental

[20] XIV, 167.
[21] XIV, 192.
[22] XIX, 18.

process was unconscious would be an all-important fact about it. Indeed, a great deal of the thrust of Freud's argument is that we pay too much attention to whether processes are conscious or unconscious: the important fact is that they can be either one or the other, not which they are. "The more we seek to win our way to a meta-psychologically real view of mental life, the more we must learn to emancipate ourselves from the importance of the symptoms of 'being conscious.' "[23]

Secondly, though Freud had thought it important to recognize that there were unconscious as well as conscious mental processes, he had never thought that, simply by paying attention to this distinction, we could arrive at—to use these terms now in a very general or over-all sense—a dynamic, as opposed to a descriptive, view of mental life. In other words, the distinction between the two types of process could not be invoked to explain the difference in their roles. At times Freud gave different explanations of inner conflict, but he never suggested that it arose between conscious and unconscious ideas *as such*. On the contrary, from the very beginning there was implicit in his thinking a view that ran totally counter to any such facile account of the matter. For Freud's preferred explanation of inner conflict was in terms of incompatibility: the incompatibility lay between certain ideas, which in consequence underwent repression, and a mental agency, which exerted repression. This agency was identified as the ego, and, as we have seen, in at least one of its activities—repression itself—Freud had long conceded it to be unconscious. Nevertheless, it took many years before the significance of this concession was fully registered. In

[23] XIV, 193.

part, the explanation is that, since, by and large, the provinces of consciousness and the ego overlapped, it had not seemed necessary to take account of discrepancies. In part—and more significantly—it was that, in the development of psychoanalysis through its early and middle phases, up till, say, the period of the First World War, when the easing-up of clinical practice encouraged Freud to return to theory, the main object of investigation had been the repressed forces, the forces of sexuality, and only cursory attention had been paid to the repressing force. "Pathological research," Freud wrote in *The Ego and the Id*,

> has directed our interest too exclusively to the repressed. We should like to learn more about the ego.[24]

For the rest of Freud's life, things were to change. But when they did—and this is the third point to bear in mind—they depended very heavily on earlier theory and earlier findings. In the last phase, the ego was placed in the forefront. Set against it was another agency, for which Freud borrowed a term from "a writer who, from personal reasons, vainly asserts that he has nothing to do with the rigours of pure science."[25] The writer was the eccentric physician from Baden-Baden, Georg Groddeck, and the term, which ultimately derived from Nietzsche, was *"das Es,"* "the id." The id, is, however, the direct heir to the system *Ucs*. And while the ego stands in opposition to the id, in what it does or dynamically, it also takes over certain conceptual features that the id has inherited from the system *Ucs*. It, too, is a system. Indeed, it is systematic in ways unknown to the

[24] XIX, 19.
[25] XIX, 23.

id. The ego is, in Freud's words, "a coherent organization of mental processes."[26] And with this phase we are taken back to some of Freud's earliest theorizing about the mind: to the "Scientific Project."

[26] XIX, 17.

The Last Phase

vii

The principal works of Freud's last phase are
Beyond the Pleasure Principle (1920), *Group
Psychology and the Analysis of the Ego* (1921),
The Ego and the Id (1923), and *Inhibitions,
Symptoms and Anxiety* (1926), but a convenient
starting point for its investigation is found
further back, in the paper "On Narcissism: an
Introduction," written in 1913–1914.

In an earlier chapter, we considered the central
thesis of this paper insofar as it contributes to
the history of infantile sexuality: namely, that
there is a phase in which the libido takes for its
object, or its proto-object, the subject's own ego.
We must now look at its more far-reaching consequences. But, first, the evidence for the thesis.

This, as Freud presented it, is threefold. First,
there is the existence of narcissism as a well-
articulated perversion, and we have seen it to be

a principle with Freud that every perversion corresponds to, or must initially be assumed to correspond to, an earlier phase of development. Secondly, there is the more oblique evidence provided by patients suffering from dementia praecox and schizophrenia. For such patients exhibit two characteristics: megalomania, and a turning away from the world. On closer inspection the latter characteristic proves to be something more specific: it is really the abandonment of erotic relations to things and to people in the world, without their replacement (as happens in hysteria or obsessional neurosis) by corresponding relations to objects in phantasy. If we now ask what happens to the libido that has been withdrawn from external objects, the patient's megalomania provides the answer, for this expresses—and also conceals—an erotic attachment to the ego. And, since this megalomania is no new creation but the magnification of an earlier condition, we are once again led to postulate a primary narcissism, which is then revived with the onset of the disorder. The disorders that provided this evidence Freud called "narcissistic neuroses," and, though his terminology is not totally consistent, he tended to think of the narcissistic neuroses as differing from the psychoses not in kind but in degree or severity. Thirdly, Freud found direct evidence for primary narcissism in the mental lives of "children and primitive people," who systematically and lovingly overestimate their own mental powers and processes.

This evidence also suggests a new and broader way of conceiving libidinal development and its relation to the ego, which Freud expressed in two favored analogies. The first is that of the ego to the amoeba.[1] Initially filled with a viscous substance (libido), the amoeba

[1] XIV, 75; XVI, 416; XVII, 139.

(ego) puts out protrusions of itself into the world (object cathexes), which it is later able to retract (object libido is transformed back into ego libido). The other, simpler analogy is of the ego as "the reservoir of the libido."[2] Both analogies are, as the editors of the Standard Edition take pains to point out, ambiguous. The second, for instance, can be ̣understood as saying that the ego is the first resting place, alternatively that it is the original source, of libido. (The former is evidently Freud's meaning, though sometimes he deviated into the latter.) And a similar ambiguity holds for the first analogy.

The hypothesis of primary narcissism gradually forced upon Freud two large issues, which came to dominate his later thought, and which he continued to grapple with after the hypothesis itself had perhaps ceased to command his full allegiance. These issues are the classification of the instincts and the nature of the ego.

I

Narcissism calls in doubt the classification of the instincts in the following way:

As we have already seen, Freud had virtually from the beginning made a distinction between two types of instinct—libido and the self-preservative instincts (or, as they were called, after 1910, the ego-instincts). On various occasions, Freud claimed for this distinction the merit of congruence with the oldest and the most familiar dichotomy noted within the appetites of man: "hunger and love." However, Freud's distinction did not merely rest on observation, it was also required by his general psychological theory, in that repression

2 VII, 218; XVII, 139; XVIII, 51; XX, 56; XXII, 103.

depended upon a duality of instinct: if not, as Freud sometimes suggested, to provide the motive for repression, then at any rate to account for its mechanism. Remove the duality, and the whole theory of the psycho-neurosis would surely crumble. And it was precisely this duality that the discovery of primary narcissism appeared to threaten. For, if there is an original libidinal attachment to the ego, is it not plausible to think that the self-preservative instincts express or derive from this attachment, and do not represent an independent or nonsexual form of drive? Might not the ego-instincts be wholly libidinal in origin?

This question is raised in "On Narcissism," and, in deciding to continue with a distinction that in the past had served well until it should be definitely disproved, Freud pointed out how the difficulty of resolving the issue was compounded by the lack of any clear method for individuating instincts. Much the same argument occurs in "Instincts and Their Vicissitudes" (1915) and in Lecture XXVI of the *Introductory Lectures*. The term "interest," which Freud had first used in the Schreber analysis, now designates the nonlibidinal components in the ego-instincts, but nothing is said to clarify their nature, or even to confirm their existence. It is only with *Beyond the Pleasure Principle* that the problem raised by primary narcissism receives its dramatic resolution. From the evident relief with which Freud presented his new position, we can infer the strain under which he and his theory had been placed these last few years.

The problem itself is stated boldly. "If the self-preservative instincts too," he wrote,

> are of a libidinal nature, are there perhaps no other instincts whatever but the libidinal ones? At all events there are none other visible. But in that case we shall

after all be driven to agree with the critics who suspected from the first that psycho-analysis explains *everything* by sexuality, or with innovators like Jung who, making a hasty judgment, have used the word "libido" to mean instinctual force in general. Must not this be so?[3]

The reply is given unambiguously. "Our views have from the very first been *dualistic* and to-day they are even more definitely dualistic than before—now that we describe the opposition as being, not between ego-instincts and sexual instincts but between life instincts and death instincts." By now, Freud was quite ready to classify the self-preservative instincts with libido, while still leaving open the possibility, on which he felt it impossible to pronounce, that there might be ego-instincts which were not libidinal. For he now thought of the central duality of instinct as lying not here at all, but between libido and the newly discerned death instinct, between Eros and Thanatos. In abandoning the traditional dichotomy between love and hunger, Freud now divided the instincts of man along the no less familiar lines of love and hate.

There are commentators on Freud who would regard his commitment to dualism as an expression of his personality or as a character trait. Any such interpretation can only be conjectural. And it would be no less unsubstantiated to think that Freud, in regarding dualism as a theoretical requirement, held this to be so in virtue of some purely *a priori* or "aesthetic" postulate that theory must satisfy. Freud's point was that any psychological theory must include some such dualism if it is to explain the facts of inner conflict, though, as we shall see, with the new dualism the pattern of conflict

[3] XVIII, 52.

is not as simple or clear-cut as it had been. In other words, Freud required of even the most abstract or speculative of his hypotheses that it should not be assessed otherwise than as part of a theory that is, in its over-all intentions, empirical.

We must now ask, Why did Freud postulate the death instinct—and, for that matter, what did he thereby postulate? The issue is very complex, and two preliminary points need to be borne in mind. The first is the distinction between the death instinct and aggression. What Freud postulated is the death instinct: that is, an aggressive instinct that is directed upon or against the subject himself. However, since a ready transformation of any instinct is a reversal of its direction, much of the evidence, and of the argument, that Freud adduced in favor of the death instinct will necessarily be indifferent between it and an externally directed instinct of aggression. Secondly, this evidence, and the argument that goes with it, are, by and large, indirect. In support of his hypothesis, Freud appealed on the one hand to something on a lower level of generality, and on the other hand to something on a higher level than the hypothesis itself. He rested his case partly on the facts of sadism and masochism, which were well attested to, though open to a variety of interpretations, and partly on the existence of certain highly general principles which regulated the mental apparatus but could only be inferred from the ordinary workings of the mind. To understand the case for the death instinct—which is presented at its fullest, though highly speculatively, in *Beyond the Pleasure Principle*, and then, more concretely but also more cursorily, in *The Ego and the Id*, *Civilization and Its Discontents*, and the *New Intro-*

ductory Lectures—we have to work our way through the two very heterogeneous types of material that Freud produced in support of it.

In the *Three Essays*, sadism, as we have seen, was classified as one of the component instincts of sexuality, and masochism was then regarded as a secondary phenomenon, or a transform of sadism. If sadism—and thus, indirectly, masochism—seemed to contain an element distinct from sexuality, in the form of a desire for mastery or subjugation, this, Freud argued, could, on biological grounds, be brought under sexuality as instrumental for obtaining sexual gratification. It was the extended concept of sexuality, to which at a later date was added the desire to counter the ideas of Adler, who, with his crude conception of "the masculine protest," wanted to oust sexuality from psychoanalytic theory, that encouraged Freud for so long not to recognize an independent instinct of aggression. "I cannot," Freud wrote in 1909, in the "Little Hans" case, "bring myself to assume the existence of a special aggressive instinct alongside of the familiar instincts of self-preservation and of sex, and on an equal footing with them." In 1923 he appended a footnote, saying that he was now obliged to assert the existence of aggression; but, he added, justifiably, "it is different from Adler's."[4]

The first shift toward the new position occurs in "Instincts and Their Vicissitudes," where Freud postulates not an instinct of aggression, but aggressiveness as a characteristic of instinct, and this he places firmly on the side of the ego-instincts. More interesting than the contention itself are two conceptual innovations on which it rests. The first is this: We have already seen that, though Freud allowed three criteria for distinguish-

[4] X, 140.

ing an instinct—source, aim, and object—it is source
that is dominant in his earlier thinking: witness his
discussion of the erotogenic instincts. However, even
within sexuality, sadism was recalcitrant to this kind of
analysis, and, apart from hunger and thirst, the criterion
of source was valueless in discussing the ego-instincts.
Accordingly, as Freud turned to aggressiveness and,
more generally, to the various ego-instincts, aim tends
to replace source as the dominant criterion. Secondly,
if sadism and masochism are increasingly taken as
providing evidence for aggression in some form or
another, Freud was not prepared to ignore the erotic
element in them, which he had previously overempha-
sized. Accordingly, he introduced a new concept of instinctual "fusion," which is instantiated in both sadism
and masochism, and this concept and its correlative,
that of instinctual "defusion," become of increasing
significance.

However, the new formulation was inherently un-
stable. For, if in studying aggression or what had been
thought of as the ego-instincts, it seemed more appropriate to employ a criterion of aim rather than of source,
it then seemed inappropriate, once this criterion had
been established, to attribute any instincts identified in
this way to the ego. For the ego itself is an agency identified by reference to aim. Accordingly, what guarantee
could there be that the aims of the ego and the aims
of the instincts attributed to it will not conflict?
From the theoretical point of view, the ego still requires
a certain fund of quantity or energy to discharge its
aims, but to equate this energy with an instinct is to
invite conceptual confusion or worse. Though Freud
nowhere explicitly disallowed ego-instincts, the notion
played less and less part in his thinking, and, more sub-

stantively, everything is now ready for the assignment of aggression, alongside sexuality, to that part of the mind which is explicitly set over and against the ego: namely, the id.

All the while, evidence for the existence of aggression had itself been accumulating. There was the evidence provided by melancholia; by the need for self-punishment, or the unconscious sense of guilt; and by the traumatic neuroses, which behaved to all intents and purposes like self-inflicted disorders. And if, in each case, there was always a sexual element present, indeed clamorous in its expression, Freud invoked, in explanation, the phenomenon of instinctual fusion.

However, all this was neutral between aggression and the death instinct. Accordingly, Freud tried to raise the probability of the latter over the former, on the one hand, by the establishment of very complex histories for phenomena like moral masochism or epilepsy, which pointed to the temporal priority of an inward over an outward form of aggression, and, on the other hand, by an appeal to very general scientific considerations: namely, that it is counter to biological sense that the organism should turn aggression upon itself unless there is a primary trend in this direction—though, of course, any such trend would itself require a biological justification.

Freud, though, never thought that these considerations were conclusive. To complete his case he looked elsewhere, and the particular direction in which he turned was ingeniously chosen.

In his earliest discussions of sexuality, Freud had distinguished between the sexual instincts themselves, pressing for discharge, and the regulatory principles under which they obtain, or are denied, discharge, i.e., the pleasure principle, or, in its modified form, the reality principle. And this distinction had itself been prefigured in the "Scientific Project," where the distinction was made between Q, or the flow of energy, and the constancy principle. However, though instincts and the regulatory principles that govern them are conceptually distinct, they are clearly not independent. For, after all, discharge is a function of tension, or of the accumulation of instinctual energy. Indeed, the only determinants of discharge other than tension are inhibitory factors as yet loosely brought together under the heading of the ego and the ego-instincts. Accordingly, the pleasure principle, and even the reality principle, bear upon them marks of the strength or import of sexuality within the mental apparatus. From the sexuality the principles regulatory of them could be inferred. In *Beyond the Pleasure Principle*, Freud constructed an ingenious and speculative argument that moved in the other direction: from regulatory principle to instinct. From a certain way in which the mind functions, Freud inferred the death instinct. Let us look at this more closely.

The regulatory principle that Freud invokes as premise to this argument is variously described: as the principle of psychic inertia, as the Nirvana principle, or as the conservatism of instinct. However, to understand its nature, we would do well, once again, to go back to the "Scientific Project." There, it will be recalled, Freud initially defined the principle governing the mental apparatus, the principle of constancy, as the tendency for the apparatus to divest itself of quantity or to reduce tension to zero. This definition, however, proved inadequate to anything but the most rudimentary cases of mental functioning, and it was revised with the notion of a minimum level of tension substituted for that of zero tension. Then in *Beyond the Pleasure Principle* Freud in effect resurrected his original definition—this time, though, not as an alternative definition of the constancy principle, but as a definition of an alternative principle. On occasions, Freud asserted, the mind acts as though it could altogether eliminate tension, as though, in other words, it could reduce itself to a state of extinction.

The key evidence that Freud produced in support of this principle is at first sight surprising, though it also goes some way toward exhibiting the rather special or idiosyncratic way in which he understood the principle. It is the compulsion to repeat, which we have already come across as not merely the core of resistance, but the secret of the neurosis itself. The two forms in which Freud considered it in *Beyond the Pleasure Principle* are the dream life of traumatic neurotics, and as the seemingly innocuous principle of children's play. In a slightly earlier essay of great charm and insight, on a childhood reminiscence of Goethe's, Freud had treated the child's tendency to repeat in play anything once found pleasurable as being itself a pleasure-seeking activity.[5] Now, however, in considering the first game played by a little boy of one and a half, in which he would get hold of a wooden reel with a piece of string tied to it, throw it over the edge of his cot so that it vanished, and then pull it back by the string, making expressive noises as it disappeared and reappeared,[6] Freud expanded his earlier view in a radical fashion. For he was now able to discern in the phenomenon of repetition two other psychic trends. In the first place, there is the mind's endeavor to work over some original

[5] XVII, 152.
[6] XVIII, 14–17.

impression, so as to master it, so as at a later stage to get pleasure from it—in other words, a principle that is prior, though not opposed, to the pleasure principle. Secondly, there is in repetition a trend that really is "beyond," i.e., inconsistent with, the pleasure principle. For, if some measure of repetition is a necessary element in the binding of energy or adaptation, when carried to inordinate lengths repetition becomes a means of throwing off adaptations and reinstating earlier or less evolved psychic positions. Combining this insight with the hypothesis that all repetition is a form of discharge, Freud arrived at the view that the compulsion (as opposed, say, to the tendency) to repeat can be seen as the effort to restore a state that is both historically primitive and also marked by the total draining of energy, i.e., death.

The compulsion to repeat, then, provided not merely evidence for the death instinct but a specific interpretation of it, an interpretation which is brought out by another of Freud's names for it: the "Nirvana principle." Freud, however, nowhere insisted on this interpretation of the principle. Indeed, he recognized the whole area as barely explored. But, given that there is some such principle operative in the mind, then, Freud argued, we can infer from it to the existence of the death instinct. For the principle and the instinct are related in much the same way as the pleasure principle is to sexuality.

A final point: about the biological justification of the death instinct. If there are both outward and inward versions of aggression, then, as we have seen, Freud had biological scruples against regarding the latter merely as a transform of the former. Yet there were obviously biological difficulties in the way of postulating the independent existence of the latter. For what biological function could the death instinct serve? Freud's

answer was to propose the hypothesis of "natural death," or of death as a point toward which the life of the individual moves. And since the survival of the species, which is the supreme biological value, is clearly independent of the non-survival of the individual, the hypothesis could not itself be faulted on any obvious evolutionary grounds.

2

The second issue raised by the hypothesis of primary narcissism is the nature of the ego. It will be apparent by now that this issue is directly linked to that of the classification of the instincts. The link may be expressed like this: The death instinct is, we have seen, in part the heir to the ego-instincts, taking over from them the contrast or opposition to sexuality which they had to abandon once their libidinal origins were clear. Nevertheless, in proposing the ego-instincts, Freud had not merely been saying that there were instincts other than the sexual. Their postulation was also a way, if a confused one, of attributing to the ego certain functions, and also the energy necessary to carry out these functions. Accordingly, once the instincts had been placed firmly on one side and the ego on the other, as happened with the reclassification of the instincts, Freud had to confront the task, towards which we have seen him moving, of defining these functions and of identifying the energy upon which they drew.

In point of fact, the functions of the ego had been slowly defining themselves ever since the "Scientific Project," which is the most sustained treatment of the topic before the late works. Roughly, these functions fall under three general headings: perception, motility, and defense. It is in virtue of the ego that we perceive the world, that we can change the world, and that we adapt to the world.

The origins of the ego, according to Freud, lie in perception, external and internal. The ego "starts out from the system *Pcpt.*"[7]

The fundamental thought here is that it is through perception that awareness develops of the difference between the outer world and the ego. But, we might ask, How could any such awareness arise through perception, unless one was already able to recognize certain things as belonging to the world and other things as belonging to the ego as and when one perceived them?—which, of course, is to assume precisely what is to be explained. But this is not Freud's point. For the distinction we make, according to him, is not between two types of perception where each type is identified by its objects, or what it is of, but between two types of perception where these differ in their nature, and it is through distinguishing the two types of perception that we then learn to distinguish their objects. And by differences in nature, Freud had in mind such facts as that some perceptions can be made to disappear by means of bodily activity on our part, whereas others are resistant. The former we come to classify as external, the latter as internal.[8] Furthermore, within many perceptions that we would classify as external, there is an element which has something of the nature of an internal perception. There is, as it were, an internal lining to many of our external perceptions: for instance, when our external perceptions give rise to pleasure or pain, or when the

[7] XIX, 23.
[8] XIV, 119, 134, 233–34; XXI, 66–68.

organ of perception makes itself felt, as invariably in touch.[9] Awareness of this division also contributes to our awareness of self.

There are three very important points implicit in this account. The first is the crucial significance that attaches to the body in our growing consciousness of the difference between the world and the ego. In many cases we rely upon bodily or kinesthetic perception, and in all cases we either move, or suppose ourselves to move, our body as an ancillary to perception, or as an aid to classifying it. Secondly, in making the distinction between the outer world and itself, the ego must not be thought of as a mere neutral or passive observer. On the contrary, it is through making this distinction, through developing an awareness of itself over and against everything else, that the ego develops. For, according to Freud, at the very beginning, in the very earliest days of infancy, there is no ego: it is only gradually, through perception, through self-awareness, that the ego emerges from the id. Thirdly, the development of the ego's self-awareness, and, in consequence, the development of the ego itself, are essentially bound up with the development of the *concept* of the ego. Without such a concept neither self-awareness nor, ultimately, existence itself could be attributed to the ego. And just as Freud could contemplate a period at which there was no ego, so he also envisaged a period at which there was no concept of the ego. Indeed, as we have seen, the distinction between autoerotism and narcissism requires there to be a moment before which the concept does not exist, and after which it does exist, in the infant's mind. However, if the concept of the ego is essential to the development of the ego, then, given the way the ego develops,

[9] XIX, 25–26; XXI, 66–68.

given the crucial role played in this development by the body, it seems to follow that the concept of the ego will have heavily corporeal overtones. If the criteria for applying this concept are ultimately bodily, how can the concept itself avoid containing bodily connotations?

Freud brings these points together in the pregnant assertion, "The Ego is first and foremost a bodily Ego."[10] The thesis of the bodily ego exercised a vast influence over a great deal of Freud's later thinking, as well as over some of his earlier, and its importance has been inadequately appreciated. It is pervasive throughout his theory of the mind.

Let us, for instance, go back and look again at Freud's account of the psychic disturbance that can arise through the sexualization of thought. This account can now be seen to rest upon two hypotheses. The first is that sexual activity can become exclusively identified with a particular bodily activity: say, gnawing, or excreting. This hypothesis derives from, or is an application of, the theory of libidinal development. The second hypothesis is that thinking can become identified with a particular bodily activity—and here we can recognize the thesis of the bodily ego. For, if the concept under which the ego develops is, to some degree or other, a corporeal concept, then it is only natural that the activities instrumental in this development should themselves be brought under the concept of corporeal activity. In seeing itself on the model of the body, the ego sees its activities on the model of bodily activity. If we now press for the detail of this process, and ask what concepts of bodily activity are employed, we shall find that here the second hypothesis draws upon the first. The corporeal concepts that the ego employs in

[10] XIX, 26.

its growing self-awareness will reflect the dominant organization of the libido. Initially they relate to the mouth, then to the anus, then to the genitals. Indeed, it is just for this reason that not merely can sexuality become equated with a particular bodily activity, and thinking also become equated with a particular bodily activity, but sexuality and thinking can become equated with one and the same bodily activity—and hence one with the other.

Nor is the influence of the corporeal upon the infantile concepts of mental activity necessarily harmful. Indeed, in an essay of 1925 entitled "Negation," Freud traced the intellectual faculty, or the capacity to assign truth or falsity to an assertion, to some very primitive movement of the mind, in which something like a thought is felt to be contained within one, and a judgment is then passed, which might be verbalized as "It shall be inside me," or "It shall be outside me."[11] The judgment "true" is like swallowing or retaining the thought, the judgment "false" like spitting it out or excreting it. More generally, it was Freud's view that once the concepts under which the activities of the ego are envisaged become too heavily corporealized, we have "the starting point of important pathological disturbances":[12] but kept in moderation, the bodily envisagement of the ego is crucial to its development.

To appreciate this last point, we must turn to the third of the functions that Freud attributed to the ego, that of defense, and look carefully at a modification within the ego—that, at any rate, is how it is initially characterized—which this function requires.

[11] XIX, 237.
[12] XXI, 68.

In the last section of "On Narcissism," Freud discussed certain phases which we all pass through, though neurotics do so in a more extreme fashion, in which at one moment we stand high in our own esteem, we have done well (we feel), and then, at another, we are thrown down and we form a harsh view of ourselves or our capacities. To account for this phenomenon, which has, Freud suggested, been thought of variously as "conscience" or "self-esteem" or "self-regard" he postulates, first, a standard, and, secondly, an agency.

That a standard is involved is evident, for it is by reference to such a standard that we are measured in the favorable or unfavorable judgments that we pass upon ourselves. This standard Freud first called the "ego ideal," though for a few years he used the term also to refer to the agency, or vehicle that carries this standard. Then, in *The Ego and the Id*, the agency is called "the Super-Ego," and this name persists. If we ask why the phenomenon with which Freud was concerned involved an agency as well as a standard, we might look at the evidence Freud cited in support of its existence. What he did was to refer to the "delusions of observation"— that is, delusions of being observed—that are common amongst paranoiacs. "Patients of this sort," he wrote, "complain that all their thoughts are known and their actions watched and supervised; they are informed of the functioning of this agency by voices which characteristically speak to them in the third person ('Now she's thinking of that again'; 'now he's going out')."[13]

Now, two objections to this as evidence immediately come to mind. In the first place, it might be said that the evidence is too narrow. Drawn exclusively from the area of the psychotic, it is inadequate to establish a

[13] XIV, 95.

general truth about the human mind. Secondly, even if the evidence were thought adequate, it would at best establish something, not about our psychic structure, but about the beliefs we have about it. The paranoiac doesn't really hear the inner voices with which he is deluded. In a single passage Freud clearly rejects both these objections. The paranoiac's complaint, he says

> is justified; it describes the truth. A power of this kind, watching, discovering, and criticizing all our intentions, does really exist. Indeed, it exists in every one of us in normal life.[14]

Against the objection that the evidence for paranoia does not admit of generalization, Freud argues that the paranoiac's experience differs from normal experience only in that the content is presented "in a regressive form." By this Freud means, first, that the experience is hallucinatory or vivid to the point of perception, and, secondly, that it reveals the origins of the judging or criticizing agency. For this agency originates from the influence of the parents, to whom are later added teachers, admired friends, the heroes of the environment, and so on—and it is their voices, and the sheer multiplicity of their voices, that is reproduced in the delusions of observation. The delusions of adult life are the phantasies of normal childhood revived.

And this puts us on the track of how Freud would deal with the second objection: that the paranoiac's delusions are evidence not for a fact about the mind, but at best for a belief about it. It is certainly true that in postulating the criticizing agency—or the superego as we may call it, in the interests of simplicity—Freud relied heavily (though as we shall see later, not ex-

[14] XIV, 95.

clusively) on the beliefs that we have about this agency.
But, if it can be shown that these beliefs are deeply
entrenched, that, for instance, they relate to the very
way in which we conceive of the activities of the mind
that correspond to this agency, then, Freud would argue,
the inference is justified. For, in part, the mind and its
activities are how we conceive them on the most fundamental level. Hence the importance for the hypothesis
of the superego of showing how it originates and how
deep are its roots in our early life.

The account that Freud gave of the origins of the
superego is something that he pieced together over the
years, and I shall examine the stages by which the
account grew. For this not merely throws light on the
superego—that is, both on the role that Freud assigned
to it and, more fundamentally, on what he intended in
postulating it—but also brings us back to the theme of
the bodily ego. In the development of the superego, the
corporeal envisagement of the ego and its activities
plays a crucial part.

For the first step in Freud's account, we must turn to
one of the great metapsychological papers, "Mourning
and Melancholia" (written in 1915, published in 1917),
from which I want to extract just one element that
occurs in the very complex and subtle analysis that
Freud provides of melancholia. A well-attested feature
of that disorder is the high degree of self-accusation in
which the sufferer indulges: high both in frequency and
in severity. The melancholic, indeed, rages against himself. However, Freud observed that these accusations
bear little relation to the melancholic himself and his
character; they are not accompanied by any particular
feelings of shame or reticence but, on the contrary,

become the occasions of persistent or compulsive self-exposure; and, though they do not correspond to the melancholic himself, there is someone whom they do fit—someone who has been loved, and whose love has been lost. To explain these facts, Freud postulated that the melancholic has established an identification with the abandoned object. "The shadow of the object," Freud wrote, in a famous phrase, "fell upon the ego."[15] The ego having been modified by the object, the melancholic, in railing against himself, rails against the loved one he has lost.

We have already encountered identification as the earliest form of, or the preliminary to, object choice, deriving from narcissism. The libido, hitherto directed exclusively upon the ego, now turns toward some other person with whom the ego has established some peculiarly intimate relation. Freud characterizes the difference between identification and object choice by saying that, whereas in the latter case the loved person is "what one would like to *have*, in the former case it is what one would like to *be*."[16] We have seen the operation of this mechanism in the case of Leonardo, who, after an unusually long and intense attachment to his mother, found himself unable either to persist in it or to renounce it, and, regressing to a narcissistic condition, identified himself with her. And in following this course, Leonardo illustrated one of the two sources of male homosexuality.

In the discussion of melancholia, Freud went beyond this, and either characterized a further and more extreme form of identification or else gave its mechanism further articulation—it is unclear which. For he now

[15] XIV, 249.
[16] XVIII, 106; XXII, 63.

appended to identification the notion of incorporation or introjection. The melancholic, in identifying himself with the lost object, takes it into himself, and, more specifically, feels himself to have devoured it.

And it is here that we return to the theme of the bodily ego. For to talk of introjection in connection with identification, or as the means by which it is secured, is, of course, to talk of a set of beliefs, or a phantasy, that a person has about his relations with another: a phantasy that has, moreover, enduring effects upon his psyche. But this phantasy is only made possible by some more general conception the person has of himself. It is in virtue of thinking of himself, or of his ego, upon the model of the body that he can then come to think of his relations with another under the guise of physically taking the other into himself. And, as we have been led to expect, the bodily conception of the ego depends for its detail, for the actual corporeal concepts under which the relation with the other is brought, upon the dominant libidinal organization. Introjection bears unmistakably the signs of the oral phase—or, more specifically, the later or sadistic part of that phase. It was from this connection, first established by the most brilliant of his disciples, Karl Abraham, that Freud inferred a characteristic that belongs to all introjected objects: namely, ambivalence. For ambivalence is itself a marked characteristic of both the oral- and anal-sadistic phases. Here again we have the influence upon a psychological state of its physiological or anatomical correlates. In a phase dominated by biting or defecating, love and hatred give way to one another with a facility borrowed from the easy and rapid transitions that these physical activities themselves can make between being gestures of love and being gestures of hate.

In "Mourning and Melancholia" Freud made only limited use of the notion of introjection: using it solely to account for the object that in melancholia is the target of the critical agency. In *Group Psychology and the Analysis of the Ego* and in *The Ego and the Id*, he vastly extended the notion. Indeed, in *The Ego and the Id* he explicitly pointed out how he had previously taken too narrow a view of its application, in that he had since come to realize that the processes of introjection and identification are integral to the development of the ego. We are, Freud says, the "precipitates" of our love relations.[17] More specifically, Freud saw that the critical agency itself, or the superego, could be accounted for in terms of introjection. In consequence, the relations between the superego and the parents or other figures of authority in the child's environment—in whom Freud had already in "On Narcissism" recognized that it originated —could now be stated with more precision. The superego derives from these figures in that it is the incorporated or introjected version of them—though, as we shall see, this does not mean that the superego reproduces them as they actually were.

The processes of introjection and identification go right back to the most primitive libidinal relations that the infant manages to establish with the outer world, and from this it might seem to follow that the superego is itself a product that evolves slowly from the earliest infancy. This, however, was not Freud's view. For, imposed upon the rhythmic sequence of introjection and projection which forms the mainstream of ordinary infantile life, there occurs a moment at which introjection of the parents takes place on such a massive scale that Freud felt entitled to see in it the origin of

[17] XIX, 19; cf. XXII, 64–65.

the superego. All that went before, significant though it might be for later developments, he assigned to the prehistory of the superego. The moment thus singled out was the moment of crisis in the web of object relations and internal conflicts that constituted the nucleus of the Oedipus complex. If, once again, we consider only the male child and concentrate upon his "positive" Oedipus complex—if, that is, we ignore all that part of the complex which derives from his feminine nature—then we are to assume a point at which the child's libidinal attachment to his mother and his powerfully ambivalent attitude towards his father reach such a peak of intensity that he is led to identify himself with his father, whom he introjects. By this means he seeks to control or avert his father's rage, and, at the same time, he secures some compensation for the erotic relations with his mother, which he has been compelled to renounce. It is this account, first set out in *The Ego and the Id*, which justifies the description, repeated by Freud on many occasions, of the superego as "the heir to the Oedipus complex."[18]

So far I have emphasized the essential link between Freud's postulation of the superego and the attribution to the individual of certain phantasies: specifically, phantasies about taking into oneself a parent at once loved and feared, and also phantasies about containing within oneself a figure of authority that watches and judges. But this does not mean that for Freud the existence of the superego was to be equated with our observed proneness to certain typical and recurrent

[18] e.g., XIX, 36, 48, 167; XX, 59, 223; XXII, 64; XXIII, 205.

phantasies. The hypothesis rests upon such observations, but it is not exhausted by them, for the significance of the superego lies, in part, in its functions and in the way in which it discharges them. The superego "confronts" the rest of the ego[19] and imposes demands upon it of a normative kind. And the two parts of the hypothesis—that concerning the individual's phantasies and that concerning his behavior and how it is controlled—are significantly connected.

In the *New Introductory Lectures* Freud explicitly considered the question whether, in postulating the superego, he was not simply reiterating what the older ethical and religious teachers had been saying when they talked of "conscience," whether his contribution to moral psychology went beyond terminological innovation. For Freud, what distinguished the hypothesis of the superego from all antecedent views about the nature of morality is that the superego has a history, moreover that it has the specific history it has. From the way in which it originates in the life cycle of the individual, it acquires a certain number of characteristics, an understanding of which can illuminate many of the paradoxes of our moral habits and our moral beliefs to which conventional or pious teaching had been singularly inadequate, either disregarding them altogether or else treating them as transient or insignificant aberrations.

First, there is the peculiar harshness of the superego, or the extreme nature of our ordinary morality. In *Civilization and Its Discontents* Freud declared his indebtedness to Melanie Klein for the observation that the severity of the superego seems in no way to corre-

[19] XIX, 34.

spond to the severity of treatment that the child has actually received,[20] and in the *New Introductory Lectures* he remarked that it was as though the superego had made "a one-sided choice" and had picked only on the parents' strictness and had ignored their feelings of love or concern. Freud explained this by the fact that, at the height of the Oedipus complex, the infant feels a deep hostility towards its parents which it knows that it must not express, both for the love it bears them and because of its physical dependence upon them. Accordingly, it projects this unconscious aggression onto its parents, and their severity is then successively compounded in its eyes: the more hostile they seem to it, the readier it is to react to them wih rage, and his rage is again projected. In consequence, when the parental authority comes to be introjected as the superego, it is invested with a double burden of aggression.[21] And now we have a total reversal of one of our conventional moral views. For it is not (as we ordinarily think) that we desist from aggression because we have a very rigorous moral ideal but, rather, we have a rigorous moral ideal just because, or to the degree to which, we have renounced aggression.[22] However, from a social or cultural point of view, there is, at any rate within limits, a merit to this arrangement, for the turning round of aggression upon itself through the vehicle of the superego is one of the few methods by which man can gain some control of his destructive instincts.[23] Internalization stands to aggression in much the same way as repression does to sexuality, and it shares in its dangers as well as its advantages.

[20] XXI, 130 and *n*.
[21] XXI, 128–30; XXII, 109–10.
[22] XIX, 54, 170; XXI, 125–26, 128–29.
[23] XXI, 123–24; XXII, 110–11.

For, if the superego is too heavily endowed with internal-ized aggression, as happens in melancholia, it can be-come, in Freud's words, "a pure culture of the death-instinct."[24]

Secondly, there is the systematic discrepancy between the standards of the individual's superego and what the individual actually does. That our behavior is widely noncompliant with our moral code has always been something of a disgrace for conventional moral philos-ophy, and notions like "weakness of will" or "bad faith" have been invoked to account for it, but, on a Freudian view, this simply reflects the different determinants or sources of, on the one hand, moral authority and, on the other, actual behavior. Indeed, for Freud, the true danger arises not from the discrepancy between what we expect of ourselves and what we do, which is in no way remarkable, but from a particular way in which the two can get linked, quite otherwise than we might ordinarily expect. As early as 1916, in the briefest of the three studies that make up "Some Character-Types met with in Psycho-analytic Work," Freud had identified what he called "criminals from a sense of guilt," which he con-nected with Nietzsche's notion of the "pale criminal," and what he had in mind were those in whom guilty feelings are so powerful that the doing of a misdeed can only bring mental relief, either because it makes those feelings rational or because of the punishment that follows in the train of the misdeed. Both in the Little Hans and in the Wolf Man cases, Freud already had clear evidence of such a tendency at work, but it was only with an understanding of the superego, more speci-fically of its origins, that he was able to explore and to generalize it. For the "unconscious sense of guilt," which

[24] XIX, 53.

Freud could now discern in the resistance to therapy as well as in the standard form of criminality, could be traced to two historic features of the superego: first, that it is the heir to an external authority; and, secondly, that it is an internalized version of that authority. From the first, it follows that we react to the superego in ways characteristic of our relations to a human being in the world: thus we display fear and, specifically, fear of the loss of love. And from the second, it follows that the superego has, or is credited with, knowledge not merely of our actions but also of our impulses or wishes. It is for these latter that we are condemned, and, when we are, our response to this condemnation is as if we confronted an external authority: we try, that is, to work our way back into its favor by any means open to us, including, most primitively, atonement through pain.[25]

Thirdly, the genesis of the superego in the individual's first, and disastrous, experience of sexual love accounts for the subtle intertwining of ethical and erotic elements which is so important and ignored a feature of our moral life. In "The Economic Problem of Masochism" (1924) Freud indicated how "moral masochism," or the way in which the ego "turns its cheek" to the attacks of the superego, may become sexualized, if the infant, in internalizing the father, is in the grip of the negative Oedipus complex: that is to say, if, either in consequence of a strong innate bisexuality or as a reaction formation under the fear of castration, the infant conceives passive homosexual feelings toward its father— a condition whose pathological consequences Freud traced with a peculiar fineness in the Schreber and the Wolf Man case histories and in the analysis of Dostoevski. Danger arises because the wish to have

[25] XIX, 48–50; XXI, 134–38.

passive intercourse with the father can so readily be represented in the infant's mind regressively by the wish to be beaten by the father. In this way, moral guilt and erotic satisfaction unite, and morality, instead of marking the transcendence of the Oedipus complex, permits a regression to it—"to the advantage neither of morality nor of the person concerned."[26] Less perversely, it is continuing evidence for the origins of the superego in the Oedipal drama that so many of the prohibitions to which the individual feels himself subject should have a partial or discriminatory character, and in this way fall short of the universality advertised by moral philosophy. And this is because the child's parent, or the parent as experienced by the child, not merely holds up as ideals some forms of behavior in which he engages, but often forbids other forms of behavior just because he engages in them himself and wishes to do so exclusively. The relation of the superego to the ego

> is not exhausted by the precept: "*You ought to be like this* (like your father)." It also comprises the prohibition: "You *may not be* like this (like your father)—that is, you may not do all that he does; some things are his prerogative."[27]

Finally, the indissoluble connection of the superego with the Oedipus complex accounts for the remarkable intransigence of morality and its comparative imperviousness to reason. Rooted as it is in what Freud had called the "infantile neurosis," it shares in the backward-looking character that we have already seen to be of the essence of the neurosis itself.

[26] XIX, 169.
[27] XIX, 34.

Quite apart from its intrinsic or substantive importance, Freud's account of the origins and development of
the ego and the superego has a great theoretical interest,
because of the vastly extended role that it assigns to
mental mechanisms, or, at any rate, to certain types of
mental mechanism. In Chapter VI we noted the first
shift in this direction when condensation and displacement, which initially appeared in psychoanalytic theory
in the closest connection with defense, were given a
further application and were recognized as the principles
of an ongoing form of mental activity, namely the system *Ucs.* Freud's account of identification and introjection in the history of the ego extends this same
process. They too have a primary application as mechanisms of defense. And since the boundary between
mechanisms of defense and principles of unconscious
thought are hard to draw, they may also be thought of
as principles of the system *Ucs.*: we may imagine identification and introjection occurring freely in the stream
of the primary process. The further application comes
about when a constructive or constitutive role is extended to these mechanisms, and they are assigned a
crucial function in the building-up of the ego.

The use of identification in defense is seen most
clearly in the phenomenon of melancholia, where the
introjection of the lost love object—against which, as we
have seen, the ego will ultimately rage—is a reaction to
deprivation, and marks an attempt on the part of the ego
to overcome or attenuate the excess of grief. In a more
complicated form, we can see the same process at work
in the formation of symptoms, particularly hysterical
symptoms, in which identification often plays a significant part. Take, for instance, the case of the woman
who carried out the elaborate obsessional ritual with

the table, the stain on the tablecloth, and the maid: or Dora's cough. In both cases, Freud pointed out, there is as part of the symptom an identification. The woman plays the part of her husband when she runs from one room into the other:[28] Dora coughs her father's cough.[29] And in each case the identification takes the place of an erotic tie which the patient wished to remain unconscious.

To some degree, the suggestion that a piece of defense could also have an integrative or constructive function in psychic life had been anticipated by Freud in his brief incursion into the study of character formation— a topic that engaged his attention for a few years immediately before the First World War, only to be abandoned. For Freud had formulated the view that a defense, originally undertaken against certain impulses or instinctual concerns, could, if systematically reiterated, lead to the establishment of permanent traits of character. So, for example, in an essay that attracted indignation and ridicule when it first appeared in 1908, "Character and Anal Erotism," Freud contended that a triad of traits—orderliness, parsimony, and obstinacy— could be regarded as the product of a sustained reaction formation against the pleasures of the anal zone or the satisfactions to be won from retaining, expelling, and playing with, the faeces. And again, in the Leonardo essay, having traced the route by which a boy may subdue and yet prolong his excessive love for his mother by identifying himself with his mother and then loving boys as she loved him, Freud went on:

By repressing his love for his mother he preserves it in his unconscious and from now on remains faithful

[28] XVI, 262–63.
[29] XVIII, 106.

to her. . . . The man who gives the appearance of being susceptible only to the charms of men is in fact attracted by women in the same way as a normal man: but on each occasion he hastens to transfer the excitation he has received from women on to a male object, and in this manner he repeats over and over again the mechanism by which he acquired his homosexuality.[30]

In other words, the man's homosexuality, or his homosexual behavior, is the reiteration, across his life, of the original piece of defense. It was on metapsychological foundations like this that Freud built up his account of the ego, the superego, and their origins.

From what has so far been said about the history of the ego and of its modification, the superego, it might be thought that the development of these agencies, though often slow and sometimes hesitant, was always forward in direction and knew checks but no reverses. This, however, is not how Freud conceived the matter. As far as the superego was concerned, he thought that at times it might be essential to healthy development that it should undergo some attenuation, and one of the tasks assigned to psychoanalytic therapy is to curb its powers when these become excessive. As for the ego, Freud's views here were rather different. He never doubted but that a strong ego was valuable. However, he thought that, quite apart from the debilitating effects of civilization, there were, in the ongoing life of the individual, experiences that could weaken or damage it. There were, in effect, Pyrrhic victories that the ego might secure over the id. In one of his last and highly suggestive papers, "Splitting of the Ego in the Process of

[30] XI, 100.

Defence," of 1937–1938, Freud connected this possibility specifically with nonrepressive forms of defense. In the course of splitting and disavowal the ego may produce within itself the same fissure that it strives to effect between itself and reality. Then in the late *Outline of Psycho-analysis*, Freud argued, more generally, that the ego is weakened by excessive defense, no matter what form this takes, if it is carried out at a period of its development when it is not ready for such expenditure of energy, and he went on to suggest that, if the child's sexual life were allowed free play, much might be avoided in the way of neurosis. In considering the possibility that defense could involve damage to, or splitting of, the ego, Freud could be seen as reviving, though now in a dynamic form, a preanalytic thesis: that is, the thesis familiar from *Studies on Hysteria* that the origins of neurosis were to be found in hypnoid states, or a special form of consciousness. However, Freud's remarks on this topic being so fragmentary, a discussion of the issue belongs more properly to the history of psychoanalysis than to a study of Freud's own thought.

Ultimately, the account that has been given must take its place inside the structural theory of the mind—the theory, that is, that explains mental phenomena in terms of id, ego, and superego. That theory is, indeed, complete when, to an account of the origins and functions of the different psychic agencies, has been added an account of the energy, or forms of energy, that drive the agencies and that are commensurable to their functions.

However, we have now reached a turning point in the theory or, at any rate, in its exposition. So far, I have emphasized an aspect often overlooked—though it has certainly been influential in the work of some of Freud's successors, notably Melanie Klein: and that is the way in which the theory not only provides a model of the mind and its workings, but also coincides with, or reproduces, the kind of picture or representation that we consciously or unconsciously make to ourselves of our mental processes. The theory, in other words, tries to catch or reproduce the fundamental concepts under which the activities of the mind occur. And one great advantage of this coincidence is that it allows a psychoanalytic interpretation, or a characterization of a certain individual's mental state derived from the theory, to have a Janus-like character. From the analyst's point of view, or objectively, it provides a description of the state of mind; whereas from the patient's point of view, or subjectively, it provides, or may provide, an explanation. It will explain the state of mind if it contains or refers to some crucial element in that state of mind of which the individual himself was unconscious—and that could most likely be the representation that he makes of it to himself. There are many reasons, as we have seen, why this is something of which the individual may wish to be ignorant.

However, when we come to Freud's account of the energies of the mental system, such a reading of the theory is no longer open to us. Everything that Freud says must be taken entirely within the context of the theory, and it can be given no subjective counterpart.

The problem of attributing energies to the various psychic agencies is, it will be appreciated, a problem that did not arise for Freud in either the early or the middle phases of the theory. For then he had to deal only with the system *Ucs.* and the ego, and each of these had, as it were, its private instinctual resources upon which it could draw: the system *Ucs.* owned the libido and the ego the ego-instincts. But with the assignment of all instinct to the id and then with the emergence of the superego by the side of the ego, the situation altered. If both the ego and the superego had defined functions assigned to them, how could they be credited with the energies necessary to discharge them?

In the case of the superego, Freud's answer was more or less straightforward. The energy of the superego is aggression. For the superego, in its confrontations with the ego, draws upon that portion of the death instinct which was projected upon the parental figure that was its prototype, either prior to, or during, its introjection and insallation. This is what Freud had in mind when he wrote, perhaps obscurely, "The super-ego merges into the id: indeed, as heir to the Oedipus complex it has intimate relations with the id."[31]

However, in the case of the ego no such ready answer was available. Accordingly, in *The Ego and the Id* Freud put forward, somewhat tentatively, the hypothesis of a neutralized, or "desexualized," libido. Precisely how this hypothesis, which has been taken up in "the ego-psychology" of Heinz Hartmann and others of the so-called New York School, is to be understood is not clear from Freud's scattered remarks. At one point he thought of desexualized libido on the model of the quality-less energy of the "Scientific Project," whereas at another his idea seemed to be of a libidinal impulse so heavily saturated in narcissism that it cannot attach itself to an outer object.[32] However, what is clear is that the hypoth-

[31] XXII, 79.
[32] XIX, 44–47; XX, 98.

esis is to be taken on a highly theoretical level, and that it has nothing to do with the observable or with behavior. More specifically, and contrary to what some commentators have suggested, nothing follows from the hypothesis about the motivation of the individual and his capacity to transcend sexuality. For desexualized libido, however it is to be taken, is a feature solely of the ego. By contrast, the motivation of the individual is a complex product which arises out of the energies of the id as these are regulated or modified by the efforts of the ego.

3

Having established the structural theory of the mind, Freud was able to produce a number of new formulations within it, which represent real advances in scope and clarity. The most striking of these was what amounted to a complete classification of mental disorder, something which Freud had not attempted since the 1890s. In a brief paper of 1923 entitled "Neurosis and Psychosis," written while convalescing from the first of the major operations he was to undergo in the last sixteen years of his life, Freud distinguished between the transference neuroses, the narcissistic neuroses, and the psychoses in the following way: "Transference neuroses correspond to a conflict between the ego and the id; narcissistic neuroses, to a conflict between the ego and the superego; and psychoses, to one between the ego and the external world"[33]—and to this the rider must be added that in the transference neuroses the ego is in the service of the superego, and in psychosis it is in the service of the id.

[33] XIX, 152.

Stated so baldly, the hypothesis may seem singularly dry. In part, the difficulty here is one that arises frequently in the understanding of psychoanalytic theory, in that it is impossible to have access to the mass of clinical evidence that a given hypothesis subsumes. Even Freud's literary genius could not encompass more than a few aspects of a particular case, and there seems no possible way of bringing out how the match of one case to a hypothesis is enhanced by a consideration of parallel cases. But this is not all there is to it, just because the value of a psychoanalytic hypothesis is not exhausted by its correspondence to known fact. In the 1923 paper Freud expressed the hope that his new hypothesis would do more than merely "enrich our store of formulas," and what he had in mind was that it should suggest new ways of looking at the facts or that it should lead on to further formulations. To see how Freud's hopes were realized is the best way of understanding or appreciating the hypothesis itself.

In "The Loss of Reality in Neurosis and Psychosis" of 1924, Freud considered an objection to the hypothesis, to the effect that the loss of reality also occurs in neurosis, so it cannot be definitive of psychosis. Freud accepted this as a fact but pointed out that it refers to a secondary stage in the development of the neurosis: to the return of the repressed. By contrast, his hypothesis refers to the origins of the disorder, of which it remains true. Freud illustrated his point by a reference to Elizabeth von R. At her sister's deathbed she had become aware of her sexual feelings for her brother-in-law. She had then completely forgotten the scene, but she had done so in the course of repressing an impulse. The psychotic reaction would have been to deny her sister's death.

In other words, Freud's new classification of mental disorder was, like his much earlier efforts in this direction, strictly genetic. Each disorder is characterized in terms of its origins, and, indeed, we may see the new hypothesis as a generalization of the view that every neurosis is dependent upon, and its nature determined by, primal repression. The generalization is twofold. In the first place, the hypothesis applies to a wider range of disorders than the psychoneuroses. And, secondly, it refers to a wider range of defenses than repression. And the two points are linked. Within the structural theory Freud was at last able to do what he had long wanted to do: to link specific disorders with specific defenses, and to show why one mechanism of defense is used rather than another. For the mechanism of defense that is invoked is that appropriate to the given form of conflict. In the transference neuroses, it is predominantly repression: in the narcissistic neuroses, it is predominantly regression: and in psychosis, it is predominantly denial or disavowal—a phenomenon that gained in significance in Freud's last writings.[34]

If, however, the new classification gave rise to a broader and more comprehensive view of mental disorder and how it arose, it also permitted a closer understanding of the particular etiological problem, or set of problems, that had engaged Freud's attention for most of his career: that is, the origins of the transference neuroses. The old issue of "incompatibility" could now be restated in terms of the superego. Repression is

[34] This kind of classification was further worked out and elaborated with great clarity and precision by Freud's daughter, Anna, in her *The Ego and the Mechanisms of Defence* (1936).

carried out by the ego upon the id, but the ego acts in the service and at the behest of the superego.[35]

This new formulation goes some way toward explaining the criteria by reference to which repression occurs, for they are the standards of the superego. And when one reflects upon the history of the superego, and how in part it is the result of massive projection by the individual of his own impulses, in particular his own aggression, we can see how, on this view, repression is still not the direct result of, yet in a very real sense is the heir to, internal conflict. More specifically, in the subservience of ego to superego, we have light thrown upon the obscure issue of the motives of repression. In working this out, Freud was led to the last and the most important of the revisions he was to make to his theory: that concerning the nature of anxiety.

Freud had been interested in anxiety from the earliest years, and his interest derived from the evidently close connection between anxiety and neurosis. However, significantly for the development of his thought, Freud held that neurotic anxiety must be studied always alongside realistic anxiety. For, roughly, it may be said that, when Freud came to change his views about neurotic anxiety, he did so by bringing them into line with what he had learned from the study of realistic anxiety.

Freud's earliest views about neurotic anxiety are already familiar to us. From two well-established premises—that neurosis originates in the repression of libido, and that neurosis is accompanied, actually or potentially, by anxiety—Freud drew the conclusion that anxiety is a transform of libido. And he found, or

[35] XIX, 52, 150; XXII, 69.

thought he found, direct support for this thesis in the actual neuroses where a change of sexual regime, from frustration to satisfaction, invariably coincided with an alleviation of anxiety. It is often said—and at one point Freud would seem to have said as much himself[36]—that the persistence of the "toxic" account of anxiety within his thinking was due to his acceptance of an economic theory of the mind. But this cannot be right, without heavy qualification. For, as we have seen, though an economic theory allows one to relate the damming up of energy or frustration at one place in the psychic apparatus with discharge at another, it does not commit one to the view that, given frustration, energy will seek discharge along all possible channels indifferently. Indeed, if the system is of any complexity, an economic theory would be virtually uninformative unless some measure of selectivity in discharge was postulated. Of course, the toxic view of anxiety fits neatly inside the economic theory, but it is not required by that theory. It is required only by the theory plus a view of anxiety as something peculiarly malleable or given to adaptation. And this view seems in turn connected with Freud's failure to see that anxiety was in any way a structured or complex condition. It is a natural concomitant of the toxic view to regard anxiety itself as a kind of free-floating mood, which descends, and then evaporates.

The correction to this lay in the study of realistic anxiety, and in the *Introductory Lectures*, where Freud elaborated on the toxic account of neurotic anxiety, there was also an extended treatment of its realistic counterpart. Realistic anxiety under analysis falls into two distinct parts. On the one hand, there is what might in some broad sense be thought of as the behavioral com-

36 XX, 161.

ponent, though Freud also called it "physiological" or "motor," and this itself is composite: it consists in a set of bodily movements, an awareness of these movements, and a feeling of unpleasure attached to this awareness. On the other hand, there is a purely psychological component, which constitutes the nucleus of the anxiety state and is in effect the re-enactment of some earlier event. For some years, Freud had been toying with the idea—to be taken up and exaggerated by Rank—that realistic anxiety was peculiarly connected with the event of birth, in that, if birth was not the ultimate object, then it was at least the prototype of all later objects, of anxiety.

This analysis certainly secured a degree of complexity for realistic anxiety and, therefore, potentially a structure: if, that is, the relations between the parts can be exhibited. However, Freud at this stage was unable to discern any comprehensible relations between the parts. Though the behavioral component seemed a response to the present situation, the psychological component referred exclusively to a past situation, and Freud concluded that, despite appearances, realistic anxiety was inexpedient. Indeed, given its predominantly backward-looking character, or the way in which it merely repeated an earlier event, he suggested that realistic anxiety could be conceived of as ultimately a derivative of neurotic anxiety.

As we have seen, there already was in Freud's conceptual apparatus a model for a kind of mental state which, while backward-looking in that it contained essentially a reference to the past, was also forward-looking, in that it used this reference with an eye to future contingencies. The conception of thought as a "trial run" combined the two temporal references, to past and future, in much this way. We revive an event that occurred in the past in order to cope with an identical event should it occur in the future. And a still closer analogy lay with the mechanism that, in the "Scientific Project," Freud had postulated for the control of the psychic apparatus by the pleasure principle. In the "Project," Freud had seen quite clearly that, if hedonism, as the principle of human action, was to mean anything more than a crude and immediate shrinking from pain or attraction toward pleasure as and when the organism is exposed to such stimuli, then the apparatus must be credited with some mechanism which allows it to anticipate the future on the basis of the past. In this way, it could steer itself toward the pleasurable and away from the painful, before either was upon it. What was required, in other words, was a signal mechanism, and Freud looked to a re-enactment of a past event, in a modified or controlled form to fill this role.

The first step, then, toward a revised account of anxiety—which was initially set out in *Inhibitions, Symptoms and Anxiety* and taken up in the *New Introductory Lectures*—consisted in making the adjustments necessary for bringing the account of realistic anxiety under the model of the "signal phenomenon." As far as the psychological component is concerned, emphasis is laid on the attenuated fashion in which the past event is re-enacted: it is remembered rather than repeated. And the behavioral component now acquires the character of expediency, in that it is it that helps to deter the individual from an actual recurrence of the event, by offering a small foretaste of what might come, and, at the same time, it helps to bind the impulse involved. The second step was to assimilate neurotic anxiety to realistic anxiety, so far as their nature or structure are concerned, and to leave the difference between the two forms of anxiety located solely in their objects, or in what they are anxiety about.

However, though Freud was prepared to do away with any essential distinction between realistic and neurotic anxiety, he nevertheless saw that the analysis he now offered could not be the sole analysis for anxiety. The break might not come where he had previously thought that it came, but this did not mean that a unitary account was possible. Freud argued for this in two stages. In the first place, anxiety, understood as a signal phenomenon, must be a secondary phenomenon. It presupposes, that is to say, some more primitive form of reaction to the situation whose repetition it signals: for in the absence of such a reaction, there would be no expediency to the signaling of the event, since there would be no motive to avoid its repetition. The primitive reaction Freud assumed to be an experience of utter helplessness, and—this is the second stage of the argument—since this experience is a constituent of the later anxiety attack, it seemed legitimate to think of it too as a form of anxiety. In other words, signal anxiety was not merely a secondary phenomenon, it was a secondary form of anxiety. So, within anxiety, Freud could now contrast what he called "reaction-anxiety" and "signal-anxiety." The former was a primitive response to a "traumatic situation" (a phrase revived), the latter a more complex reaction to a "danger situation." And just as signal anxiety presupposed reaction anxiety, so danger situations derived from traumatic situations. And in drawing the distinction within anxiety as he now drew it, Freud, it is interesting to observe, was going back to a distinction originally made in the "Project" along much the same lines, between the initial experience of pain, which hits the system like "a stroke of lightning," and the fresh release of unpleasure from the key neurons, which warned of the likely return of pain.

What now remained was to clarify the distinction between the objects of realistic anxiety and the objects of neurotic anxiety, and to specify the latter. Freud's answer to the first problem was simple: "A real danger is a danger which threatens a person from an external object, and a neurotic danger is one which threatens him from an instinctual demand."[37] And if it now seems questionable how a purely internal process, like the development of an instinct, could constitute a danger, Freud's thinking here proceeded along lines that we have seen were laid down in his earliest writings. An internal danger is, in the first instance, to be understood in purely quantitative terms, as the excessive accumulation of amounts of stimulation. The individual is, or feels himself to be, overwhelmed from within. This is "the traumatic situation." However, internal dangers readily associate themselves in the early mind with external dangers, through the intermediate notion of an object or agency that could relieve this tension. For, if this object is itself exposed to danger, the stimulation will not be discharged. Accordingly, the next step is for neurotic anxiety to be experienced as the fear of the loss of, or of separation from, an object whose presence could put an end to the dangerous situation against which the infant is helpless. As to what the object is, this is determined by the instinctual development of the infant. Out of this Freud devised a genetic account of the various forms that neurotic anxiety assumes. "Each period of the individual's life has its appropriate deter-

[37] XX, 167.

minant of anxiety."[38] There is, first, the fear of birth: secondly, the fear of separation from the mother: thirdly, the fear of castration: and, finally, the fear of the super-ego, experienced initially as the fear of its anger, or of the loss of its love, and then as the fear of death. Freud thought that these objects of anxiety would not necessarily attain consciousness, and therefore he thought it correct, though derivative, further to distinguish neurotic from realistic anxiety as anxiety about an unknown danger as opposed to anxiety about a known danger.

If, however, neurotic anxiety acquires, by a certain associative mechanism, a set of external objects, it still retains the marks of its internal origin. The objects are never more than proxies for inner states, and this manifests itself in a number of ways which set neurotic anxiety apart from realistic anxiety. In the first place, the object of neurotic anxiety would not be a danger if it were not for certain impulses that we entertain. To take Freud's example: a wolf would most likely attack a man irrespective of what the man does, but, when we fear loss of love or the threat of castration, these dangers would never arise if we did not entertain certain feelings or intentions. Accordingly, we feel it natural or appropriate to "proceed against the external danger by taking measures against the internal ones."[39] In other words, in the case of neurotic anxiety we commit ourselves to a policy of defense rather than flight. But there are two respects in which defense is at a disadvantage compared with flight. In most cases of defense, it is not enough for us simply to evade the danger (which is what flight effects), but we must in some way close with it and overcome or deflect it. And, where defense is appropriate,

[38] XX, 142.
[39] XX, 145.

we are invariably implicated with the danger, since we and the impulse, unlike the man and the wolf, are both parts of the same organization.

Freud, as we have seen, treated the various forms in which neurotic anxiety expresses itself as successive, or phase-specific. Nevertheless, he was insistent that there is considerable superimposition in that earlier fears can underlie later fears, and later fears can conjure up earlier fears. Much of the richness and complexity of the infant's emotional life derives from this fact. So, for instance, fear of the loss of the mother can intensify fear of castration, since the penis guarantees one way in which the infant can be united to (or to a substitute for) his mother: that is, in copulation. Or, again, the fear of castration can reactivate the fear of birth; for the infant, identifying himself with his penis, or thinking of his penis as himself, can now feel himself forever cast out from where he wishes to be: in (or in the entrance to) her womb.[40]

However, the important issue is not simply that these phases overlap, or that one object of neurotic anxiety persists into a phase more properly dominated by another. That would account for disturbances of childhood. But what is serious is that these anxieties can persist from childhood, from the phases to which they belong, throughout the individual's life, to some degree or other. Sometimes, for instance, the object of the anxiety will undergo disguise, as when fear of castration is retained in the guise of fear of syphilis. Fear of the superego, however, persists in its original form. So we must ask, Why does this phenomenon, which has no real value in itself and runs counter to the movement of life, survive in this way? In the last section of

[40] XVII, 100–102; XX, 138–39.

Inhibitions, Symptoms and Anxiety, Freud sketched an answer. He enumerated the three types of factor that have to be taken into account: biological, phylogenetic, and psychological—and he insisted, as he had throughout his work, that the quantitative issue is paramount. Nevertheless, he was not prepared at this stage to go beyond generalities. For, as he put it:

> we have once more come unawares upon the riddle which has so often confronted us: whence does neurosis come—what is its ultimate, its own peculiar *raison d'être*? Aften tens of years of psycho-analytic labours, we are as much in the dark about this problem as we were at the start.[41]

In this passage we are brought up against what is, from the point of view of Freud's theory as a whole, the most arresting feature of the new account of anxiety: the reversal it achieves in what had for so long been held to be the relations between anxiety and neurosis. After re-examining two of his most important case histories, Little Hans and the Wolf Man, Freud concluded, "It was anxiety which produced repression and not, as I formerly believed, repression which produced anxiety."[42] Neurotic anxiety, in other words, is so called because of its effect, not because of its cause. And, having made this suggestion, Freud then went beyond it, and hinted at a solution not merely for the etiology of neurosis but, once again, for the choice of neurosis. For the various transference neuroses might be explicable in terms of the forms of neurotic anxiety from which they emerge, and Freud proposed specific links between hysteria and fear of the loss of love, between the phobias

[41] XX, 148–49.
[42] XX, 108–109.

and fear of castration, and between obsessional neurosis and fear of the superego.

Not merely does the new hypothesis about anxiety and neurosis fit excellently into the structural theory of the mind, but it also, Freud contended, makes better sense of the evidence from which he had originally argued for anxiety as the transform of libido. For, as we have seen, Freud was heavily influenced in adopting this hypothesis by the concomitance of neurosis and anxiety and, more specifically, by the fact that, if the symptoms of a neurosis are suppressed, anxiety appears. An agorophobic patient who is left alone in the street, or an obsessional neurotic who is prevented from washing his hands, becomes a prey to unbearable anxiety. But as things stand, we have here a bare conjunction. If, however, we add a third term, and assign to the anxiety an object, in the form of a situation of danger, then the position gains in intelligibility. For now we can say that the symptom was formed in order to fend off the situation of danger, and that, if the symptom is not allowed to form, the danger in fact materializes, or threatens to materialize, and it is this threat that accounts for the generation of anxiety. But this in turn presupposes that the anxiety existed prior to the symptom formation or, for that matter, to the onset of neurosis.

This account of the relation of the neurosis to anxiety is certainly clearer than anything that Freud had achieved earlier, and it had the effect of putting the problem of anxiety in the forefront of scientific attention. To trace the natural history of anxiety, to see what part is played in its formation by instinct, by the controlling activity of the ego, and by the internalized aggression of the superego, and to assess whether, as Freud hoped, all could be ultimately traced to "the dreaded economic situation"[43]—these were the immediate tasks that Freud bequeathed to his successors.

One question remains: If repressed libido is not transformed into anxiety, what becomes of it? In the *New Introductory Lectures*, Freud gave it as his "modest reply" that "what happens to it is probably not always the same thing."[44] On one point on which Freud had not always been quite explicit, he was now clear: and that is, that the fate of a certain emotion and the fate of a certain quantity of instinctual energy could not be identified. For an emotion is something structured, something laced around with thoughts or ideas, and one common effect of repression, indeed of all the defenses, is to undo this structure. In the great metapsychological papers, Freud had confessed to some conceptual unease in talking about unconscious emotions, as though emotions could survive intact in the unconscious. To this original unease, Freud could now add theoretical, and indeed empirical, considerations.[45] Our unconscious life may be powered by strong bursts of energy, it may contain rigid and deathless concatenations of belief and desire, but it seems not to be the locus of complex or evolved emotions. For emotions, like traits of character, like man's cultural capacities, evince the workmanship of the ego. In consequence, when they undergo repression, the chances are that they also suffer inhibition: that is, their development is damaged, and their function is impaired.

[43] XX, 138.
[44] XXII, 91.
[45] XX, 142*n*.

4

For the last sixteen years of his life Freud was a dying man, coexisting painfully with "the mysterious process," as he called it,[46] from which he was eventually to die on September 23, 1939. Cancer of the mouth was diagnosed in the spring of 1923, and, before it ran its course, Freud had undergone thirty-three operations, many of them grave and some inept. In an appendix to his biography of Freud, Ernest Jones has provided a case history of the disease, from which we can see the cruelty of its progress and Freud's heroism in the face of it.

Freud never ceased to work. Some of his finest and most audacious books were written while he was in intense pain, and he continued his psychoanalytic practice, taking as many as four patients a day, until he was quite near the end. Any public appearance became impossible for him after 1923 because of the deterioration of his speech. In 1932, to bring the popular presentation of his ideas up to date, as well as to try and aid the failing finances of the psychoanalytic publishing house, Freud wrote the *New Introductory Lectures*, which he modeled upon the original set. But he knew that he could never deliver them. If, as he put it, he once more took his place in the lecture room, it was "only by an artifice of the imagination."[47]

In the summer of 1938 Freud was forced to leave Vienna and settle in London. Through the good offices of friends and admirers—notably Ernest Jones, William Bullitt, the American ambassador in Paris, and the

[46] Zweig, p. 175.
[47] XXII, 5.

Princesse Marie Bonaparte—the move was accomplished as painlessly as possible. However, by the time of his exile, Freud felt himself quite estranged from the two societies to which he was tied by birth and upbringing: Vienna, and Judaism. For Vienna he had always expressed intense dislike, and he found it hard to bear the facile judgment of the world that psychoanalysis owed everything to a city from which he, in point of fact, had never experienced anything except indifference, hostility, or rejection. There may also have been some feelings of affection for his native city. As to Judaism, his attitude was, at once, more respectful and more distant. He was proud of the high ethical standards of the Jewish tradition and felt that he owed much to them, but the historic preoccupation of Judaism with religious over other cultural concerns daunted him. "Palestine," he wrote to Arnold Zweig, contrasting it with the rest of the eastern Mediterranean, for which he felt such deep attachment, "has never produced anything but religions, sacred frenzies, presumptuous attempts to overcome the outer world of appearance by means of the inner world of wishful thinking."[48] The opposition, as he saw it, of Jewish scholarship to *Moses and Monotheism*, the love child of his old age, and the nationalistic tendencies of Zionism only alienated him further. If he belonged anywhere at all, it was to the psychoanalytic community from which, throughout his life, he had suffered so much in the way of secessions, feuds, painful quarrels, and many personal tragedies. The prospects for psychoanalysis itself he always found somber. On his eightieth birthday he received many tributes, but, as he wrote, again to Arnold Zweig,

[48] Zweig, p. 40.

Numerous articles in newspapers at home and abroad expressed their repudiation and hatred clearly enough. One could thus establish with satisfaction that honesty has not yet quite vanished from the earth.[49]

Freud was never a lover of humanity, but he did as much for it as any other human being who has lived. And, if he could find little evidence for the goodness, he had a sense, as no one else before him, of the richness and mystery, of the psyche. Amongst the last things Freud ever wrote, we find, "Mysticism is the obscure self-perception of the realm outside the ego, of the id."[50]

[49] Zweig, p. 127.
[50] XXIII, 300.

Civilization and Society

viii

To try to find in Freud's writings an articulated
or coherent social theory or ethic, an enterprise
to which some of the most speculative minds of
our day have committed themselves, is a vain
task. For Freud had no such theory and no such
ethic: as he himself was able to recognize.

There were, of course, many aspects of society
and its institutions in which he was deeply interested, and, if we look for a pervasive concern,
we can find it in the hold exerted over him by
any issue to do with social origins or with the
beginnings of a particular social or cultural
phenomenon. The origins of morality, of religion,
of social institutions in general and of political
authority in particular were questions to which
he constantly reverted, and his major writings on
society—*Totem and Taboo, Group Psychology
and the Analysis of the Ego, The Future of an*

Illusion, Civilization and Its Discontents, and *Moses and Monotheism*—are largely composed out of bold and highly speculative answers to these questions. In part, this concern corresponded to something deep in Freud's nature: a characteristic preoccupation with the primitive and the archaic not only dominated his scientific work, but manifested itself in his general reading and in the art that he collected. One of Freud's favored similes for his own work, for the work of psychoanalysis, was that of archaeological investigation.[1] And, in turn, this preoccupation with the past was reinforced by a somewhat outmoded conception to which Freud clung, according to which there is a match between what is early historically, or in the life of the species, and what is early psychologically or in the life of the individual. However, contrary to what is sometimes said, Freud never committed the fallacy of thinking that there was a direct relation between the antiquity of an institution and either its social desirability or its social necessity. This is to be seen most clearly in Freud's discussion of religion in *The Future of an Illusion.* Religious belief, according to him, was ancient, baneful, and eradicable.

However, on the most general issues of social organization, Freud had not read deeply nor did he aim at holding any systematic or entrenched opinions. Audacious as he was within the field of science and impatient always to push its frontiers outward, he was deeply averse, both by nature and by intellectual training, to the formation of beliefs or principles that went beyond comprehension or analysis as he felt himself to possess them. Discussing the differences between the methods of religion and science, Freud wrote:

[1] E.g. IX, 40, 51; X, 176–77; XXI, 69–71; XXIII, 259–60.

In its third function, in which it issues precepts and lays down prohibitions and restrictions, religion is furthest away from science. For science is content to investigate and to establish facts, though it is true that from its applications rules and advice are derived on the conduct of life.[2]

This somewhat austere view of inquiry fitted in not only with Freud's scientific world picture but also with his temperament. There are few things that so effectively divide him from our own more enthusiastic age than his refusal to believe that it is in any way the mark of a good or generous mind to give way to hope. On the contrary, Freud thought that mankind collectively had most to fear from the phenomenon of "illusion": that is to say, from beliefs molded by wishes.

I

There was one issue on which Freud did think that his scientific work gave him a right to pronounce, even if he himself felt unable to reach a definitive opinion, and that issue was nothing less than the value or ultimate justification of civilization itself.

In a paper of 1907 entitled "Obsessive Actions and Religious Practices," we find Freud already committed to the idea of an inherent conflict between civilization and instinctual pleasure, as though the former were built upon a progressive renunciation of the latter. The question then arose whether the price of civilization, calculated in instinct, was not too high, and it was this question—roughly, whether civilization was worth it— that Freud felt his clinical experience put him in a favored position to answer. In a paper of the following

[2] XXII, 162.

year he wrote, "We may well raise the question whether our civilized 'sexual' morality is worth the sacrifice which it imposes on us, especially," he adds drily, "if we are still so much enslaved to hedonism as to include among the aims of our cultural development a certain amount of satisfaction."[3] And years later, at the age of seventy-three, by which time few men are still prepared to raise fundamental questions about the organization of life, he wrote:

> I can at least listen without indignation to the critic who is of the opinion that when one surveys the aims of cultural development and the means it employs, one is bound to come to the conclusion that the whole effort is not worth the trouble and that the outcome of it can only be a state of affairs which the individual will be unable to tolerate.[4]

The question is clearly bold, yet, on closer inspection, we can see that certain difficulties or obscurities attach to it. Two of them can rather neatly be brought into focus by asking, Why did Freud think that his clinical experience specifically equipped him to deal with this question? To this the obvious answer might be that what seemed to Freud relevant in his clinical experience was the insight it had permitted him into the ill-effects of sexual repression. But surely the issue of instinctual renunciation is larger than that of sexual repression— and along two dimensions. First, there can be renunciation of non-sexual instincts, and, secondly, there can be forms of renunciation other than repression. Accordingly, if the answer that I have suggested for Freud is the correct one, then was Freud in effect denying that

---

[3] IX, 204.
[4] XXI, 144–45.

these possibilities were realized in the course of cultural advance—or did he simply overlook them?

On the first possibility Freud, it is true, had very little to say—so long, that is, as he continued to identify the nonsexual instincts with the ego-instincts. Once Freud admitted aggression alongside sexuality, then, as we shall see, it was a matter of some moment to consider how far its renunciation entered into the costs of civilization. Until then, Freud probably thought that he had little to contribute to the ordinary estimate of how much of that price was paid in ego-instincts.

On the second possibility, the issues are more complex, and Freud was somewhat elliptical in what he said. One evident misunderstanding of Freud is to suppose that he thought of sexual repression as the natural instrument by which civilization maintained itself in the cultural domain, parallel to its employment to political repression in the civil domain. For, among other errors, this interpretation suggests that instinctual renunciation is exacted only from the oppressed classes; whereas it was Freud's view that oppressors and oppressed alike are made to pay. Indeed, the oppressors pay more heavily. Where injustice arose, in Freud's view, was in the fact that only the oppressors stand to gain from this imposition, for it is only they who share in the benefits of civilization.

The alternative to repression as the possible means by which civilization might secure instinctual renunciation were (roughly) frustration, sublimation, and rational rejection. Rational rejection, or judgment as Freud called it, he equated with the liberated morality, that is, the morality freed from anxiety—but he clearly did not think that it was as yet within the capacities of any but a comparative few: quite apart, of course, from the question whether it could be rational judgment to reject instinct to the measure that civilization demanded. The same held good for sublimation. Moreover, both sublimation and frustration were quantitative matters, and both had an upper limit set to them: only a certain amount of instinctual energy could be sublimated, and only a certain amount of frustration could be tolerated. For this reason, the question of the extent to which civilization makes use of repression in controlling the instincts is bound up with the question how heavily such control is exercised, or the scale of the instinctual renunciation that civilization involves.

There is another factor that bears upon this. The principal vehicle by which the demands of civilization are carried is, of course, morality; and morality, as we have seen, is, in large part, an internalized process. Morality is internalized along with the superego and contributes generously to the standards or norms to which repression strives to make the instincts of the individual conform. However, just as there is a point beyond which frustration cannot be tolerated, so—it seems to have been Freud's opinion—there is a point beyond which a repressive, or at any rate an arbitrarily repressive, morality cannot be internalized.

In the paper of 1908 whose title is " 'Civilized' Sexual Morality and Modern Nervous Illness," Freud envisaged three different stages at which society might be as far as its moral attitude to sexuality is concerned.[5] The first is one where the sexual instinct may be freely satisfied; the second is one where the sexual instinct may be satisfied only if it serves the aim of reproduction; and the third is one where the sexual instinct may be satisfied only if it serves the aim of legitimate reproduction—that

[5] IX, 189.

is, reproduction within institutionalized marriage. Freud thought that the society in which he lived was at the third stage—though, of course, when it came to living up to its morality, hypocrisy intervened. And such a morality, it was clear to Freud, was intolerable except for the strongest spirits. For not merely was the instinctual burden of its demands exorbitant, but the arbitrariness of the demands themselves made it harder for them to be internalized. Contemporary sexual morality, then, rested upon a combination of repression and frustration, and, insofar as repression failed or frustration proved excessive, it gave rise to two characteristic practices—both of which Freud thought baneful—by which it was at once maintained and evaded: prostitution and masturbation.

We are now in a position to see that Freud, in claiming that his clinical experience entitled him to a view on the ultimate value of civilization, and whether it was worth the price it demanded, did not have in mind solely what he had learned about the ill effects of sexual repression. He relied as much upon the study of the actual neuroses as upon the study of the psychoneuroses. For in the actual neuroses Freud had found evidence—or so he thought at the time—for the harm caused by sexual abstinence or an impoverished sexual life. Frustration, in other words, even without repression, could give rise to anxiety. At the time, it is true, Freud's view of the actual neuroses was closely connected with his equation of anxiety with transformed libido, and, when he later came to doubt this equation, he never returned to the problem of the actual neuroses or reformulated his view of them. Indeed, by this point of time the actual neuroses had ceased to interest Freud. But the explanation for this seems to be that Freud had come to think of the actual neuroses as invariably resting upon a sub-strate of psychoneurosis. Accordingly, there was no need for Freud to revise his estimate of the pathogenic character of frustration: but its pathogenic character now derived from the way in which it worked in conjunction with, or reactivated, repression.

There remains a difficulty with the question that Freud raised about the value of civilization. As the quotation I cited earlier made clear, Freud thought that it is our hedonism that makes us doubt whether civilization is worth while. So long as we continue to desire pleasure, we must wonder whether we are right to renounce it on so massive a scale as civilization requires. And yet, if we really are hedonists, if we really do place such a supreme value upon pleasure, how is it that we have ever come to accept a form of life that exacts such a heavy toll in pleasure—unless it be that, though civilization asks us to renounce pleasure in one form, it does so only to make it more secure for us in some other form? Indeed, taking up this last point, we might ask whether Freud has not falsified the issue by presenting us only with the cost of civilization, and concealing what we gain from it. If we could see both sides of the account, might it not be that we should find an over-all balance in favor of pleasure—as indeed we should expect, given that man is a pleasure-seeking animal?

At this point Freud drew a distinction which, though common form among those who subscribe to a hedonistic theory of human nature, acquires a special importance within his thinking.[6] Instinctually, it is true, man pursues pleasure. Yet he is so made that he can experience pleasure rarely, at some difficulty to himself,

[6] XXI, 76–85.

and only by contrast with the general tenor of his life. On the other hand, he is placed in the world in such a way that he can experience pain very readily. There are three sources from which pain derives and to which he is constantly exposed: his body, the external world, and, "as a kind of gratuitous addition,"[7] his relations with others. In consequence, the task of avoiding pain acquires a priority over that of obtaining pleasure, and it seems to have been Freud's view that, if man in his private existence remains a pleasure-seeking animal, in his civil existence he is more concerned with avoiding pain. If civilization demands a massive instinctual sacrifice, what it offers in return is not so much security of pleasure as the absence of suffering. The sources of suffering being what they are, this absence can be achieved only through the forgoing of instinctual satisfaction and work. Since neither of these two things is inherently agreeable, coercion is necessary. Nevertheless, all these factors admit of degree, and, though Freud sometimes posed the question of civilization dramatically, as though it were a matter of all or nothing, at his more realistic he saw the problem as one of evaluating the most favorable balance or equation between the different factors than can be achieved at a given historical moment. So, for instance, Freud, in talking of assessing the Russian Revolution, made the suggestion that the verdict of the future may well be

> that the experiment was undertaken prematurely, that a sweeping alteration of the social order has little prospect of success until new discoveries have increased our control over the forces of Nature and so made easier the satisfaction of our needs. Only then perhaps may it become possible for a new social order

[7] XXI, 77.

not only to put an end to the material need of the masses but also to give a hearing to the cultural demands of the individual.[8]

"Even then," Freud went on, "we shall still have the struggle for an incalculable time with the difficulties which the untameable character of human nature presents to every kind of social community."

An originality of Freud's approach to the problem of civilization is this: having posed the question as one whether the burden or price of civilization is worth it, whether the pleasure that it asks us to renounce is compensated for by the suffering that it saves us, he went on to suggest that the discontents or *malaise* of civilization should be assessed from the point of view of those who stand to gain most from it. For, if they remain dissatisfied, this points to fundamental or inherent defects in our social arrangements. Of course, Freud thought it to be a major task of any civilization that hoped to endure that it should incorporate the greater part, if not the totality, of its members into what it had to offer. "If," Freud wrote,

a culture has not got beyond a point at which the satisfaction of one portion of its participants depends upon the suppression of another, and perhaps larger, portion—and this is the case in all present day cultures—it is understandable that the suppressed people should develop an intense hostility towards a culture whose existence they make possible by their work, but in whose wealth they have too small a share. . . . The hostility of these classes to civilization is so obvious that it has caused the more latent hostility of the social strata that are better provided for to be overlooked.

[8] XXII, 181.

It goes without saying that a civilization which leaves so large a number of its participants unsatisfied and drives them into revolt neither has nor deserves the prospect of a lasting existence.[9]

Nevertheless, Freud was clear that any attempt to extend or open up the benefits of civilization that did not take into account its inherent limitations, as these were exhibited in what it managed to offer to the most favored sections of the community, could only perpetuate illusion. For so often, in the denunciation of this or that historical form of society, what was being attacked was something essential to society itself.

2

And now we might put a question which takes us to the heart of Freud's estimate of civilization: Granted that the avoidance of pain is a project of overwhelming significance for man, granted that this project can be carried through with any measure of success only inside a society that is held together by common ties, why does this unification have to rest upon massive instinctual renunciation backed by coercion? Is it not possible that the ties that link society should be based upon instinct rather than run counter to it? More specifically, might not that complex balance of impulses —erotic and affectionate, direct and inhibited, outward-flowing and narcissistic—which we call love, be sufficient to hold together the members of a society, without the use of political oppression and a harsh morality? In *Civilization and Its Discontents*, Freud raised the question whether there could not be a society in which the

[9] XXI, 12.

social bond was preponderantly erotic, and the basic unit was the couple brought and held together by sexual attraction. Having talked of the power of sexual love between two persons, Freud asked whether it was too fanciful to envisage

> a cultural community consisting of double individuals like this, who, libidinally satisfied in themselves, are connected with one another through the bonds of common work and common interests.[10]

Moreover, the question that is here explicitly raised can never have been very far from Freud's mind when he turned to social or political issues, and it comes most naturally out of his whole thinking about man and his place in society.

Yet Freud's response to this idyllic conception of civilization, in which Cythera provides the model of human society, is undoubtedly skeptical. Initially, it is true, civilization is prepared to tolerate love. Indeed, it never ceases to esteem it or to rank it among the highest values of culture. But, increasingly, according to Freud, its place is diminished, and the attitude of civilization ceases to be altogether friendly.

> In the course of development the relation of love to civilization loses its unambiguity. On the one hand love comes into opposition to the interests of civilization; on the other, civilization threatens love with substantial restrictions.[11]

Even within the charmed circle of privilege the rights of love are systematically abrogated.

If we now ask why this process occurs, why society cannot rest upon love but must conflict with it, Freud's

[10] XXI, 108.
[11] XXI, 103.

answer was, in part, that it is love that is inherently subversive. Sexual love is a relation between two persons to which a third must be either superfluous or disturbing. But the more important part of Freud's answer was that civilization needs the sexuality that is spent between two lovers so as to diffuse it over the other members of the society and compose from it the ties of friendship and community that constitute the social nexus. It has, of course, been a commonplace among political thinkers—since, say, the discussions of Plato and Aristotle on communal marriage—that there exists some kind of proportionality, of an inverse order, between private passion and public feeling. Freud, however, advances the discussion by suggesting the psychic mechanism by means of which the ratio is maintained. His argument, which is to be found in *Group Psychology and the Analysis of the Ego*, requires a reconsideration of certain phenomena, such as identification and love, which we have already looked at, but now in their social context. For it is in terms of them that the social equation, as we might call it, is to be understood.

True to a style of thinking that was already a trifle outmoded, Freud sought to explain the advanced looseknit society of his own day by reference to the closer, more homogenized groups characteristic of earlier times and exhibited, in the modern age, in somewhat peripheral institutions like the army or the Roman Catholic Church and, more transiently, in crowds or revolutionary mobs. In such groups, Freud argues, two traits have been observed and commented on by nearly all those who have given the matter attention: they may be thought of as contagion and suggestion. Contagion is a relation between members of the group, and suggestion is a relation between the members of the group and someone outside it, who can conveniently be called "the leader."[12]

Freud then tried to explain both these traits, and the difference between them, by reference to identification. There are many circumstances—some of which we have already looked at—in which an individual, in phantasy, takes an object, generally an object that he has lost or that he fears to lose, into himself and makes it part of his inner world. In such cases he is enriched. There are, however, other cases, which bear a resemblance to these, save in the outcome. In these cases the individual is noticeably impoverished. He exhibits excessive humility, he is worthless in his own eyes, and at the same time he overvalues or idealizes the object that he has internalized. The first type of case Freud called identification: for the second type of case he had no specific name, but he recognized it in the phenomena of hypnosis and of being in love—particularly unhappily in love. And in the one case, Freud argued, the object has been put in the place of the ego, in the other it has been put in the place of what he still called "the ego-ideal."[13]

As the use of this phrase indicates, Freud's discussion of contagion and suggestion and the difference between them antedated—by two years, in point of fact—his developed account of the superego, which is given in *The Ego and the Id*. And in that account the origin of the superego is specifically linked with identification. Here, however, we hear of a multiplicity of objects being set up internally as the result of identification. Is this a discrepancy, and, if so, how is it to be accounted for? The answer is, I think, that we are to take seriously a distinction implicit, in what Freud said, between the

[12] XVIII, 95.
[13] XVIII, 114, 116.

internalized object being set up as the superego and the internalized object being set up in the place of the super-ego. In other words, Freud was thinking of hypnosis and unhappy love as phenomena superimposed on, and to some degree effacing, the results of normal development: although, of course, the fact that such effacement can happen shows that the development was not robust.

Identification, then, is the source of the social tie. In virtue of it, members of a group model themselves upon each other, they tend to think and to feel alike, and it is only an extreme variant of this phenomenon that we find in the contagion endemic in mobs or crowds convulsed by passions of the moment. And so we need to ask what are the circumstances that favor identification.

We have some idea of the answer that Freud would give as far as the development of the individual is concerned. Identification belongs to the phase before object choice has been established, and in consequence it characteristically appears whenever there is a regression to this early phase. However, there is another set of circumstances in which identification can occur, of less importance in itself but highly significant for group psychology. The reason why these circumstances are less important, is that then identification occurs as a secondary phenomenon. The example that Freud gave[14] is that of a girl in a boarding school who receives a letter from someone with whom she is secretly in love: the letter, for some reason, arouses her jealousy, and she reacts with a fit of hysterics: then the chances are that some of the girl's friends who know of the incident will catch the fit, by "mental infection." Here is a case of identification, but the identification arises because of a common emotional quality. The girl's friends identify

[14] XVIII, 107.

with her on the basis of another, and deeper, tie:
for they desire to have the kind of relation that she
is supposed to have with the man who has made her
unhappy. In this kind of situation, peripheral for the
study of identification but central for the study of
society, we find what Freud called "the formula for the
libidinal constitution of groups."[15] Groups, Freud suggests, consist in *a number of individuals who have put
one and the same object in the place of their ego ideal
and have consequently identified themselves with one
another in their ego.*" In other words, of the two traits
that are characteristic of groups, suggestion and contagion, there is a dependence of the latter upon the
former. The emotional link within the group derives
from, and is sustained by, the emotional link between
the group and its leader. This point Freud put forcefully
by saying that man is not a herd animal, but a horde
animal.[16]

Of course, what is true of the group is not necessarily
true of advanced societies. Freud recognized this.
Nevertheless insofar as the lineaments of the older forms
of social organization are still discernible within our
own, to that degree the libidinal formula holds. And this
has two aspects. In the first place, the social tie is dependent on the link to the leader. The leader is not
simply an external agent who polices the society and
preserves it from disunity. Rather, it is in obedience to
him that the society finds its existence. Social cohesiveness is rooted in political subjection. Secondly, the social
tie is secured at the expense of instinctual satisfaction.
In the doctrine of Universal Love organized society pays
its final respects to the human instinct of love, for

[15] XVIII, 116.
[16] XVIII, 121.

in instituting the doctrine it vanquishes the instinct.

The question therefore arises how far the older or closer form of society is simply a historical phenomenon arising out of the exigencies of primitive life, which will disappear as they are overcome. Are the traditional forms of socialization relative to the stage of human need and weakness, and will they naturally be attenuated as mankind gains control over his environment? It was only by the time he came to write *Civilization and Its Discontents* that Freud felt ready to take on this question, and by this time he had an answer. The commandment "Love thy neighbor as thyself" had a perennial appeal just because nothing else runs so directly counter to the natural tendencies of man.[17] The diffused erotic ties between members of a society, depending at once on a self-effacing attachment to authority and a massive renunciation of direct satisfaction, are barriers against the most potent and implacable enemy of civilization: the death instinct in its outward manifestation of aggression. "The meaning of the evolution of civilization," Freud wrote,

> is no longer obscure to us. It must present the struggle between Eros and Death, between the instinct of life and the instinct of destruction, as it works itself out in the human species. This is what all life essentially consists of, and the evolution of civilization may therefore be simply described as the struggle for life of the human species. And it is this battle of the giants that our nurse-maids try to appease with their lullaby about Heaven.[18]

The central problem, on which any estimate of the value of human civilization must ultimately depend, is how

[17] XXI, 111, 143.
[18] XXI, 122.

aggression can be controlled, and whether the machinery
built into the traditional society provides the only means
of achieving this result.

Freud enumerated four ways of controlling aggression.
The first two are manifestly social in that they involve
the institutions of society. As we have seen, aggression
can be regulated by intensifying communal feeling
through the attachment to a leader. But apart from the
sacrifices that any such society will demand from its
members, there is the further disadvantage that the
strengthening of communal feeling goes along with an
increasing intolerance of everyone outside the community. And this intolerance does not require that each
society should be very clearly demarcated from the
others. On the contrary, through the operation of what
Freud called "the narcissism of small differences,"[19]
feelings of hatred and envy can be readily mounted
against outsiders who in many ways resemble the society
whose hostile attention they attract. Again, to some
degree at any rate, aggression can be controlled by
removing the occasions of aggression, and in this connection Freud looked with evident favor upon attempts
to abolish or to attenuate the institutions of nationhood
and property.[20] Indeed, Freud's main objection to such
measures, as they were for instance attempted in Russia
in the 1920s, was to the state of mind in which they
were carried out, dominated, as he saw it, by the false
and quite dangerous belief that the fundamental problems of human society are due to society, rather than to
human nature. "I too," Freud wrote in *Civilization and
Its Discontents*, "think it quite certain that a real change
in the relations of human beings to possessions would

[19] XI, 199; XVIII, 101; XXI, 114; XXIII, 91.
[20] XXI, 143; XXII, 181, 207–208.

be of more help in this direction than any ethical commands: but the recognition of this fact among socialists has been obscured and made useless for practical purposes by a fresh idealistic misconception of human nature."[21]

That measures of institutional reform, however far-reaching, tend to give rise to illusion, if they are treated as panaceas, derives from the fact, which it also attests to, that aggression cannot adequately be controlled through purely social means, and that any radical treatment of the problem must recognize it to be one in individual psychology—though, of course, the individual's attempt to regulate his aggression can be helped, or hindered, by the kind of social arrangement that prevails. Freud conceived of two ways in which this attempt can be made. Aggression can be internalized, in that the superego can be invested with the instinct that the individual renounces in his own person. Or there can be the replacement of instinct by intellect.

Both these two methods belong to civilization only in its higher reaches. They presuppose a conjunction of many favorable circumstances. Moreover, they are both essentially linked to the resolution of what was for Freud the major social issue: whether civilization could incorporate everyone into its benefits, or whether it must remain a source of gratification only for a favored section of society. For the internalization of aggression, or the development of a strong superego, required on the part of the individual some measure of acceptance of the standards of the environment. And this was not conceivable unless the fruits of civilization were distributed in a way that was not blatantly unjust.[22] The

[21] XXI, 143.
[22] XXI, 12.

other method that Freud proposed, the replacement of instinct by intellect, does not so much presuppose, as conduce to, a society of equal men. For it is an idea, thrown out by Freud though never developed, that, in the future at any rate, an ideal, or more specifically, the ideal of reason, might play the role filled in more traditional societies by the leader. In *New Introductory Lectures* and in an exchange of letters with Einstein, Freud talked of "the dictatorship of reason" as the principle of the society to come.[23] Writing in the 1930s, he was fully aware of the ironical coloring of this phrase: it exhibited, we might say, to a high degree, the provocativeness inherent in all thought.

Freud believed in reason. "In the long run," he wrote in *The Future of an Illusion*, "nothing can withstand reason and experience."[24] He believed, that is, that the mind of man is so attuned that it is swayed by arguments and rational considerations once it listens to them. But just because arguments and rational considerations have such power over him, he will, when comfort demands it, do all he can not to listen to them. Freud's life work, we might say, was a research into the deafness of the mind. Freud was a rationalist, but not an optimist. He thought that ultimately reason will prevail, but he saw no reason to form an opinion when the ultimate would come about, or what might happen first. And he thought it inconsistent with the scientific oulook to convert the generalized assurance that one day humanity would listen to reason into a faith in the foreseeable future. There were justifiable grounds for action and for the pursuit of knowledge, but not for

[23] XXII, 171–72, 213; cf. XXI, 53–56.
[24] XXI, 54.

hope. "I have not," Freud wrote, and we can see this as his envoi,

> the courage to rise up before my fellow-men as a prophet, and I bow to the reproach that I can offer them no consolation; for at bottom that is what they are all demanding—the wildest revolutionaries no less passionately than the most virtuous believers.[25]

No greater disservice can be done to Freud than by those who, in the interest of this or that piety, recruit him to the kind of bland or mindless optimism that he so utterly and so heroically despised.

[25] XXI, 145.

SHORT BIBLIOGRAPHY
INDEX

SHORT BIBLIOGRAPHY

Anyone who sets out to write on Freud owes his primary debt to three important works. First, and most heavily, to the great *Standard Edition of The Complete Psychological Works of Sigmund Freud* (New York: Macmillan, 1964–   ), under the general editorship of James Strachey, in collaboration with Anna Freud, assisted by Alix Strachey and Alan Tyson. The degree to which their editorial labors, their introductions, notes, and voluminous cross-reference, have abridged my work is incalculable. Secondly, to Ernest Jones, *Sigmund Freud: Life and Work* (New York: Basic Books, 1953–57), a three-volume biography, which not merely contains a vast storehouse of information, but admirably relates, as the subtitle promises, the two sides of the man. Thirdly, to *The Origins of Psycho-analysis*, edited by Marie Bonaparte, Anna Freud, and Ernst Kris (New York: Basic Books, 1954), which contains the greater number of Freud's letters to Wilhelm Fliess, along with numerous drafts and notes (including the *Scientific Project*) that formed part of the correspondence.

Another important source of information is Freud's letters to his friends and colleagues. In addition to the Fliess correspondence found in *The Origins of Psycho-analysis*, the following volumes have appeared:

Abraham, Hilda C., and Freud, Ernst L. (eds.). *A Psychoanalytic Dialogue: The Letters of Sigmund Freud and Karl Abraham*. New York: Basic Books, 1965.

Freud, Ernst L. (ed.). *Letters of Sigmund Freud 1873–1939*. New York: McGraw-Hill, 1964.

————. *The Letters of Sigmund Freud and Arnold Zweig*. New York: Basic Books, 1970.

Meng, Heinrich, and Freud, Ernst L. (eds.). *Psychoanalysis and Faith: The Letters of Sigmund Freud and Oskar Pfister. New York*: Basic Books, 1963.

On the personal side, the Jones biography may be supplemented by:

Freud, Martin. *Sigmund Freud: Man and Father*. New York: Vanguard, 1958.

H.D. *Tribute to Freud*. New York: Pantheon, 1956.

Leavey, Stanley A. (ed.). *The Freud Journal of Lou Andreas-Salomé*. New York: Basic Books, 1964.

Roazen, Paul. *Brother Animal: the Story of Freud and Trausk*. New York: Alfred A. Knopf, 1969.

Sachs, Hanns. *Freud: Master and Friend*. Cambridge: Harvard University Press, 1944.

Two useful summaries of Freud's theories are:

Brenner, Charles. *An Elementary Textbook of Psychoanalysis*. New York: Doubleday Anchor, 1957.

Hall, Calvin S. *A Primer of Freudian Psychology*. New York: New American Library, 1954.

The best introduction to Freud's work is provided by Freud himself in the brilliant *Five Lectures on Psychoanalysis*, based on lectures he gave at Clark University, Worcester, Massachusetts. From these the reader might move on either to the *Introductory Lectures on Psychoanalysis* or to some more specific works, such as *The Interpretation of Dreams* (New York: Avon, 1967) and the *Three Essays on the Theory of Sexuality* (New York: Avon, 1962). Throughout his career, Freud wrote works which, though often inspired by some polemical or propagandist motive of the moment, were in effect summaries of his work as it stood to date. In addition to the two sets of lectures just mentioned, these include *On the History of the Psychoanalytic Movement* (1914; New York: Norton, 1966), "Psychoanalysis" and "The Libido Theory" (1922), "A Short Account of Psychoanalysis" (1923), *An Autobiographical Study* (1924; New York: Norton, 1963), *The Question of Lay Analysis* (1926; New York: Norton, 1949), and the *New Introductory Lectures* (1932; New York: Norton, 1965). *An Outline of Psychoanalysis* (1938; New York: Norton, 1949) is not the elementary work that the title suggests.

The reader may sometimes feel himself in need of an accompaniment to Freud's text in the form of a glossary to the concepts that the text employs. The Hampstead Clinic Psychoanalytic Library sets out to satisfy this need with a series of volumes, each dealing with an important part of Freud's theory. So far two volumes have appeared: Volume I, entitled *Basic Psychoanalytic Concepts on the Libido Theory* (London: George Allen & Unwin, 1969), and Volume II entitled *Basic Psychoanalytic Concepts on the Theory of Dreams* (London: George Allen & Unwin, 1969), both edited by Humberto Nagera. A far more modest work is Charles Rycroft, *A Critical Dictionary of Psychoanalysis* (London: 1968). However, when a really difficult problem of interpretation arises, the reader is likely to find that the answer remains locked in Freud's words, to which he must return.

As far as the development of Freud's thought is concerned, the following are valuable:

Andersson, Ola. *Studies in the Prehistory of Psychoanalysis.* New York: Humanities Press, 1962.

Bernfeld, Siegfried. "Freud's Earliest Theories and the School of Helmholtz." *Psychoanalytic Quarterly*, XIII (1944), 341–62.

Bibring, Edouard. "The Development and Problems of the Theory of the Instincts." *International Journal of Psychoanalysis*, XXII (1941), 102–31; also L (1959), 293–308.

Dorer, Maria. *Historische Grundlagen der Psychoanalyse.* Leipzig: 1962.

Hartmann, Heinz. "The Development of the Ego Concept in Freud's Work." *International Journal of Psychoanalysis*, XXXVII (1956), 425–38. Reprinted in his *Essays in Ego-Psychology*. London: Hogarth, 1964.

Hartmann, Heinz; Kris, Ernst; and Loewenstein, Rudolph M. *Papers on Psychoanalytic Psychology*. New York: International Universities Press, 1964.

Madison, Peter. *Freud's Concept of Repression and Defense*. Minneapolis: University of Minnesota Press, 1961.

Nunberg, Herman (ed.). *Minutes of the Vienna Psychoanalytic Society*. New York: International Universities Press, 1962–1967.

Pribram, Karl H. "The Neuropsychology of Sigmund Freud." *Experimental Foundations of Clinical Psychology*, edited by Arthur J. Bachrach. New York: Basic Books, 1962.

Stewart, Walter A. *Psychoanalysis, The First Ten Years, 1888–1898*. New York: Macmillan, 1967.

Otherwise there is a massive literature on Freud, most of which, insofar as it does not make a direct contribution to psychoanalysis itself, is not of great value.

INDEX